*Robert Penn Warren*

# Robert Penn Warren
## A COLLECTION OF CRITICAL ESSAYS

*Edited by* JOHN LEWIS LONGLEY, JR.

NEW YORK UNIVERSITY PRESS    1965

© 1965 BY NEW YORK UNIVERSITY
LIBRARY OF CONGRESS CATALOG CARD NUMBER: 65–13207
MANUFACTURED IN THE UNITED STATES OF AMERICA

*For Taow, Michie, and Johnny*

# ACKNOWLEDGMENTS

ACKNOWLEDGMENT is made to periodicals and authors for permission to reprint the following:

"Robert Penn Warren's Novels: The Symbolic and Textual Patterns," by John M. Bradbury. Reprinted from *Accent* (Spring, 1953). © 1953 by Accent. © in part 1958 by the University of North Carolina.

"The Art of Fiction XVIII: Robert Penn Warren." Reprinted from *Paris Review* IV (Spring-Summer, 1957). © 1957 by The Paris Review, Inc.

"Robert Penn Warren's *Night Rider:* The Nihilism of the Isolated Temperament," by Alvan S. Ryan. Reprinted from *Modern Fiction Studies* VII (Winter, 1961). © 1961 by the Purdue Research Foundation.

"Self-Knowledge, the Pearl of Pus, and the Seventh Circle," by John Lewis Longley, Jr. Originally printed in a somewhat different form in *Modern Fiction Studies* VI (Spring, 1960). © 1960 by the Purdue Research Foundation.

"*All the King's Men:* The Matrix of Experience," by Robert Penn Warren. Reprinted from *Yale Review* (Winter, 1964). © 1964 by Robert Penn Warren.

"Melpomene as Wallflower: or, The Reading of Tragedy," by Robert B. Heilman. Reprinted from *Sewanee Review* LV (January-March, 1947). © 1947 by the University of the South.

"Tangled Web," by Robert B. Heilman. Reprinted from *Sewanee Review* LIX (Winter, 1951). © 1951 by the University of the South.

"Mr. Warren and the Reviewers," by F. Cudworth Flint. Reprinted from *Sewanee Review* LXIV (Autumn, 1956). © 1956 by the University of the South.

"Miscegenation as Symbol: *Band of Angels*, by Leonard Casper. Reprinted from *Audience* I (Autumn, 1959). © 1959 by the Audience Press, Inc.

"Journey to the Interior," by Leonard Casper. Reprinted from *Modern Fiction Studies* (Spring, 1960). © 1960 by the Purdue Research Foundation.

"Trial by Wilderness: Warren's Exemplum," by Leonard Casper. Reprinted from *Wisconsin Studies in Contemporary Literature* III (Fall, 1962). © 1962 by the *Wisconsin Studies in Contemporary Literature*.

"The Burden of the Literary Mind: Some Meditations on Robert Penn Warren as Historian," by William C. Havard. Reprinted from *The South Atlantic Quarterly* LXII (Autumn, 1963). © 1963 by Duke University.

"Psychology and Theme in *Brother to Dragons*," by Frederick P. W. McDowell. Reprinted from *Publications of the Modern Language Society* LXX (Winter, 1955). © 1955 by The Modern Language Association of America.

"Warren's Later Poetry," an original essay, written for inclusion in this collection, by George P. Garrett. © 1964 by George Garrett.

"Knowledge and the Image of Man," by Robert Penn Warren. Reprinted from *Sewanee Review* LXII (Spring, 1955). © 1955 by the University of the South.

NOW THAT Faulkner and Hemingway are gone, Robert Penn Warren is clearly America's most distinguished man of letters, especially so if the term is used in the European sense of a person established in significant literary genres and easily at home in the various philosophical fashions that come and go. The bare record of Mr. Warren's literary achievement is more than adequate to establish the contention. There is first of all his dazzling virtuosity: in an age of one-book, middle-aged *enfants terribles*, he has published eight novels, a body of short fiction, lyric poetry, major criticism, drama, and one of the more important book-length poems of the twentieth century. His work is philosophic, which is to say that, beyond the brilliance of surface and the tortured unwinding of motive and consequence, the major concern is with whatever is grave and constant in the human condition. In this late period of our waist-high culture, Mr. Warren's personal style has been a shining exception, being lofty, noble, jazzy, or colloquial as occasion requires.

Purely creative work aside, there are his studies of segregation, and in *The Legacy of the Civil War* what is quite possibly the only truly original contribution to our thinking on that subject yet to emerge from the hullabaloo of the Centennial. The textbooks he and Professor Cleanth Brooks wrote many years ago radically changed the teaching of literature in America and elsewhere. This association flourished also in the founding and editing of *The Southern Review*, which was during its brief lifetime one of the distinguished literary quarterlies of the world. Recognition has not been altogether withheld. Mr. Warren has been awarded the highest literary prizes America has to offer, being the only person thus far to receive a Pulitzer Prize in both fiction and poetry. Public recognition has come in due course. He has written serious fiction that turned out to be bestsellers. His status is secure in every place that ultimately matters. But this is perhaps not the immediate problem. The immediate problem is the one to which this collection of essays addresses itself.

The very richness and variety of Mr. Warren's creation has complicated an easy understanding of it; still, this need not be a permanent obstacle. His poetry is not as "difficult" as that of Eliot, for instance, nor his prose as experimental as that of Gertrude Stein. The problem is that of finding a profitable critical orientation.

As recently as 1961, Professor Louis Rubin observed [1] that Warren has been the victim of some of the most slipshod literary journalism of his day. He noted also how it seems impossible for a newspaper or magazine reviewer to read a book by Warren without cutting loose a barrage of irrelevant, ideological and sociological prejudgment. It would be a happy task to be able to say that the reception of *Flood* (1964), Warren's most recent novel, has been different. But such is not the case.

II

An instrument which offers even tentative guidance through the tangle of Warren commentary should state its criteria and presuppositions early. The present collection is a modest one. The major limiting factor has been that of space: for every essay here, there are at least two I keenly regret having to leave out. Thus no claim could be made that the collection offers a final insight into the canon of Warren criticism, or even an adequate one. Before detailing the criteria of selection, it should be stated that the process of rejection was much simpler. All ephemera were discarded as such. The various examples of irrelevance were weeded out, even those which show a naive enthusiasm. Mr. Warren is a particularly articulate critic and teacher of literature. His own comment about his major aims, procedures, and presuppositions has appeared a number of times in print, and would be discovered in the course of even a casual scholarly search. When a commentator

1. Louis D. Rubin, Jr., *"Theories* of Human Nature: Kazin or Warren?" The *Sewanee Review* LXIX (1961), 501.

manages to indicate that he is ignorant of these statements, he is simply confirming his right to amateur standing. When a commentator pretends ignorance of these statements for the purpose of extending an established critical distortion, the result is deliberate obfuscation. As Professor Rubin noted, every serious Warren critic has had to begin again each time by laboriously clearing away the journalistic debris of irrelevant and idiotic objections.[2] The present collection is no exception. The most it can do is get the Augean stables cleaned up enough to reveal the general shape of the building.

The best general introduction to Warren's work at this date is Leonard Casper's *Robert Penn Warren: The Dark and Bloody Ground*.[3] The recent (1964) pamphlet by Paul West, *Robert Penn Warren* (University of Minnesota Pamphlets on American Writers, Number 44), is an excellent introduction and easily available. Both contain excellent bibliographies, as does the all-Warren issue of *Modern Fiction Studies* (Spring, 1960). The present volume begins with Bradbury's essay on the major themes in Warren's fiction. The 1957 *Paris Review* interview, which is reprinted in its uncut version, is the most extensive body of commentary by Mr. Warren yet to appear on his own working habits, attitudes, and theories. His comment ranges over many subjects and offers a fascinating insight into matters which reappear in *The Legacy of the Civil War* (1961) and *Flood* (1964). Following this preliminary orientation, the various essays consider the major novels in turn. In each case, the editor was forced to make a selection from a number of excellent possibilities. Not surprisingly, the Pulitzer Prize novel *All the King's Men* has received the widest attention from critics and reviewers alike. Many excellent studies of it exist, including Professor Rubin's chapter on Burden's Landing in his *The Faraway Country: Writers of the Modern South*.[4] Professor Heilman's essay evaluates and counters much of the early commentary on the novel. Mr. Warren's most recent account of the origin and growth of the novel is given, comple-

2. Ibid.
3. Leonard Casper, *Robert Penn Warren: The Dark and Bloody Ground* (University of Washington Press, 1960).
4. Louis D. Rubin, Jr., *The Faraway Country: Writers in the Modern South* (University of Washington Press, 1963).

menting the Introduction to the Modern Library edition. Professor Heilman next attempts to untangle some of the misunderstanding surrounding *World Enough and Time,* and Professor Flint points out why *Band of Angels* is not the pornographic potboiler it has sometimes been called. One essay each is printed for *The Cave, Wilderness,* and *Flood.*[5] Professor Havard, a historian and political scientist, assesses Mr. Warren's "reliability" in matters of historical accuracy and concludes he is very reliable. The poetry is given far fewer pages than it deserves, again for reasons of space. This lack is partly offset by the thoroughness of Professor McDowell's analysis of *Brother to Dragons* and George Garrett's lively original essay on the later poetry. The book concludes with Mr. Warren's own quietly eloquent statement, given ten years ago at a symposium at Columbia University, which is almost a personal testament of faith. As stated, this collection is hardly the totality of Warren commentary. But, taken together with the items in the selected bibliography, it perhaps does constitute a beginning.

III

What emerges in the collection is the portrait of a major writer and the world of his creative imagination. In his justly famous essay on Conrad, Warren states that the philosophical novelist is one "for whom the documentation of the world is constantly striving to rise to the level of generalization about values, for whom the image strives to rise to symbol, for whom images always fall into a dialectical configuration, for whom the urgency of experience, no matter how vividly and strongly experience may enchant, is the urgency to know the meaning of experience." In his own practice this striving often emerges as conflict; not merely the conflict between Warren the sophisticated critic and teacher versus Warren the Southerner, nourished on spread-eagle rhetoric and the haunting historical

5. Since my own essay on *Flood* was written, Professor Arthur Mizener has written an excellent essay review of that novel, "The Uncorrupted Consciousness," *Sewanee Review* LXXII (Autumn, 1964).

consciousness natural to his personal background. There are as well the clash and clang of violence, guilt, escapism, responsibility, time, will, and the search for identity; jagged at times, but at their best a beautifully orchestrated and sustained, perfected achievement. The man who emerges is seen to be neither a bigot, a racist, nor an apologist for Fascism, as reviewers with a strong socio-economic preoccupation were often able to believe.

What then can we be certain of in the Warren canon? Ten years ago Professor Leslie Fiedler said:

Robert Penn Warren occupies a unique and baffling position in the history of our recent literature . . . He represents a line of development which begins with Faulkner's vision of the South as the landscape proper to the terror of us all . . .

Warren, however, manages to preserve the shrillness of the Faulknerian tone, the provinciality of his diction and the sense of a rhetoric more controlled by passion than design. He is, indeed, the only serious contemporary writer I know able to achieve the typical Faulknerian corkscrew motion of action, the inward and downward circling toward a climax of horror, which makes of plot an outward symbol of our inward flight from and attraction toward a revelation of guilt . . . We should be aware . . . that Warren's turning to the Historical Romance is an accomodation neither mercenary nor naive; he exploits it for sophisticated and strategic ends.[6]

What is excellent in this brief quotation is the clear grasp of one way Warren is not Faulkner (so clear to Fiedler, so difficult for so many others), how the two writers are similar in their power and terror, but the one not thereby a pallid imitation of the other. I personally would only add that often the typical spiral action works both ways—often it sweeps upward and outward from the terror of personal guilt to embrace and include all humanity, living or dead. Warren's passion has always been not merely to document the characteristic experiences of our time, but above all else to give them meaning in a largely meaningless world. To repeat his comment on the practice of Conrad, the duty of the novelist remains—no matter how vividly and strongly experience may enchant—to know

6. Leslie A. Fiedler, "Romance in the Operatic Manner," *New Republic* CXXXIII (September 6, 1955), 28–29.

the meaning of experience. This urgency, which both writer and reader must share, is the only avenue to that essential concern which is most urgent of all: self-knowledge. Often this urgency leaps from the page with an immediacy that is undeniable.

. . . the clammy, sad little foetus which is you way down in the dark which is you too lifts up its sad little face and its eyes are blind, and it shivers cold inside you for it doesn't want to know . . . It wants to lie in the dark and not know, and be warm in its not-knowing. The end of man is knowledge, but there is one thing he can't know. He can't know whether knowledge will save him or kill him.[7]

Every soul is valuable in God's sight, and the story of every soul is the story of its self-definition for good or evil, salvation or damnation . . . Each of us longs for full balance and responsibility in self-knowledge, in a recognition and harmonious acceptance of our destiny. Saints and sages may achieve that harmonious sense of destiny . . . But we lesser and more fumbling mortals may find at least some intimation of it in the unfolding patterns, however modest, of our own effort toward knowledge.[8]

With only this much as a beginning, the reader may be ready to move, as Mr. Warren so steadily does, from practice to theory and from theory to a personal understanding of practice. Through such a journey, the reader may acquire an adequate familiarity with the clash of theme and counter-theme which are the polarities of Warren's power: the incredibly realistic creation of the physical world—men, action, speech. Each seeks for meaning in the long search for self-identity and self-knowledge; the commitment to an idea, political or other; the recognition of self-complicity; the dead weight of tradition and the intolerable burden of history; the tragic vision which often takes the form of human greatness, attempting to create within a frame of reference that is itself corrupt or absurd, and above all, (what the greatest of writers can sometimes do), the elevation of history into the kind of myths men live and die by. To repeat, man cannot know if

7. Robert Penn Warren, *All the King's Men* (New York: Harcourt Brace, 1946), pp. 11–12.
8. Robert Penn Warren, "Knowledge and the Image of Man," *Sewanee Review* LXIII (Winter, 1955), 182, 189–190.

knowledge will save him or kill him, but know he must. Like it or not, every soul is at every moment moving in history, and no man, whatever theory of self-exculpation he may devise, is ever outside that awesome responsibility.

J. L. L. JR.

*Charlottesville and New York*
*Summer, 1964*

CONTENTS

PART TWO     FICTION—Continued

* A new essay written for this volume.

* A new essay written for this volume.

*Part One*      *Themes*

John M. Bradbury

# 1·Robert Penn Warren's Novels:
## The Symbolic and Textural Patterns

IN THEIR RECENT ANTHOLOGY, *The House of Fiction*, Allen Tate and Caroline Gordon through a series of analyses have defined a fictional technique which can only be called "symbolic naturalism." "If the art of naturalism consists mainly in making *active* those elements which had hitherto in fiction remained *inert*, that is, description and expository summary, the further push given the method by Joyce consists in manipulating what at first sight seems to be mere physical detail into dramatic symbolism." For the editors it is evident that this is entirely a, but *the* technique of great fiction. This verdict may well be questioned, but there can be no doubt that symbolic naturalism has dominated at least one important sector of modern fiction, that in our southern literary renaissance.

In such a writer as Faulkner the symbolic or mythic aspect may predominate with characters, events and style subject to portenteous heightening; or the naturalism highly elective and active may predominate as in Eudora Welty. Tate's own novel, *The Fathers*, approaches the norm of the definition, not without self-consciousness. But in Robert Penn Warren's fiction the balance is achieved with no sacrifice of individuality and human warmth.

Warren's novels, pegged to the "naturalism" of historic events, localities and characters, and patterned to the archetypal quest motif, are created, from the structural skeleton up, to the Tate-Gordon specifications. On the structual surface a sharply observed and colloquially recorded realism consorts

3

with rich rhetoric and a profuse imagery, which is restrained and directed by the patterns of its symbolic extensions.

On the whole, the textural organization of the novels, as distinguished from the structural and ideological organizations, appears strongly influenced by that of Elizabethan drama, particularly as interpreted by modern "expanded metaphor" analysis.[1] Each of the novels is dominated by sets of images which undergo variations and expansions in conjunction with thematic developments. At the same time, a more specialized imagery often attaches to individual characters, whose particularity is thereby given symbolic extension. Finally an independent localized imagery wells up in a spontaneous flow, as if to give body to Ransom's theory of textural irresponsibility—the *"id"* element of poetry.

The conceptual method is that of the poetic drama conceived both as "metaphysical" poem and as "romantic" tragedy. As a technique for the novel, such a method has many advantages. It permits, even requires, a plot of action, hence a melodramatic appeal on the primary level. Like Shakespeare and many of his contemporaries, Warren derives his plots largely from historic events of a violent nature. Again on the level of the pit (though the appeal is by no means so limited) he is enabled to indulge an earthy humor and salty wit. At the same time, he can introduce bold rhetoric in soliloquies and scenes of high emotional stress. Yoking together such opposites, he preserves unity through the control and extension of the major symbolism. In prose form, therefore, Warren's dramatic symbolic naturalism embodies all the chief fugitive poetic theories: Ransom's doctrine of "metaphysical" poetry, Tate's "tension" between intensive and extensive factors, and his own concept of "impure" poetry.[2] Each of the novels, premised on the dualism of fact and idea, probes human experience in both of its aspects (physical and Platonic, intensive and extensive, naturalistic and symbolic) in order to "earn" its insights or tensions.

---

[1] Slim Sarrett's brief critique of Shakespeare in *At Heaven's Gate* offers a kind of "figure in the carpet" for Warren's novels, both thematically and texturally.

[2] Robert Penn Warren: "Pure and Impure Poetry," *Kenyon Review* (Spring, 1943).

Warren's first published novel, *Night Rider*, establishes its basic imagetic patterns in the opening scenes. The crowd and the crowd pressure to which Percy Munn is subjected on the opening page as he prepares to leave his train fix one symbolic pole—the political one—for the novel's action: "The gathering force which surged up the long aisle behind him like a wave took and plunged him hard against the back of the next man."

After the crowd on the streets and the subsequent group pressure which forces his commitment to the mass movement of the Association, and his too successful speech, Munn recalls "how incredibly brilliant and empty had been the sky from which the light poured over the landscape and the innumerable faces." The emptiness which is attached here as a corollary of the crowd symbol (of the light as well) gradually takes form, or at least outline, in the figure of Senator Tolliver, who is seen almost at once staring at a "blankly sunlit wall." Tolliver is a moral hollowness surrounded by political man, and it is finally with Tolliver that Munn is forced to identify himself. Equivocal, like all of Warren's symbols, the crowd represents the true reality which Munn seeks and at the same time the image of his own emptiness.

More obvious, as well as more complex, is the pervasive symbolism of light and dark, and its extension in terms of warmth and coldness. In the main, the day-night pattern reflects Warren's fact-idea dualism, and it is closely allied, as in the quotation above, with the political symbols. The first "glare of the morning sun . . . half-blinding him after the dim interior of the coach," marks Munn's emergence from the cocoon of his marriage into a world of fact and activity. But the full glare of responsibile public action for Percy Munn hardly survives his maiden speech. From the moment of his complete involvement in the Association, he becomes a creature of the night. The first evening in the hotel he cannot sleep and rises to watch and listen to the crowd—with "disgust not only for them but for himself." The revulsion he feels for the men and for his own act of identification with them is balanced by a new wave of exultation, an orator's gesture in the night—he would "tell them what he knew to be the truth." The accompaniment of this commitment to "the Word" is the singing in the streets below to the tune of "John Brown's Body," a significant reference since Warren's early biography of Brown pictures him as an archetype of man given over to abstraction. Munn's gesture becomes his renunciation of his own essential humanity and of his proper self-realization.

After the inauguration of night-riding tactics, every important event in Munn's life occurs under the aegis of night, with the coldness of stealth, lust, and violence gradually mastering every phase of his activity. Only occasional flickers of light and warmth penetrate to Munn through the body of the novel until the climax of night-riding brings the great burst of flame from dynamited warehouses. But the moment of fulfillment which this artificially enkindled light and heat provide for Munn is soon itself a cold, blackened ruin. On a grander scale, it is the empty oratorical gesture in the hotel room.

In addition, the false heat and light of the fires parallel the love affair of Munn and Lucille Christian. Their desperately sought fulfillment is a clandestine, violent, and empty action, like that of the night riders, and it ends in the destruction of a true center of warmth, Lucille's father, simultaneously with the destruction by fire of Munn's home. The double catastrophe by night and fire discovers to the lovers their essential coldness, isolation, and emptiness.

The imagetic pattern is completed with "the blunt, frayed flame" of Munn's pistol punctuating the night, the pistol with which he had been symbolically unable to kill his hollow father-surrogate and alter ego, Tolliver. For the trapped and dying Munn, the final scene is a reversion to childhood innocence, with the voices of his assassins sounding to him "like the voices of boys at a game in the dark." Thus the symbolism which began with the dimness of Munn's emergence from innocence comes full circle, back through night abstraction with its false lights to the dark womb of innocence and death.

Warren's second novel, *At Heaven's Gate*, is ideologically a study of modern "freedom"; hence the ironic title, applying primarily to Sue Murdock—"my lady sweet, arise"—but to the other major characters as well in their attempts to escape the ties of "evil" family and tradition. This is Warren's only city novel, and its central imagery reflects the agrarian's judgment against a form of life dominated by finance capitalism and cut off from its roots in the soil. The novel develops two large symbolic clusters: those relating to decay, disease, deformation, and the like; and those which may be grouped as unreality images. The focus of the first group is the fiigure of Lemuel Murdock, whose murder of a rival politician in defense of his honor, as he and his code understood honor, has left him "mountainously decayed, sagging from the big maned head, the gray streaked yellowly as by old rust stains, the whole mass sagging, as by long slip and erosion." Symbolically, he is the tradition itself, the South, a monstrous ruin in the new order. Similarly, the backgrounds of the younger characters abound in images of decay and deformation. In Jerry Calhoun's agrarian home there are cripples, foulness, rot; in Dorothy Murdock's peeling family house rotting Revoluntionary War boots; in Duckfoot Blake's slum bungalow a "distorted parody of an old man"; in Sweetwater's decaying family home "dust-smelling horsehair furniture" and "gray-faced old ladies" whose breaths smell "like stale cooked turnips."

These insistences from the past are more than balanced by images of filth, crippling, and disease in the city life of the younger generation. While the repulsive heritage represented by Lemuel Murdock may be taken as sufficient excuse for the unprincipled, artfully smooth, and attractive surface life which his son creates, the moral emptiness and human coldness of that life is sufficient to drive the daughter, Sue, to a restless career which reflects distortedly, invertedly, the images projected directly by the figures of decayed tradition. Sue's city world is dominated by the overt images of the cripple, Rosemary, of Sarrett's ambiguous sex, of Sweetwater's scars, Blake's splay feet and farts. But it is the inverted reflection of these pictures that gives them symbolic weight. Sue must compel Jerry to take her on the cripple's bed, and he must feel "as though he clasped that other body, small, bony, twisted." She must wear Rosemary's dress and sleep on her bed in her patch of warmth, and call Jerry an "emotional cripple." The characters "pick" their psychological "scabs," "boil out" their mental "pus," exhibit their ambitions "like boils"; they need to squeeze their emo-

tional "pimples," they slobber and vomit or feel like it, spit or
"dribble saliva." Art in Sarrett's circle becomes a growth out of
"dung and offal," poetry "the glitter of pus," criticism "at its
worst . . . an attempt to disintegrate the rose into the dung
which fertilized the root," and discovery of a sympathetic role
in the theatre "like first menstruation."

Art, particularly theatre art, along with sport, comprises a
major division of the unreality images, which symbolize a contrasting but intimately related aspect of traditionless lives. The
specific unreality images revolve largely about two centers: Bogan Murdock, who is a "solar myth" or "just a dream Bogan
Murdock had" ("When Bogan Murdock looks in the mirror,
he doesn't see a thing"); and Slim Sarrett, persuasive exponent
of the reality principle, but himself a whole-cloth creation. Bogan personifies the chimera of finance capitalism, a "wonderful
idea" without tangible reality. It is Bogan's moral nonexistence
(reflected also in the sport-for-appearance images surrounding
him) which gradually steals from his wife her sense of reality
and which, by its specious glitter, attracts Jerry Calhoun, only
to leave him with the memory of "events and persons . . . as
shadowy as frosted breath on the air." And it is this blank
heritage which Sue, as the modern questing spirit, attempts to
fill with a series of liaisons: first, with the American dream hero,
up from poverty through football to success (Jerry); then with
irresponsible estheticism (Sarrett); finally with Communism
(Sweetwater).

Sarrett personifies the artistic-intellectualist denial of the
world of fact. His attributes, the strict athlete's discipline, the
hard surface and penetrating insight, the androgynous character,
the alienation from and by society, and the retaliatory attack
upon society, are those of art itself. Sue, attached to Sarrett's as
well as to Murdock's unreality center, experiences her most
significant moments in non-self-identifications: on the stage,
particularly as the innocent victim, Cordelia; in the utterly detached artificiality of her participation in Sarrett's parties; in the
self-forgetfulness of drink and sex; and in her times of pure
emptiness, when her overpowering urge to be loved and to be
identified through love has left her. The numerous images of
gold and glitter link her with her father's world, those of free-

dom, power, and powerlessness with her attempt to find a self in the world of abstractions bounded by Jerry, Sarrett, and Sweetwater. To the end of her cry, that of the "freed" generation, is " 'Oh, what am I?' "

*All the King's Men* is a novel of redemption and the only one of Warren's four which permits the protagonist, who is again like Sue Murdock a symbol of modern man in quest of self-identification, to emerge from his ordeal to the hope of a new life. The symbolic fable of this book embodies the world of reality in Willie Stark and the world of idea or abstraction in Adam Stanton, while the Eves of the piece, Anne Stanton and Sadie Burke, are the agents by which knowledge (of fact or evil) is transmitted.

The pervasive imagery of this novel enforces the redemption-rebirth theme, as Norton Girault has noted, and the related Eden-fall-knowledge motif to which the title obliquely refers. The early episodes dealing with the childhood idyl of Adam, Jack Burden, and Anne are heavily saturated with water imagery. The womb-innocence connotations are underscored by the numerous childlike features and attitudes which Jack notes in Anne. But the major image of Anne, that of lying back gazing into the bright sky or with closed eyes, whether she is floating on water or reclining on the seat of the roadster or waiting naked on Jack's bed, is one of expectancy and receptivity to real experience. Jack's preservation of this image, which he understands only in its aspect of innocence, and his inability to violate it are the indices of his subconscious urge to hold to or return to the womb state. So Jack is thinking in terms of an "aqueous green" forest coolness with himself as a bird diving into it, while Anne is destroying his memory picture by accepting Stark (fact) as a lover, embracing the realities which Jack shuns. When he discovers the violation, for which the receptive aspect of the image should have prepared him, the water symbol becomes "green scum on the shrunk pool around which the exposed earth cracks and scales like a gray scab." (Jack is still unprepared in a final sequence when Anne opens her door for him with, " 'Of course I'd let you in.' ")

The rebirth symbols appear on several levels and in various

tones throughout the novel. The episode of Willie Stark's enlightenment, when he changes from a "country sap" into an
astute politician, is dominated by images of conversion, ritual
killing, and revival. Stark had heard the call to politics "as for
a saint," had been "the little white lamb of God." In the crucial
scene, he becomes "the sacrificial goat . . . the ram in the
bushes," passes out to be called "the remains" with a "face pale
and pure." Jack's morning midwifery produces "a high and pure
and transparent look like a martyr's face," and Jack can soon
comment that "he's been on the road to Damascus and he saw
a great light." The scene ends with Willie's eyes shining "and
over him God's bright, brassy, incandescent sky." All this forms
an ironic prelude to the final enlightenment and rebirth of
Jack himself. Willie is reborn into "realism," and it is under
the aegis of Willie and realism in its various forms that Jack
is to live. On one level, this novel is a testing of philosophic
realism—as *World Enough and Time* is a testing of romantic
idealism.

As early as page 11, Jack's resistance to the rebirth which
comes from knowledge has been presented in a graphic image:
"But the clammy, sad little foetus which is you way down in
the dark which is you too lifts up its sad little face and its eyes
are blind. . . . It wants to lie in the dark and not know and be
warm in its not-knowing." [3] (The contrasting image for Willie
in his pre-Damascus phase is: "inside himself . . . something
was swelling and growing painfully and dully and imperceptibly
like a great potato in a dark, damp cellar.") Jack's progress
toward enlightenment is a reverse movement, marked by running away images and by the womb returns called "Great
Sleeps." The climax of this process occurs in Jack's mechanistic
phase—the Sleeps separate his adoptions of various "realistic"
philosophies. He watches Adam perform a prefrontal lobotomy,
designed to provide the patient with a new personality by purely
mechanical means, an operation, Jack thinks, "more radical even
than what happened to Saul on the road to Damascus." Like
Willie's, this ironic conversion-rebirth previews Jack's, but now
more explicitly, for the imagetic paraphernalia includes the

3 Robert Penn Warren, *All the King's Men* (New York: 1946), pp.
11–12. All quotations in this essay are from this edition.

"white nightshirts" of a revivalist baptism and Jack's insistence
that the patient "is born again and not of woman. I baptize thee
in the name of the Great Twitch, the Little Twitch, and the
Holy Ghost. Who, no doubt, is a Twitch, too."

One further false rebirth symbol is associated with Jack's
"father," the Scholarly Attorney. Here the religious aura, the
"hanged man" symbol (George, the more or less adopted son of
the Scholarly Attorney, was "the man who got hanged" in the
circus), the bed wetting, the "maternal little noises," the
metaphor of a "saint" to describe George's masticatory bliss—
all support a downward-to-false-innocence redemptive regeneration. And since George has become the stand-in for Jack in
a doubly false or unreal situation, the ironic application of the
scene is clear.

With this preparation, the true redemption of Jack Burden
occurs, but only after he has recognized his responsibility for
the deaths of both his father-imago and his real father. The
ritual shedding of the father's blood has purchased knowledge,
for all knowledge that "is worth anything . . . has cost some
blood, and knowledge is redemption," and "the truth always
kills the father."

Jack's rebirth is heralded by his mother's scream, "which
snatched [him] from sleep" with its "bright, beautiful, silver purity of feeling," by her moaning and drugged behavior. Her revelation of a capacity to love gives Jack not only a new father and
a new mother, but "a new picture of the world." At the same
time, Willie Stark's "greatness," which "perhaps he spilled
. . . on the ground," as Onan his seed, has a dubious rein-
carnation in the illegitimate perhaps grandchild whom Lucy
adopts and names "Willie Stark." The contrast and irony are
complete with the paralleling of this offspring of spilled seed
with Jack's hard birth into responsibility.

*World Enough and Time,* a novel in which Warren tests
various versions of philosophic idealism, offers a symbolic pattern oriented about primitivistic ritual, centered in the sacrificial shedding of blood, and the ritual's idealization in romantic
tragedy. The key image for the former aspect is developed
from the Indian conception of Kentucky, defined by Warren

as the "Dark and Bloody Ground . . . a holy land . . . a land of mystery . . . for the gods lived here." The principal dramatic images reflect Jeremiah Beaumont's view of himself "mounting the high stage" to perform a "noble" tragic action.

Blood imagery dominates the early wilderness scenes in which Jeremiah's character is formed, the climactic episodes involving the sacrificial killing of Col. Fort, Jeremiah's father-surrogate, and the final retributive section. The development of this blood motif culminates in the symbolic hacking off of Jerry's head—the final Platonic severance which Ransom has brilliantly exploited in his poem, "Painted Head." The blood pattern is initiated with a description of the acres of wild strawberries on the father's home site, so thick that "his boots were red and bright with juice as with blood." Jeremiah adds: "But I remember from my own time how they were sweet to the tongue." This association of sweetness with the blood image is indicative of Jeremiah's—and romanticism's—distortion of natural violence, and it sets the referents for the following religious conversion scene. The revivalist's sermon, visualizing God as a great bear whose "fangs drip wrath" and the victim-to-be-saved as a lamb offering its throat so that its blood will spurt under the divine jaws, is prefaced by words touching "for their sweetness," and followed by the exhortation: "let there be sweetness in your terror." At this point there recurs to Jeremiah an ambiguous sacrificial and sadistic image from early childhood of a young woman martyr at the stake in flames. Thus the symbolic complex of sweetness, blood-sacrifice, and "high stage" is completed.

As Jeremiah approaches his sacrificial murder of Fort, the revivalist imagery controls his thinking. "The blood of Fort would clear him. . . . He would bathe in it and be clean." He goes off on his "errand of blood" like a knight of romance, with a red ribbon "the color of blood" to fly "as a pennon for victory." When the deed is done, the thought of his own blood to be shed in retribution starts a sudden feeling of "great lightness and cleansing, as though he . . . *was* innocent and could trust his innocence."

The final sequence begins with Jeremiah's flight to the West (a constant false innocence motif in Warren). Here the

God-bear image recurs, but now ironically twisted, as Jeremiah
seeks an animal-innocence in the body alone. His guide,
"smeared and stained" with juice of the wild grape, seems
"savagely painted for ritual, or as though [he] had fed on drip-
ping flesh and the waste blood had caked about the muzzle."
In the retreat of the Gran Boz, where Rachel wears a red
ribbon on her hair to greet the monster, the religious ritual
is perverted to drunken fornication at the side of a man bleed-
ing to death—and Jeremiah contracts a venereal disease from
the "corrupt blood" of the woman. After the severance of head
from body and the burial of "ideal" head alone, a final note
of irony is appended when Willkie Barron, who personifies
the way of the world, shoots himself so "tidily through
the heart" that he leaves not "a single spatter of blood on the
floor."

The dramatic symbolism, representing Jeremiah's idealistic
version of his own action and later Rachel's forced version of
hers, plays a constant accompaniment to the blood-sacrifice
motif. For Jeremiah in his first retreat with Rachel, the world
of affairs is a "mock-show," but soon it is a "flight from another
more dire mock-show" of his own intimate life of mind. From
this perception, Jeremiah rises to picture and then to enact
his "secret drama," in which Fort is the villain and he the hero.
But it must all be played in the dark, out of the light of realism,
and he must draw Rachel onto the romantic shadow stage with
him. The high tragedy has its ironic climax when poison fails
to produce more than a violent retching sickness: "So after the
fine speeches and the tragic stance, the grand exit was muffed.
The actors trip on their ceremonial robes, even at the threshold
of greatness, and come tumbling down in a smashing pratt-fall,
amid hoots and howls from the house. . . ."[4]

The world of reality has the last laugh. The primitive ritual
of hunting and bloodshed—the pure earth-born violence apos-
trophized by Faulkner and Hemingway—is perverted through
the three stages of Jeremiah's errors until it ends in pratt-falls
and animal reversion and corruption. In contrast, realism, trium-

4 Robert Penn Warren, *World Enough and Time* (New York: Random House, 1950), pp. 401–402. All quotations in this essay are from this
edition.

phantly managing its entrances and exits, bows off to applause—
and in the wings accomplishes its own bloodless defeat.

The "rhetoric" of Warren's novels, particularly that of
*All the King's Men*, has been harshly treated by several competent critics. "Rhetoric" is a much abused term, but it is the
proper one for Warren if it be understood in its Elizabethan
and baroque-metaphysical sense. In literary temperament Warren is much closer to sixteenth- and seventeenth-century ideals
than to modern simplicity cults which have attached pejorative
connotations to a word once denoting the effective use of language.

Warren's normal prose style derives from the Ransomic
dualism which underlies his own theory of "impure" poetry.
To do justice to the "complexities and contradictions of experience," language must, he feels, reflect in a constant counterpoint both the ideal-romantic aspect of man's dual nature and
the crude fact-animalism. To disallow either of these aspects
of Warren's writing—critics have referred to them as "fancy
writing" and "vulgarity," thereby revealing much of their own
temperaments—is to rule out Warren's philosophic and literary
premise. These stylistic extremes are not what the critics imply,
lapses of taste or indulgences, but technique, and technique
that has been fully integrated with conception.

Each of the novels is, in fact, a different stylistic, as well
as symbolic, compound. *Night Rider*, the least complex of the
books, told from a single point of view, proceeds largely in
graphic and forceful, but always decorous, style, slightly elevated
to the tone of the idealistic southern landholder. (The constant
use of titles for the characters, especially the author's consistent
reference to his protagonist as "Mr. Munn," is largely a tonal
device.) Counterpoint to this normal style, which is often
poetically heightened in Munn's thought monologs, is supplied
chiefly by the dialogue: the colorful, earthy comments and
explosions of Bill Christian, the only less vivid realism of Dr.
MacDonald, and the dialects of the farmers and Negroes, in
particular the finely sustained tale of Willie Proudfit.

*At Heaven's Gate*, with its shifting multiple viewpoints,
employs a rich variety of styles, from the densely metaphoric

mountain-evangelist dialect of Ashby Windham to the brittle nervous language of the Slim Sarrett episodes or the tough-gentle humor of Sweetwater's. Through such ground styles as these play such variations as Blake's gamey naturalism and Uncle Lew's rural crudities, the hysterical ritualistic dialect of Negroes in torture-sport and in fear, Murdock's pretentious self-salesmanship, and Sarrett's modernist poetry. In this Babel of speeches, reflecting the city setting with its confusion of purpose and creed, there is no center. There is, instead, a gradual intrusion of an impersonal, yet cynical, news-reporter style which ends by dominating the closing sections. The abstract beliefless voice of the city prevails finally.

Both the rhetoric and the "smart-aleck" commentary of *All the King's Men* have been roundly condemned by critics, usually without reference to their functional significance. Once the role of Jack Burden, the narrator, is seen in its true centrality, with his dual nature objectified on the one side in Willie Stark's factualism, on the other in Adam's abstract idealism, the necessity for the stylistic devices becomes evident. The cynical "smart-aleck" pose is Jack's defense against an alien world, the "fancy writer" the smothered and hence exaggerated ideal of himself. These two continually warring elements are further overlaid by the retrospective reflections of the mature philosophic Jack of the book's end. Most characteristic of this counterpointed style is the appended tag which snatches a sharp insight, a lush description, or an indulged emotion from its heights and debases it in the manner of Eliot's "The Waste Land." Or again the brilliantly mixed descriptions of scenes and people, such as the one which opens the book, recklessly paced kaleidoscopic successions of imagery and metaphor, quick observation and comment, humor and vulgarity and beauty. This is Jack (and perhaps Warren) letting himself go, but it is also, functionally, the hectic symbol of the Willie-Adam "terrible division of our age."

Extended philosophic passages, in this book always metaphorical and often racy, and the paced speculative formality of the Cass Mastern story reveal new stylistic veins that come to dominate *World Enough and Time*. This fourth novel, despite its quadruple perspective—the historian's that of the documents, those of Jeremiah present and reflective—offers a more even tonal surface than any of the earlier books. Jeremiah's formal vocabulary is modified in the historian's controlled language, but there is no real contrast. Similarly, the speculative bent, marked in both styles, has only been purged of its emotional ingredient in the historical commentary, without loss of essential resemblance.

As in *Night Rider*, the "world of fact" contrast is supplied largely in the dialogue. The ready spittle-punctuated realism of the common speech and its dialectal color comes through unpurged in Jeremiah's report, where it stands as the groundling commentary on the "high stage" performance of Jeremiah and his peers. There is nothing in this story of the racy cynicism of Jack Burden, none of the Babel of competing voices which characterizes *At Heaven's Gate*. It is an index of Warren's stylistic versatility and mastery that he is able in this novel to capture the somewhat stilted tone of abstract speculative and dated language without losing dramatic appeal—the book has even been called a "Hollywood thriller." No other writer of our time, with the possible exception of W. H. Auden, has exhibited such fluency and narrative ability in so many styles. Only Faulkner has approached his mastery of colorful vernacular speech, and even Faulkner, whose highly personal flavor so permeated everything he wrote, did not achieve the individualized authenticity or the variety of Warren's dialects.

Warren's ear is uncommonly acute, but the most valuable faculty he possesses is human insight, a shrewd and at the same time sympathetic ability to penetrate imaginatively into the inner life of his characters. In the most caustic vignette offered through Jack Burden's squinted eyes, the pity of human wastage is never lost. Warren's sense of "irreducible evil" and of human frailty permits an extremely wide range to a natural sympathy that is completely devoid of sentimentalism—ironic in the Richards sense that it is immune to irony. The sympathy does have limits, marked at one end by a Bogan Murdock and at the other by a Carlos Bumps, the upper and lower cases of the dollar sign. But the humanism that can embrace Senator Tollivers, Uncle Lew Calhouns, Sugar Boys, and Sadie Burkes, and Percival Skroggs gives to the intellectual and symbolic dialectic of the novels a warm and vibrant concretion.

Warren as a writer of fiction cannot be better described than in his own definition of the philosophical novelist:

one for whom the documentation of the world is constantly striving to rise to the level of generalization about values, for whom the image strives to rise to symbol, for whom images always fall into a dialectical configuration, for whom the urgency of experience, no matter how vividly and strongly experience may enchant, is the urgency to know the meaning of experience. . . . For him the very act of composition [is] a way of knowing, a way of exploration.

# 2·The Art of Fiction XVIII:
## *Robert Penn Warren**

(THIS INTERVIEW takes place in the apartment of Ralph Ellison at the American Academy in Rome: a comfortable room filled with books and pictures. Mr. Penn Warren, who might be described as a sandy man with a twinkle in his eye, is ensconced in an armchair while the interviewers, manning tape recorder and notebook, are perched on straight-back chairs. Mrs. Ellison, ice bowl tinkling, comes into the room occasionally to replenish the glasses: all drink *pastis*.)

INTERVIEWERS: First, if you're agreeable, Mr. Warren, a few biographical details just to get you "placed." I believe you were a Rhodes Scholar . . .

WARREN: Yes, from Kentucky.

INT: University of Kentucky?

WARREN: No. I attended Vanderbilt. But I was Rhodes Scholar from Kentucky.

INT: Were you writing then?

WARREN: As I am now, trying to.

INT: Did you start writing in college?

WARREN: I had no interest in writing when I went to college. I was interested in reading . . . oh, poetry and standard novels, you know . . . my ambitions were purely scientific but I got cured of that fast by bad instruction in freshman chemistry and good instruction in freshman English.

* Original, uncut transcript of interview published in *Paris Review* IV (Spring–Summer, 1957).

INT: What were the works that were especially meaningful for you? What books were—well, doors opening?

WARREN: Well, several things come right away to mind. First of all when I was six years old, *Horatius at the Bridge* I thought was pretty grand.

INT: And others?

WARREN: Yes, *How They Brought the Good News from Aix to Ghent* (at about the age nine). I thought it was pretty nearly the height of human achievement. I didn't know whether I was impressed by riding a horse that fast or writing the poem. I couldn't distinguish between the two, but I knew there was something pretty fine going on . . . Then *Lycidas.*

INT: At what age were you then?

WARREN: Oh, thirteen, something like that. By that time I knew it wasn't what was happening in the poem that was important—it was the poem. I had crossed the line.

INT: An important frontier, that. What about prose works?

WARREN: Then I discovered Buckle's *History of Civilization.* Did you ever read Buckle?

INT: Of course, and Motley's *Rise of the Dutch Republic.* Most southern bookshelves contain that.

WARREN: . . . And Prescott . . . and *The Oregon Trail* is always hovering around there somewhere. Thing that interested me about Buckle was that he had the one big answer to everything: *geography.* History is all explained by geography. I read Buckle and then I could explain everything. It gave me quite a hold over the other kids, they hadn't read Buckle. I had the answer to everything. Buckle was my Marx. That is, he gave you one answer to everything, and the same dead-sure certainty. After I had had my session with Buckle and the one-answer system at the age of thirteen, or whatever it was, I was somewhat inoculated against Marx and his one-answer system when he and the depression hit me when I was about twenty-five. I am not being frivolous about Marx; but when I began to hear some of my friends talk about him in 1930, I thought, "Here we go again, boys." I had previously got hold of one key to the universe. Buckle. And somewhere

along the way I had lost the notion that there was ever
going to be just one key. But getting back to that shelf
of books, the Motley and Prescott and Parkman, and so
on, isn't it funny how unreadable most history written now
is when you compare it with those writers?

INT: Well, there's Samuel Eliot Morison.

WARREN: Yes, a very fine writer. Another is Van Woodward,
he writes very well indeed. And Bruce Catton. But Catton
maybe doesn't count, he's not a professional historian. If
he wants to write a book on history that happens to be
good history and good writing at the same time, there
isn't any graduate school to try to stop him.

INT: It's very interesting that you were influenced by historical
writing so early in life. It has always caught one's eye how
history is used in your work, for instance *Night Rider*.

WARREN: Well, that isn't a historical novel. The events belonged
to my early childhood. I remember the troops coming in
when martial law was declared in that part of Kentucky.
When I wrote the novel I wasn't thinking of it as history. For one thing, the world it treated still, in a way survived. You could still talk to the old men who had been
involved. In the 1930's I remember going to see a judge
down in Kentucky—he was an elderly man then—a man of
the highest integrity and reputation—who had lived through
that period and who by common repute had been mixed up
in it—his father had been a tobacco grower. He got to
talking about that period in Kentucky. He said, "Well,
I won't say who was and who wasn't mixed up in some
of those things, but I will make one observation: I have
noticed that the sons of those who were opposed to getting
a fair price for tobacco ended up as either bootleggers or
brokers." But he was an old-fashioned kind of guy, for
whom bootlegging and brokerage looked very much alike.
Such a man didn't look "historical" thirty years ago. Now
he looks like the thigh bone of a mastodon.

INT: Beyond the question of the historical, from the first your
work is very explicitly concerned with moral judgments.
This during a period when much American fiction was
concerned with moral questions only in the narrow way

of the "proletarian" and "social realism" novels of the
1930's.

WARREN: I think I ought to say that behind *Night Rider* and
my next novel, *At Heaven's Gate,* there was a good deal of
the shadow not only of the events of that period but of the
fiction of that period. I am more aware of that fact now
than I was then. Of course only an idiot could have not
been aware that he was trying to write a novel about, in one
sense, "social justice" in *Night Rider,* or for that matter,
*At Heaven's Gate.* But in some kind of a fumbling way I
was aware, I guess, of trying to find the dramatic rub of the
story at some point a little different from and deeper than
the point of dramatic rub in some of the then current
novels. But what I want to emphasize is the fact that I was
fumbling rather than working according to plan and already
arrived at convictions. When you start any book you don't
know what, ultimately, your issues are. You try to write to
find them. You're fiddling with the stuff, hoping to make
sense, whatever kind of sense you can make.

INT: At least you could say that as a southerner you were more
conscious of what some of the issues were. You couldn't,
I assume, forget the complexity of American social reality,
no matter what your esthetic concerns, or other concerns.

WARREN: It never crossed my mind when I began writing fiction that I could write about anything except life in the
South. It never crossed my mind that I knew about anything else; know, that is, at the level you know something
to write about it. Nothing else ever nagged you enough to
stir the imagination. But I stumbled into fiction rather late.
I've got to be autobiographical about this. For years I
didn't have much interest in fiction, that is, in college. I
was reading my head off in poetry, Elizabethan and the
moderns, Yeats, Hardy, Eliot, Hart Crane. I wasn't seeing
the world around me—that is, in any way that might be
thought of as directly related to fiction. Be it to my ever-
lasting shame that when the Scopes trial was going on a
few miles from me I didn't even bother to go. My head
was too full of John Ford and John Webster and William
Blake and T. S. Eliot. If I had been thinking about writing

novels about the South I would have been camping in
Dayton, Tennessee—and would have gone about it like
journalism. At least the Elizabethans saved me from that.
As for starting fiction, I simply stumbled on it. In the spring
of 1930 I was in Oxford, doing graduate work. I guess I
was homesick, and not knowing it. Paul Rosenfeld, who
with Van Wyck Brooks and Lewis Mumford, was then
editing the old *American Caravan*, wrote and asked me why
I didn't try a long story for them. He had had the patience
one evening to listen to me blowing off about night-rider
stories from boyhood. So Oxford and homesickness, or at
least back-homeward-looking, and Paul Rosenfeld made
me write *Prime Leaf*, a novellette, which appeared in
the *Caravan* and was later the germ of *Night Rider*. I
remember playing hookey from academic work to write
the thing, and the discovery that you could really enjoy
trying to write fiction. It was a new way of looking at
things, and my head was full of recollections of the way
objects looked in Kentucky and Tennessee. It was like
going back to the age of twelve, going fishing and all that.
It was a sense of freedom and excitement.

INT: When you started writing, what preoccupations, technically and thematically, had you in common with your
crowd?

WARREN: I suppose you mean the poets called the Fugitive
Group, in Nashville—Allen Tate, John Crowe Ransom,
Donald Davidson, Merrill Moore, and so on?

INT: Yes.

WARREN: Well, in one sense, I don't know what the group had in
common. I think there is a great fallacy in assuming that
there was a systematic program behind the Fugitive Group.
There was no such thing, and among the members there
were deep differences in temperament and esthetic theory.
They were held together by geography and poetry. They
all lived in Nashville, and they were all interested in poetry.
Some were professors, some businessmen, one was a banker,
several were students. They met informally to argue philosophy and read each other the poems they wrote. For
some of them these interests were incidental to their main

concerns. For a couple of others, like Tate, it was poetry
or death. Their activity wasn't any "school" or "program."
Mutual respect and common interests—that was what held
them together—that and the provincial isolation, I guess.

INT: But did you share with them any technical or thematic
preoccupations?

WARREN: The answer can't, you see, apply to the group. But
in a very important way, that group was my education. I
knew individual writers, poems, and books through them.
I was exposed to the liveliness and range of the talk and
the wrangle of argument. I heard the talk about techniques
but techniques regarded as means of expression. But most
of all I got the feeling that poetry was a vital activity, that
it related to ideas and to life. I came into the group rather
late. I was timid and reverential I guess. And I damned
well should have been. Anyway, there was little or no
talk in those days about fiction. Some of the same people,
a little later, however, did give me in a very concrete way
a sense of how literature can be related to place and history.

INT: It's very striking when you consider writing by southerners before the 1920's. There were few writers as talented
or as competent, or as confident as today, when writers
seem to pour out of the South. This strikes me as a very
American phenomenon in spite of its specifically regional
aspects. Because when the South began to produce writers
in great numbers they emerged highly conscious of craftsmanship, highly aware of what literature was about, how
to relate it to society and philosophy, and so on. Would
you say that this was a kind of repetition of the cultural
phenomenon which occurred in New England, say during
the 1830's?

WARREN: Yes, I do see some parallel between New England
before the Civil War and the South after World War I
to the present. The old notion of a shock, a cultural shock,
to a more or less closed and static society—you know, what
happened on a bigger scale in the Italian Renaissance or
Elizabethan England. After 1918 the modern industrial
world, with its good and bad, hit the South and all sorts
of ferments began. As for individual writers, almost all

of them of that period had had some important experience
outside the South, then returned there—some strange mixture of continuity and discontinuity in their experience—a
jagged quality. But more than mere general cultural or personal shocks, there was a moral shock in the South, a tension that grew out of the race situation. That moral tension
had always been there, but it took new and more exacerbated forms after 1920. For one thing, through the growing
self-consciousness of the Negroes was involved the possibility of expanding economic and cultural horizons. The
southerner's loyalties and pieties—real values, mind you—
were sometimes staked against his religious and moral sense,
those real values. There isn't much vital imagination, it
seems to me, that doesn't come from some sort of shock,
imbalance, need to "relive," redefine life.

INT: Would you say that by the time you were editing the
Southern Review, the between the wars period, that this
moral shock was making itself felt in writing?

WARREN: Well, the Review started in 1935 and went on till '42.
So it was late for the first ferment of things. But there were
a lot of good young, or younger, writers in it. Not all southern either.

INT: I remember that some of Algren's first work appeared
there.

WARREN: Oh yes, two early stories, for example; and a longish
poem about baseball.

INT: And the story "A Bottle of Milk for Mother."

WARREN: And the story "Biceps." And three or four of Eudora's
first stories were there—Eudora Welty—and some of Katherine Anne's novelettes—Katherine Anne Porter.

INT: There were a lot of critics in it—young ones too.

WARREN: Oh yes, younger then, anyway. Kenneth Burke, F. O.
Matthiessen, Theodore Spencer, R. P. Blackmur, Delmore
Schwartz, L. C. Knights.

INT: Speaking of critics reminds me that you've written criticism
as well as poetry, drama, and fiction. It is sometimes said
that the practice of criticism is harmful to the rest. Have
you found it so?

WARREN: On this matter of criticism, something that appals me is the idea going around now that the practice of criticism is opposed to the literary impulse. Is *necessarily* opposed to it, in an individual or period. Sure, it *may* be a trap, it may destroy the creative impulse, but so may drink or money or respectability. But criticism is a perfectly natural human activity and somehow the dullest, most technical criticism may be associated with full creativity. Elizabethan criticism is all, or nearly all, technical—meter, how to hang a line together—kitchen criticism, how to make the cake. People deeply interested in an art are interested in the "how." Now I don't mean to say that that is the only kind of valuable criticism. Any kind is good that gives a deeper insight into the nature of the thing—a Marxist analysis, a Freudian study, the relation to a literary or social tradition, the history of a theme. But we have to remember that there is no *one, single, correct* kind of criticism—no *complete* criticism. You only have different kinds of perspectives, giving, when successful, different kinds of insights. And at one historical moment one kind of insight may be more needed than another.

INT: But don't you think that in America now a lot of good critical ideas get lost in terminology, in its gobbledy-gook style?

WARREN: Every age had its jargon, every group. When the jargon runs away with the insight, that's no good. Sure, a lot of people think they have the key to truth if they have a lingo. And a lot of modern criticism has run off into lingo —into academicism—the wrong kind of academicism, that pretends to be unacademic. The real academic job is to absorb an idea, to put it into perspective of other ideas, not to dilute it to lingo. As for lingo, it's true that some very good critics got bit by the bug that you could develop a fixed critical vocabulary. Well, you can't, except within narrow limits. That is a trap of scientism.

INT: Do you see some new ideas in criticism now emerging?

WARREN: No, I don't see them now. We've had Mr. Freud and Mr. Marx and—

INT: Mr. Fraser and *The Golden Bough.*

WARREN: Yes, and Mr. Coleridge and Mr. Arnold and Mr. Eliot

and Mr. Richards and Mr. Leavis and Mr. Aristotle, and so on. There have been, or are, many competing kinds of criticism with us—but I don't see a new one, or a new development of one of the old kind. It's an age groping for its issue.

INT: What about the New Criticism?

WARREN: Let's name some of them—Richards, Eliot, Tate, Blackmur, Winters, Brooks, Leavis (I guess). How in God's name can you get that gang into the same bed? There's no bed big enough and no blanket would stay tucked. When Ransom wrote his book called the *New Criticism* he was pointing out the vindictive variety among the critics and saying that he didn't agree with any of them. The term is, in one sense, a term without any referent— or with too many referents. It is a term that belongs to the conspiracy theory of literary history. A lot of people— chiefly aging, conservative professors, scared of losing prestige or young instructors afraid of not getting promoted— middle-brow magazine editors—and the flotsam and jetsam of semi-Marxist social-significance criticism left stranded by history—they all have a communal nightmare called the New Criticism to explain their vague discomfort. I think it was something they ate.

INT: What do you mean—conspiracy?

WARREN: Those folks all had the paranoidal nightmare that there was a conspiracy called the New Criticism, just to do them personal wrong. No, it's not quite that simple but there is some truth in this. One thing that a lot of so-called New Critics had in common was a willingness to look long and hard at the literary object. But the ways of looking might be very different. Eliot is a lot closer to Arnold and the Archbishop of Canterbury than he is to Yvor Winters, and Winters is a lot closer to Irving Babbitt than to Richards, and the exegeses of Brooks are a lot closer to Coleridge than to Ransom, and so on. There has been more nonsense talked about this subject than any I can think of (and I don't want to add to the burden of history right now).

INT: Well, getting back to your own work, there is, for us, an exciting spiral from *I'll Take My Stand* through the novels to *Segregation.* It would seems that these works mark stages in a combat with the past. In the first, the point of view seems orthodox and unreconstructed. How can one say it? In recent years your work has become more intense and has taken on an element of personal confession which is so definite that one tends to look, for example, on *Segregation* and *Brother to Dragons* as two facets of a single work.

WARREN: You've thrown several different things at me here. Let me try to sort them out. First you refer to the southern agrarian book *I'll Take My Stand,* of 1930, and then to my recent little book *Segregation.* My essay in *I'll Take My Stand* was about the Negro in the South, and it was a defense of segregation. I haven't read that piece, as far as I can remember, since 1930, and I'm not sure exactly how things are put there. But I do recall very distinctly the circumstances of writing it. I wrote it at Oxford at about the same time I began writing fiction—the two things were tied together—the look back home from a long distance. I remember the jangle and wrangle of writing the essay and some kind of discomfort in it, some sense of evasion, I guess, in writing it, in contrast with the free feeling of writing the novelette *Prime Leaf,* the sense of seeing something fresh, the holiday sense plus some stirring up of something inside yourself. In the essay I reckon I was trying to prove something, trying to find out something, see something, feel something—exist. Don't misunderstand me. On the objective side of things, there wasn't a power under heaven that could have changed segregation in 1929 —the South wasn't ready for it, the North was not ready for it, the Negro wasn't. The Court, if I remember correctly, had just reaffirmed segregation, too. No, I'm not talking about the objective fact, but about the subjective fact, yours truly, in relation to the objective fact. Well, it wasn't being outside the South that made me change my mind. It was coming back home. In a little while I realized I simply couldn't have written that essay again. I guess trying to write fiction made me realize that. If

you are seriously trying to write fiction you can't allow yourself as much evasion as in trying to write essays. But some
people can't read fiction. One reviewer, a professional
critic, said that *Band of Angels* is an apology for the
plantation system. Well the story of "Band" wasn't an
apology *or* an attack. It was simply trying to say something
about something. But God Almighty, you have to spell
it out for some people, especially a certain breed of professional defender-of-the-good, who makes a career of holding
the right thoughts and admiring his own moral navel. Well,
that's getting off the point. What else was it you threw at
me?

INT: Would you say that each book marks a redefinition of
reality arrived at through a combat with the past? A development from the traditional to the highly personal of
reality?

WARREN: Yes, I see what you mean. But I never thought of a
combat with the past. I guess I think more of trying to
to find what there is valuable to us (the line of continuity
to us, and *through* us). The specific southern past, I'm
now talking about. As for combat, I guess the real combat
is always with yourself, southerner or anybody else.

INT: Well that may bring up another of the four things I threw
at you—the increasing element of personal confession in
your work which is so serious that one tends to look, for
example, on *Segregation, Brother to Dragons*, and *Band of
Angels* as parts of one work. Or maybe this is doing violence to them?

WARREN: Not at all. But it wouldn't have occurred to me. You
fight your battles one by one and do the best you can.
Whatever pattern there is, develops—it isn't projected—
really basic patterns, I mean, the kind you live into. As
for confession, that wouldn't have occurred to me either,
but I do know that in the last ten years or a little more
the personal relation to my writing changed. I never both-
ered to define the change. I quit writing poems for several
years, that is, I'd start them, get a lot down, then feel that
I wasn't connecting somehow. I didn't finish one for several
years, they felt false. Then I got back at it, and that is

the bulk of what I've done since—*Band of Angels*, and a new book of poems which will be out in the summer. But cutting back to where we started—the confession business. When you try to write a book—even objective fiction— you have to write from the inside not the outside—the inside of yourself—you have to find what's there—you can't predict it—just dredge for it—and hope you have something to work the dredging. That isn't "confession"—that's just trying to use whatever the Lord lets you lay hand to. And of course you have to have common sense enough and structural sense enough to know what is relevant. You don't choose a story, it chooses you. You get together with that story somehow . . . you're stuck with it. There certainly is some reason it attracted you and you're writing it trying to find out that reason; justify, get at that reason. I can always look back and remember the exact moment when I encountered the germ of any story I wrote —a clear flash . . .

INT: What is your period of incubation? Months? Years?

WARREN: Something I read or see stays in my head for five or six years. I always remember the date, the place, the room, the road, when I first was struck. For instance, *World Enough and Time*. Katherine Anne Porter and I were both at the Library of Congress as Fellows. We were in the same pew, had offices next to each other. She came in one day with an old pamphlet, the trial of Beauchamp for killing Col. Sharp. She said, "Well, Red, you better read this." There it was. I read it in five minutes. But I was six years making the book. Any book I write starts with a flash but takes a long time to shape up. All of your first versions are in your head so by the time you sit down to write you have some line developed in your head.

INT: Speaking of crafts, how conscious are you of the dramatic structure of your novels when you begin? I ask because in it there is quite a variety of subforms, folklore, set pieces like the "Ballad of Billy Potts" or the Cass Mastern episode in *All the King's Men*. Are these planned as part of the dramatic structure, or do they arise while you are being carried by the flow of invention as it falls into form?

WARREN: I try to think a lot about the craft of other people—
that's part of my long years of teaching. When you've been
explaining things like how the first scene of *Hamlet* gets
off . . . thinking of how things have been done . . . and
when it comes to work you have made some objective decisions, like who is going to tell the story. That's a prime
question, a question of control. You have to make a judgment. You find one character is more insistent, he's more
sensitive and more pointed than the others. But as for
other aspects of structure and craft, I guess, in the actual
process of composition or in preliminary thinking, I try
to immerse myself in the motive and *feel* toward meanings
rather than plan a structure or plan effects. After a thing
is done, then I try to get tough and critical with myself.
But damn it, it may sometimes be too late then. But that
is the fate of man. What I am trying to say is that I try
to forget the abstractions when I'm actually composing a
thing. I don't understand other approaches that come up
when I talk to other writers. For instance, some say their
sole interest is experimentation. Well, I think that you
learn all you can and try to use it. I don't know what is
meant by the word "experiment"; you ought to be playing
for keeps.

INT: Yes, but there is still great admiration of the so-called
experimental writing of the '20's. What of Joyce and Eliot?

WARREN: What is "experimental" writing? James Joyce didn't
do "experimental" writing—he wrote *Ulysses*. Eliot didn't
do "experimental" writing—he wrote "The Waste Land."
When you fail at something you call it an "experiment,"
an elite word for flop. Just because lines are uneven or
capitals missing doesn't mean experiment. Literary mag-
azines devoted to experimental writing are usually filled
with works by middle-aged or old people.

INT: Or middle-aged young people.

WARREN: Young fogeys. But to come back to the experimental
business. In one way, of course, all writing that is any good
*is* experimental; that is, it's a way of seeing what is possible
—what poem, what novel is possible. Experiment—they
define it as putting a question to nature, and that is true of

writing undertaken with seriousness. You put the question to human nature—and especially your own nature—and see what comes out. It is unpredictable. If it is predictable —not experimental—then it will be worthless.

INT: What about the use of history in your fiction? Obviously you don't write "historical" novels: they are always concerned with urgent problems, but the awareness of history seems to be central.

WARREN: I'm gonna jump back . . . something is hanging on the edge of my mind . . . about planning . . . I try to, awful hard. At some point, you know, you have to try to get one with God and *then*, take a hard cold look at it— and try again on it afterwards and plan to take it, trusting in your viscera and nervous system and your previous efforts as far as they've gone. The hard thing, the objective thing, has to be done before the book is written. And if anybody dreams of *Kubla Khan*, it's going to be Coleridge. If the work is done the dream will come to the man who's ready for that particular dream; it's not going to come just from dreaming in general. About historical novels; I don't think I write historical novels. I try to find stories that catch my eye, stories that seem to have issues in purer form than they come to one ordinarily.

INT: A kind of unblurred topicality?

WARREN: I wrote two unpublished novels in the '30's. *Night Rider* is the world of my childhood. *Heaven's Gate* was contemporary. My third published, *All the King's Men*, was worlds I had seen. All the stories were contemporary.

INT: *Brother to Dragons?*

WARREN: This last belonged to a historical setting but I don't see any break myself. A matter of dealing with issues in a more mythical form. The novel I'm writing now, and two I plan, are all contemporary. I hate costume novels, but maybe I've written some and don't know it! I have a romantic kind of interest in the objects of American history: saddles, shoes, figures of speech, rifles, and so on. They're worth a lot. Helps you focus. There *is* a kind of extraordinary romance about American history. That's the only word for it . . . a kind of self-sufficiency. You know, the grandpaws and the great grandpaws who carried the assumption that somehow their lives and their decisions were important, that as they went up, down, here and there, such a life was important and a man's responsibility to live it.

INT: In this connection, do you feel that there are certain themes which are basic to the American experience, even though a body of writing in a given period might ignore or evade them?

WARREN: First thing, without being systematic, that comes to mind without running off a week and praying about it, would be that America was based on a big promise—a great big one: the Declaration of Independence. . . . When you have to live with that in the house, that's quite a problem —particularly when you've got to make money and get ahead, open world markets, do all the things you have to, raise your children, and so forth. America is stuck with its self-definition put on paper in 1776, and that was just like putting a burr under the metaphysical saddle of America—you see that saddle's going to jump now and then and it pricks. There's another thing in the American experience that makes for a curious kind of abstraction. We had to suddenly define ourselves and what we stood for in one night. No other nation ever had to do that. In fact, one man did it. One man in an upstairs room, Thomas Jefferson. Sure, you might say that he was the amanuensis for a million or so people stranded on the edge of the continent and backed by a wilderness, and there's some sense in that notion. But *somebody* had to formulate it—in fact, just overnight, whatever the complicated background of that formulation—and we've been stuck with it ever since. With the very words it used. Do you know the Polish writer Adam Gurowski? [1] Of a high-placed Polish family, he came and worked as a civil servant in Washington, a clerk, a kind of self-appointed spy on democracy. His book *America*—of 1856, I think—begins by saying that America is unique among nations because other nations are acci-

[1] Adam Gurowski (1805–66). Author of *America and Europe* (1857) and *My Diary: Notes on the Civil War* (1866).

dents of geography or race, but America is based on an idea. Behind the comedy of proclaiming that idea from Fourth of July platforms there is the solemn notion, *Believe and ye shall be saved.* That abstraction sometimes does become concrete, is a part of the American experience.

INT: What about historical time? America has had so much happening in such a short time.

WARREN: Awful lot of foreshortening in it. America lives in two times, chronological time and history. The last widow drawing a pension from the War of 1812 died just a few years ago. My father was old enough to vote when the last full-scale battle against Indians was fought—a couple of regiments of regulars with artillery.

INT: You had a piece in the *New Republic* once where you discuss Faulkner's technique. One of the things you emphasize is Faulkner's technique of the "still moment." I've forgotten what you called it exactly; a suspension, in which time seems to hang.

WARREN: That's the frozen moment. Freeze time. Somewhere, almost in a kind of pun, Faulkner himself uses the image of a frieze for such a moment of frozen action. It's an important quality in his work. Some of these moments harden up an event, give it its meaning by holding it fixed. Time fluid vs. time fixed—In Faulkner's work that's the drama behind the drama. Take a look at Hemingway; there's no time in Hemingway, there are only moments in themselves, moments of action. There are no parents and no children. If there's a parent he is a grandparent off in America somewhere who signs the check, like the grandfather in *A Farewell to Arms.* You never see a small child in Hemingway. You get death in childbirth but you never see a child. Everything is outside of the time process. But in Faulkner there are always the very old and the very young. Time spreads and is the important thing, the terrible thing. A tremendous flux is there, things flowing away in all directions. Moments not quite ready to be shaped are already there, waiting, and we feel their presence. What you most remember about Jason in *The Sound and the Fury,* say, is the fact that he was the treasurer when the children made and sold kites, and kept the money in his pocket. Or you remember Caddy getting her drawers muddy. Everything is already there, just waiting to happen. You have the sense of the small becoming large in time, the large becoming small, the sweep of time over things. That, and the balance of the frozen, abstracted moment against violent significant action. Those frozen moments are Faulkner's game. Hemingway has a different game. In Hemingway there's no time at all. He's out of history entirely. In one sense, he tries to deny history, he says history is the bunk, like Henry Ford.

INT: This intrigues me very much because we reach a moment in American history where we have a man like Twain coming along who is highly moral and who is a humorist. He's master of moral literature, of native folklore, and though some people miss his mastery of literary technique he was highly conscious of technique, and he was certainly conscious of language, of how it operates, what it means.

WARREN: He's a great inventor of language. He made a language.

INT: You have Hemingway taking up that language side of his work and emphasizing it and extending it while he muted down, inverted Twain's moral questioning. And you have Faulkner picking up both that side, the inventiveness, plus the explicit concern with moral continuity. It seems that this comes back to the southern experience. Due not to anything that comes in the blood, not through any intention either, but to the fact that something shocking, something traumatic had occurred. We were all there and we had certain beliefs and certain conflicts of belief and certain conflicts between our beliefs and our actions and history was alive. It wasn't a matter of abandoning a central issue after Reconstruction or after the Hayes-Tilden Compromise, shall we say, and then saying, "Now these issues are no longer important."

WARREN: That was said elsewhere. On Wall Street, to be exact. History didn't stop that day south of the Mason-Dixon line. Of course the big split in American life is that history *did* stop for certain other people at a certain date. It stopped for the happy children of the gilded age. They settled down to making money and getting those railroads built out West and digging the gold out and speculating in land and watering stock and developing a continent, and on the way sometimes looting it and a fair percentage of their fellow-citizens. The heroic effort and the brigandage are both in the brew. But for a variety of reasons, history didn't stop for certain other people. Down South they were stuck with it, sometimes for some very poor reasons, including stupidity. But one good and sufficient reason was that the South was stuck with a lot of unresolved issues, including the question of the relation of the South to the rest of the country—for one thing, the relation of the economy of the South to that of the rest of the country—and including the race question. To sum up, you might say that the South got bogged down in history —in time—and the North got bogged down in nonhistory —non-time—and that split is the tragic fact of American life.

INT: Switching to something which might be related to this— there seems to be in the early Hemingway a conscious effort *not* to have a very high center of consciousness within the form of the novel. His characters may have a highly moral significance, but they don't talk about things. They seldom discuss issues. They prefer to hint. Thus distinctions may be lost in the oversimplification of gesture. In the underplaying of important lines.

WARREN: Sure, Hemingway sneaks it in, but he is an intensely conscious and, even, philosophical writer. When the snuck-in thing, or the gesture works, the effect can be mighty powerful. But in general, I was in no sense making an invidious comparison between the two writers—or between their special uses of time. They are both powerfully expressive writers. But it's almost too pat, you know, almost too schematic, the polar differences between those two writers in relation to the question of time. Speaking of pairs of writers, take Proust and Faulkner. There may be a lot written on the subject but I haven't encountered much of it. They'd make a strange but instructive pair to study—in relation to time. I want to go back to something—the question of the center of consciousness. French fiction, it has been said, usually has a hero who deals very consciously with the issues. He is his own chorus to the action, as well as the man who utters the equivalent of the Elizabethan soliloquy. But in our fiction of the 20's, in Hemingway, for instance, you had these matters sneaked in. You had hints or you had the issues left out completely, especially among those writers who didn't know what was going on anyway, who didn't know what Hemingway knew very well. By contrast, nineteenth-century fiction could deal with the issues. Those novels could discuss them in terms of a man's relation to a woman, or in terms of whether you're going to help a slave run away. Or in terms of what to do about a man obsessed with fighting evil, nature, what have you, in the form of a white whale.

INT: Well, your own work seems to have this explicitly, and without being literal Jack Burden in *All the King's Men* is a conscious center and he is a highly conscious man. Furthermore, he's not there as an omniscient figure, but, like each of us, is urgently trying to discover something. He is involved.

WARREN: Burden got there by accident. He was only a sentence or two in the first version—the verse play from which the novel developed.

INT: Why did you make the change?

WARREN: I don't know. He was an unnamed newspaper man, a childhood friend of the assassin, an excuse for the young doctor, the assassin of the politician, Willie Stark, to say something before he performed the deed. When after two years I picked up the verse version, and began to fool with a novel, the unnamed newspaper man became the narrator. It turned out, in a way, that what he thought about the story was more important than the story itself. I suppose he became the narrator because he gave me the kind of interest I needed to write the novel. He made it possible for me to control it. He is an observer, but he is involved.

INT: To follow this line a little farther, I was struck by the great flexibility of method you allowed yourself in *Brother to Dragons*. With ghosts coming back and re-enacting their lives, and commenting on the action. You have several worlds of reality operating there. Everyone spoke, if I remember correctly, but the slaughtered slave. Why is he silent?

WARREN: He did have three lines toward the end:

> I was lost in the world and the trees were tall.
> I was lost in the world, and the dark swale heaved.
> I was lost in my anguish and did not know the reason.

Then Jefferson says, "Reason, my son . . . how could I show you the light of reason, when I had lost it when your blood ran out."

INT: I'm probing here—maybe the character of RPW in the poem spoke for him, too, in the scheme of the book?

WARREN: I didn't want George, the slave boy, *not* to be there, *not* to speak. I wanted him to be there all the time. I wanted his presence to speak, his experience to speak. I wanted the fact of his experience to ricochet off something. I wanted to make a bank shot like in billiards. The relation of George's experience to other people, not the experience itself, merely, was what I wanted to play up. If somebody, a character, is in the position of George, is pure victim, what can he say? He has nothing to say. All you can do is bounce him off other people, those with various kinds of moral involvements and responsibilities. But—to change the subject perhaps—those three lines which George does speak were the first lines of *Brother to Dragons* that I composed—four years before I began the consistent composition of the poem.

INT: Would you say that you really come to grips with the problem of George in *Band of Angels*, in the person of Manty?

WARREN: No, I don't see it that way. George is just a boy caught in a maniacal piece of direct brutality. He had had a world to live in, with relations he could accept. It was a world he knew. Then suddenly it was upside down, and he was caught in the increasing terror and couldn't understand it.

INT: And Manty?

WARREN: Oh, she's different. One difference is the degree of consciousness. Manty has read books, is educated. For another thing, she has—or I tried to make her have—an inside story. She is striving for identity, for enlightenment. George, however, is not highly conscious, and he has no inside story. He is victim. Manty is, of course, a victim too, but in one perspective at least, her view of herself as victim is what stands in the way of her achieving identity. But George—he isn't a subject for a story, has no personality, no problem. He's just a little boy caught in a terrible fix. *Brother to Dragon* isn't *about* him.

INT: Well, what about Manty's problem in her relationship to Hamish Bond (Alex Hinks)? So, here is a young girl trained as a white gentlewoman who suddenly finds herself on the slave block where she is bought by a man bearing a false name and who, though wealthy through his own efforts, is escaping from his mother, who in her turn is obsessed by her myth of aristocracy.

WARREN: About that mother, I had somebody in mind—a real person, as I don't usually do—but I'm not going to tell you who it was.

INT: Were you implying here that both Manty and Bond have false identities, especially Bond?

WARREN: Yes, and even the false name and false identity were forced on him by his mother.

INT: His mother who insists that she is by birth an aristocratic Buckhampton, who were great slave owners.

WARREN: That's her myth. The stick she beats husband and son with. So the son's going to fix her, he says. He's going to get a million slaves, he says. He's going to be "ass-deep in niggers," he says. Bond makes her lie come both true and untrue. He sinks himself into the lie in order to escape from it—and to explore it, to know the truth of the lie. And of course, he is out to avenge himself on his mother for giving him a false identity, and on his father for being a weakling, for having no identity to give him, to give the son.

INT: That's a great scene where the boy makes the morose and beaten old father laugh by denouncing and rejecting the mother.

WARREN: Bond has to escape them both. He gets away from her by making the lie come true, but true in some shocking not respectable way that would violate her need for respectability. He becomes a slave-runner, and isn't respectable, even though he is a king of the coast. But somehow he can't quite get away from her. He has to become respectable in the end, blackmail his way into New Orleans society. Stuck with his lie he has to live it all the way through before he can speak an honest word, even though he's an old man.

INT: It sounds like the last part of your book on *Segregation* where you speak of the necessity of achieving moral identity.

WARREN: I hadn't thought about it that way. Maybe it's in the cards, though.

INT: Another thing that strikes me about Hamish Bond is that he has know-how. He has initiative, he is inventive, self-assertive. Capable of great violence and revulsion from that violence.

WARREN: If it hadn't been for his mama he might have gone West.

INT: Is it significant that he gets his start by tying in with an old Yankee slave-runner?

WARREN: To mention that in the book was just Confederate nastiness. [*Laughter*]

INT: But would it be historically true? The Yankee slave-runners?

WARREN: Would it! I guess the last of the numerous breed was a man named Gordon hanged in 1863 in New York. He was, by the way, the only one they ever got around to hanging. But in 1863 they, and Gordon, were sort of stuck with it.

INT: Do you feel that in terms of national morality that we're the oldest country rather than the New World—that we've become the Old World in the sense that we've been grappling longer with the problem of industrialization, the increasing anonymity of the individual, plus the tortures of the race problem in its most intense and intimate form. Aren't we the Old World now in the sense that we've

been coming to grips with these problems which European
nations are only now beginning to encounter in their
crucial forms?

WARREN: We've been through some things, or are deeper into
some things, that are just beginning for some other nations.
In industrialization, for instance, France and Italy haven't
even touched problems that we've got to the other side of,
by luck and national resources, I guess. Not that I want to
say we're home free. I've got my fingers crossed.

INT: For ten years or more it has been said in the United States
that problems of race are an obsession of Negro writers
but that they have no place in literature. But how can a
Negro writer avoid the problem of race?

WARREN: How can you expect a southern Negro not to write
about race, directly or indirectly, when you can't find a
southern white man who can avoid it?

INT: I must say that it's usually white northerners who express
this opinion, though a few Negroes have been seduced by
it. And they usually do so on esthetic grounds.

WARREN: I'd like to add to that here what I said about the
historical element seems important. The Negro who is
writing protest *qua* protest strikes me as anachronistic. Protest *qua* protest denies the textures of life. The problem is
to permit the fullest range of life into racial awareness. I
don't mean to imply that there's nothing to protest about,
but aside from the appropriate political, sociological, and
journalistic concerns, the problem is to see the protest in
its relation to other things. Race isn't an isolated thing—I
mean as it exists in the U.S.—it becomes a total symbolism
for every kind of issue. They all flow into it. And out of it.
Well, thank God. It gives a little variety to life. At the
same time it proclaims the unity of life. You know the
kind of person who puts on a certain expression and then
talks about "solving" the race problem. Well, it's the same
kind of person and the same kind of expression you meet
when you hear the phrase "solve the sex problem." This
may be a poor parallel, but it's some kind of a parallel.
Basically the issue isn't to "solve" the "race problem" or

the "sex problem." You don't solve it, you just experience it. Appreciate it.

INT: Maybe that's another version of William James' "moral equivalent of war." You argue and try to keep the argument clean, all the human complexities in view.

WARREN: What I'm trying to say is this. A few years ago I sat in a room with some right-thinking friends—the kind of people who think you look in the back of the book for every answer—attitude A for situation A, attitude B for situation B, and so on for the damned alphabet. It developed that they wanted a world where everything is exactly alike and everybody is exactly alike. They wanted a production belt of human faces and human attitudes.

INT: Hell, who would want such a world?

WARREN: "Right-thinkers" want it, for one thing. I don't want that kind of world. I want variety and pluralism—and *appreciation*. Appreciation in some sort of justice and decency and freedom of choice in conduct and personal life. Man is interesting in his differences. It's all a question of what you make of the differences. I'm not for differences *per se*, but you just let the world live the differences, live them out. I feel pretty strongly about attempts to legislate *undifference*. That is just as much tyranny as trying to legislate difference. Apply that to any differences except between healthy and unhealthy, criminal and noncriminal. Furthermore, you can't legislate the future of anybody, in any direction. It's not laws that are going to determine what our great-grandchildren feel or do. And you can't legislate virtue. The tragedy of a big half of American liberalism is to try to legislate virtue. You can't legislate virtue. You should simply try to establish conditions favorable for the growth of virtue. But that will never satisfy the bully-boys of virtue, the plug-uglies of virtue. They are interested in the production-belt stamp of virtue, attitude A in the back of the book, and not in establishing conditions of justice and decency in which human appreciation can find play.

INT: Getting back to fiction—what's the relation of sociological

research and other types of research to the forms of fiction,
to the writer's view of social reality?

WARREN: I think it's purely accidental. For one writer a big dose
of such stuff might be fine, for another it might be poison
. . . I've known a good many people, some of them writers,
who think of literature as *material* that you "work up." You
don't "work up" literature. But they point at Zola. But
Zola didn't do that. Nor did Dreiser. They must have
thought they did, but they didn't. They weren't "working
up" something—in one sense, something was working them
up. You see the world as best you can—with or without the
help of somebody's research, as the case may be. You see
as much as you can, and the events and books that are interesting to you should be interesting to you because you're
a human being, not because you're trying to be a writer.
Then those things may be of some use to you as a writer
later on. I don't believe in a schematic approach to material.
The business of researching for a book strikes me as a sort
of obscenity. What I mean is, researching for a book in the
sense of trying to find a book to write. Once you are engaged by a subject, are in your book, have your idea, you
may or may not want to do some investigating. But you
ought to do it in the same spirit in which you'd take a
walk in the evening air to think things over. You can't research to get a book. You stumble on it. Or hope to. Maybe
you will, if you live right.

INT: I see certain parallels between the development of your
work and its movement from *I'll Take My Stand* to *Band
of Angels* and *Segregation,* and Faulkner's Lucas Beauchamp. He appears first as an aged and lecherous coachman
who molests young maids and cooks, and who eats ice
cream with either spinach or turnip greens. Then in his
final metamorphosis he is an estimable symbol of human
courage.

WARREN: Total courage and dignity.

INT: This you have to pay something for, don't you? For a view
of the world that's that complicated. Is this something arrived at through taking a liberal stance, or is it a product of

what Henry James called "felt life," a wrestling with reality?

WARREN: Not long ago a very bright, well-informed lady was talking to me about some novels by southerners. She finally burst out: "Well, I think it's far too high a price to pay for good books to have people live like that, the way they live down there." That lady, I reckon, would "approve" of Lucas Beauchamp as heroic symbol—but I bet she'd stop that nonsense of eating ice cream and turnip greens mixed up and pinching the housegirl on the can.

INT: Turnip greens and ice cream and all, elements of stereotypes and individual complexity and ambiguousness, Lucas Beauchamp comes out as one of the most dignified men in the Faulkner gallery. This seems to me to be a question that has been confronted by most writers whether they know it or not—you start out with certain assumptions given you by the culture into which you're born, and——

WARREN: You're stuck with certain things. Either you can see them and appreciate them or you can't. By the way, Lucas reminds me of something. More than twenty years ago I spent part of a summer in a little town in Louisiana, and like a good number of the population, whiled away the afternoons by going to the local murder trials. One case involved an old Negro man who had shot a young Negro woman for talking meanness against his baby-girl daughter. He had shot the victim with both barrels of a twelve-gauge at a range of eight feet, while the victim was in a crap game. There were a dozen witnesses to the execution. Besides that he had sat for half an hour on a stump outside the door of the building where the crap game was going on, before he got down to business. He was waiting, because a friend had lost six dollars to the intended victim and had asked the old man to hold off till he had a chance to win it back. When the friend got the six dollars back, the old man went to work. He never denied what he had done. He explained it all very carefully, and why he had to do it. He loved his baby-girl daughter and there wasn't anything else he could do. Then he would plead "Not Guilty." But if he got tried and convicted—and they couldn't fail to convict—he would get death. If, however, he would plead guilty to manslaughter he could get off light. But he wouldn't do it. He said he wasn't guilty of anything. The whole town got involved in the thing. Well, they finally cracked him. He plead guilty and got off light. Everybody was glad, sure—they weren't stuck with something, they could feel good and pretty virtuous. But they felt bad, too. Something had been lost, something a lot of them could appreciate. I used to think I'd try to make a story of this. But I never did. It was too complete, too self-fulfilling, as fact. But to get back to the old man. It took him three days to crack, and when he cracked he was nothing. Now we don't approve of what he did—a status homicide the sociologists call it, and that is the worst sort of homicide, worse than homicide for gain, because status homicide is irrational, and you can't make sense of it, and it is the mark of a low order of society. But because status homicide is the mark of a low order of society, what are we to think about the old man's three-day struggle to keep his dignity? And are we to deny value to this dignity because of the way "they live down there?"

INT: You feel then that one of the great blocks of achieving serious fiction out of experience is a sort of self-righteousness, the assumption that you're on the right side, that you're without sin?

WARREN: Once you start illustrating virtue as such you had better stop writing fiction. Do something else, like Y work. Or join a committee. Your business as a writer is not to illustrate virtue but to show how a fellow may move toward it—or away from it.

INT: Malraux says somewhere in his essays that "one cannot reveal the mystery of human beings in the form of a plea for the defense."

WARREN: Or in the form of an indictment, either.

INT: What about the devil's advocate?

WARREN: He can have a role, he can be Jonathan Swift, or something.

INT: Well, back to what you call the "right-thinkers." I wonder what these people think, well, they confront a Negro, say, the symbol of the underdog, and he turns out to be a son-of-a-bitch. What do they do—hold a conference to decide how to treat him?

WARREN: They must sure have a problem.

INT: The same kind of people, they have to consult with themselves to determine if they can laugh at certain situations in which Negroes are involved. Like minstrel shows. A whole world of purely American humor got lost in that shuffle along with some good songs. Some American art forms have been lost for the same reason.

WARREN: It's just God-damned hard, you have to admit, though, to sort out things that are symbolically charged. Sometimes the symbolic charge is so heavy you have a hard time getting at the real value really there. You always can, I guess, if the context is right. But hell, a lot of people can't read a context.

INT: It's like the problem of Shylock in *The Merchant of Venice*.

WARREN: Yes, suppress the play because it might offend a Jew. Or *Oliver Twist*. Well, such symbolic charges just have to be reckoned with and taken on their own terms and in their historical perspective. As a matter of fact, such symbolic charges are present, in one degree or another, in all relationships. They're simply stepped up and specialized in certain historical and social situations. There are mighty few stories you can tell without offending somebody—without some implicit affront. The comic strip of *Li'l Abner*, for instance, must have made certain persons of what is called "Appalachian white" origin feel inferior and humiliated. There are degrees as well as difference in these things. Context is all. And a relatively pure heart. *Relatively* pure—for if you had a pure heart you wouldn't be in the bookwriting business in the first place. We're stuck with it in ourselves. What we can write about, if anything. What you can make articulate. What voices you have in your insides—and in your ear.

*Part Two*        *Fiction*

*Alvan S. Ryan*

# 3·Robert Penn Warren's *Night Rider:*
## The Nihilism of the Isolated
## Temperament

IN TAKING my subtitle from one of Mr. Morton Zabel's essays
on the fiction of Joseph Conrad, I want to suggest that the
similarity often noted between the themes of Conrad and Warren furnish a valuable clue to the interpretation of Warren's
first novel, *Night Rider.* The context of Zabel's phrase is his
essay on *The Nigger of the "Narcissus,"* one of Conrad's earliest
works. Zabel calls it "the work in which Conrad first defined the
central motives of his art" and finds in it several of "the primary conceptions that were to be developed and given their full
complexity of realization in his future novels." Similarly, *Night
Rider* can be said to define the central motives of Warren's art,
and I would add, too, that while the "full complexity of realization" found in Warren's later novels is not here, there is
nevertheless an impressive unity of structure, a concentration
and focus, that has its own artistic justification.

Zabel sees as central to *The Nigger of the "Narcissus":*

that drama of man's destiny which Conrad repeatedly emphasized:
the conflict between his isolation as an individual, the incom-
municable secrecy of the self which begins and ends in loneliness,
and his need to share his life with others, the force of that "solidarity" which Conrad insistently invoked as a human necessity, a
mode of salvation from the nihilism of the isolated temperament.
An "unavoidable solidarity," he called it, "the solidarity in mysterious origin, in toil, in joy, in hope, in uncertain fate, which binds
men to each other and all mankind to the visible world." [1]

---

1 *Craft and Character in Modern Fiction* (New York: 1957), p. 182.

I would call attention especially to the word "nihilism" in this
passage, because at least one critic (Norman Kelvin, in *College
English*, April 1957) has called Warren a "moral nihilist,"
whereas a careful reading of *Night Rider* shows that while the
protagonist's nihilistic attitude is of central importance, this attitude is not at all to be equated with the novelist's vision. As I
hope to show, the protagonist is torn by the conflict Zabel
speaks of, and attempts to escape from loneliness and isolation.
His failure is that he embraces a false solidarity, and, paradoxically, in so doing only increases his sense of isolation.

The theme of the novel is the search of the hero for self-
definition and self-knowledge. This is Warren's first treatment
of a theme that has freqently been pointed out as central to all
of his fiction. The hero's discovery, under the pressure of moral
choice and action, of what kind of man he is, of the terms
within which he can act, and of what fulfills or destroys his
search for meaning and significance, is the burden of the novel.
From the outset Mr. Percy Munn is set apart from the other
characters; he is always an isolated man. The theme is embodied
in the action of the novel in a powerfully ironic way, for the
action traces Munn's progressive discovery that in allying himself with political and economic association calling itself a
"Brotherhood" he discovers only his own emptiness in his relations with his mistress, Lucille Christian, and finally the very
basis of his sense of selfhood, the relation between his present
actions, his past, and a possible future, disintegrates completely.

What kind of man is Mr. Munn? The essential thing is
that he is a divided man who does not know himself and the
terms within which he can act. Yet he struggles toward this
knowledge and broods over his acts after they are committed. It
is, in fact, Munn's relentless self-scrutiny that makes him a
character of essential dignity, and gives to the novel much of its
impact. But his failure is due to a deep inner nihilism that is a
kind of darkness. Images of darkness, of night, or of loneliness
and isolation are associated with all of Munn's broodings, and
perhaps nowhere more effectively than in the symbolic image of
the grackles that opens Chapter 9:

One clear afternoon, as he walked down a quiet street between the
rows of dull-colored brick houses, the grackles came sweeping over

the roofs, not flying very high, and settled in the trees of a little park just ahead. He stopped stock-still, one hand on the iron fence in front of a narrow dooryard. Then, slowly, he walked on down the street, toward the little park where the grackles were. In the over-mastering loneliness of that moment, his whole life seemed to him nothing but vanity. His past seemed as valueless and as unstable as a puff of smoke, and his future meaningless, unless—and the thought was a flash, quickly dissipated—he might by some unnamable, single, heroic stroke discover the unifying fulfillment.[2]

His urge toward community with other men is counterpointed against this sense of isolation. What he does not learn until too late—yet, as I read the novel, he does at last learn it—is that the anarchic and immoral actions of the Association, however just the claim for a fair price for their tobacco crop, are only a travesty of the true search for community. The community or solidarity he wants is one that respects the individual human person and the imperatives of his sole self, not one that swallows up the individual in some absolute. Hence, as the action unfolds, Munn, far from being drawn closer to other men, is able only to give himself to the abstract idea of the Association of Growers of Dark Fired Tobacco, and his isolation is increased rather than diminished.

The opening incidents of the novel reveal an uncertainty in Mr. Munn that is immediately felt as having tragic possibilities. He is drawn into a leading role in the Association by a series of maneuvers which he momentarily resists, then gives in to. He is drawn in by the firm wills of other men, men like Mr. Christian and Senator Tolliver. He comes in to Bardsville for a meeting, but he does not want to be there; he resents the physical pressure, the pushing of the crowd to get out of the train, and we are soon aware that he gives way to a series of pressures, not of bodies but of wills, that are just as insistent. And the opening scene becomes an image of Munn's situation, of his essential isolation even when he is in the midst of men, and of his failure to define the way in which he would assert either his own identity, or his "solidarity," in Conrad's sense, with other men.

When Mr. Christian calls the first meeting of the Association, and asks Munn to come along, Munn at first protests, but

2 Robert Penn Warren, *Night Rider* (New York: Random House, 1939), p. 208. All quotations in this essay are from this edition.

on Mr. Christian's assurance that "it's not official or anything" (p. 12) he assents. (Mr. Christian's daughter Lucille has already made the first advances toward Munn that foreshadow her own way of manueuvering him.) Christian breaks down Munn's resistance by flattery. "You're a smart man, Perse . . ." (p. 12). Later, Christian uses the same tactics to persuade Munn to join him, Senator Tolliver, and Captain Todd at dinner. We now see the root of Munn's conflict in his musing on what he wants from life. He is attracted to a life deeply rooted in southern tradition, to a life of politics combined with the law and the management of his farm. Yet "if he desired anything of life, that thing was to be free, and himself" (p. 13). From the dinner he goes to the mass meeting, in which he has no intention of taking an active part. Yet he is ushered up to the platform, and in a state of bewilderment as to how he has been so deftly manipulated, he even makes a speech.

Later in his hotel room Munn thinks back on the speech and decides that "he had been drunk. . . . He felt cheated and betrayed" (p. 30). The two scenes suggest an undefined emptiness in Munn, even a readiness to be the prey of another's will. His passivity leads him away from the desire he had expressed "to be free and himself."

Munn takes a further step into the organization when he accepts membership on the board of directors of the tobacco growers' association. Yet here again he tries to refuse; and for months afterwards he speculates as to why he had not been firm in his refusal. "Mr. Munn's common sense, his logic, had conspired with his friends to force his acceptance. Such chances to get along didn't turn up every day to a young man of thirty. He had better grab it" (pp. 32–33). His response, however, is not this simple, but curiously ambivalent, for he also remembers months later—and the mood is precisely like the one that gripped him after his first speech—that in accepting "he felt unmanned and ashamed, as though an unsuspected weakness had betrayed him" (p. 33). When he tells his wife, May, that he has been named to the board, and she expresses pleasure at the news, he is disappointed at her response. Yet why should he expect her to detect the false impulse at the root of his acceptance if he could not define it himself? For Munn, there is defeat involved in his activities with the Association long before he has taken part in any violence. Even the rain on the roof over their heads at one of the meetings seems to beat on his mind, "dulling him, conquering him, and those other men, into a kind of immemorial passivity and acceptance" (p. 39).

It is a mark of Mr. Munn's inner division that another response, quite different, alternates with this one. He is frequently seized by a sense of exaltation and elation. As he watches farmers signing their names and joining the association, he experiences "the grip of an absolute, throbless pleasure in which he seemed poised out of himself and, as it were, out of time" (p. 37). He lives in a state of excitement although "poised on the brink of revelation"; his energy "seemed boundless" (p. 45). Why this elation comes to him he does not know, and when he tries to define it to his wife the words fail him. Here Warren touches on one of the deep moral issues involved in influence and persuasion, for Munn is not simply avid for power. On the contrary, it is usually his vision of some single person in his audience, his recognition of one man's significance as a man, that frees his tongue. It is this that he tries to tell his wife. But this sense of persons, which would have been Munn's salvation had he held onto it, is obscured by the clearer impulse toward power. Munn, in fact, is trying to define himself by his power over others. If he cannot see this himself, it is because of his infatuation. His elation comes from a sense of power over others, sense that he is influencing their wills—even as his own is being swayed. And in this elation he forgets, or fills temporarily, the loneliness and emptiness within him. He is unaware of the irony of his inner division, of the fact that the elation he feels as others join the Association is the same sense of power felt by those like Senator Tolliver and Mr. Christian, who are using him; while, if he feels that another part of his being is betrayed, he is yet unaware that he must also in his success be betraying others. How much these pragmatic conquests mean to Munn is clear on the night when he is unable to persuade anyone to join. "It had gone black out for him, as suddenly and as irrelevantly as the man's face above the lamp the instant the flame was extinguished. . . . At what moment could a man trust his feelings, his convictions?" (pp. 40–41)

The conflict of two selves in Munn is given dramatic form
by his relationship to two men, Captain Todd and Senator Tolliver, who represent the two paths open to him from the outset
of the action. The way which he rejects by a series of bad decisions is that of Todd, who has the "deep, inner certainty of
self" (p. 43) which Munn aspires to but lacks. Todd is firm in
his moral decisions. He is not an opportunist, and he will neither
abrogate nor abdicate his freedom of decision and his sense of
justice. Tolliver is the opportunist, the compromiser. His flattery
probes and finds Munn's weakness, which is his inability to
decide between his desire "to be free and himself" and his desire
for public acclaim and for a political career like Tolliver's, even
at the cost of compromise.

The scene early in the novel (Ch. 4), in which the members of the Association Board meet at Senator Tolliver's house,
shows Munn poised between Todd and Tolliver, and fatally
erring in his judgment of the latter. The bond linking Tolliver
and Munn is Munn's ambition. Just as Tolliver, as a young
lawyer, had been advised to enter politics, so Munn, himself a
lawyer and thirty years old, has been tempted against his better
judgment to accept a position on the board because it is too
good a chance to miss. Now the Senator's flattery further in-
fatuates Munn. When Tolliver introduces him as "my good
friend Percy Munn" and adds, "We'll have him in Congress
yet" (p. 93), Munn is pleased by the empty words and the hand
on his shoulder. His moral vision obscured by flattery, Munn
later sits at the meeting looking from the Senator to Captain
Todd, and decides that "he was a good man, the Senator, but
Captain Todd was a better. The best of the lot. But the Senator
was a good man" (p. 95).

In this same scene Munn's uncertainty is again shown by
his apologetic tone when he discusses with Captain Todd's son,
Benton, his own decision to begin law practice, not away from
home, as the young man decides to do, but in Bardsville. Perhaps, he says, it was a mistake. And when Benton compliments
him on his speech at the mass meeting, Munn dismisses it as
"an accident" and muses on "the accidents which were his
history" (p. 103).

Looking back on this crucial Christmas meeting, Munn

realizes that "he had been taken in" by Senator Tolliver. But it is important to notice that in spite of his frequent references to "accident" he does not call this accident. Only for a moment had he been struck by "the force of accident and change." "Later, he was to curse his blindness, his stupidity, and his vanity" (p. 113). He had not known himself, so how could he know the others? But this clear vision of his own weakness is after the event, and it does not govern his response to those of the same kind that follow. For when in early spring the association receives the rigged offers of several large buyers, Munn votes with Tolliver to accept them, though the vote is carried against acceptance. The Senator's subsequent resignation from the board and the discovery that he has been bought off are deeply disillusioning to Munn. Yet his response is ironically self-destructive, and a further evidence of Tolliver's role as his alter ego. Musing, on his return home, that Tolliver "was out to break what he had made" ("To destroy what you create —that was the power, the fullest manifestation. . . . The last vanity" [p. 126]), Munn purposely breaks the news to his wife in the most unsettling way possible. He realizes that he wants to make her suffer, yet he "enjoyed the moment, postponing consideration of the event, and of the judgment which, he knew, he would later bring to bear bitterly against himself" (p. 128).

Thenceforth Mr. Munn more and more gives himself to the "idea" of the Association, doing things he hates, yet doing them nonetheless. His awareness of his self-betrayal is shown by a whole pattern of incidents and images. He acts joylessly, reluctantly, often petulantly. He sullenly performs acts he does not believe in, and his inner division is made manifest in the physical revulsion of his own nerves and body. His nausea, his retching, and, after the lynching of Bunk Trevelyan, his vomiting show the price Munn is paying for his failure of moral will. Looking for a scapegoat, Munn comes to see in Tolliver the enemy on whom he would have revenge. His wife sees the change in him and though she senses its cause she no longer can reach him, while he knows that he is "destroying the promise of happiness" she had given him (p. 160).

With the formation of the Protective Brotherhood, farmers

who refuse to join are forced at gunpoint to scrape their own
plantbeds, and the violence of the night rider activities increases. Barn burnings and the dynamiting of warehouses are
followed by the retaliatory burning of houses. Here again, the
relation of Tolliver and Munn is developed through symbolic
incident and through the very structure of the novel. Tolliver,
now in the service of the buyers, makes a public address denouncing the night riders. Munn listens, and as he looks at the
"somewhat stooped, sallow" man on the baggage platform he
feels "the firmness of the hatred within himself" (p. 301), and
relishes it as something he can depend on and cling to and
cherish "as one fingers a token or a keepsake, which is nothing
in itself, but which means the reality of one's past, . . . the
fact of one's identity" (p. 302). Yet as Munn reflects on the
change in Tolliver from the day of the first rally, he realizes how
much he, too, has changed. "He hung poised on the brink of
that thought, as on the brink of blackness" (p. 302). (The
sentence echoes with an ironic change the earlier one, describing his feelings as he watched men joining the association, when
Munn felt "poised as on the brink of revelation.")

That same night the Senator's house, Monclair, is burned
to the ground, and Munn's place is next. This suggestion of the
intertwining of the fates of the two men foreshadows the final
confrontation between them. From the window of Mr. Munn's
office Dr. Ball, in Munn's absence, fires from Munn's rifle the
shot that kills Turpin, and the blame is placed on Munn. So
Munn, who is certain it was his bullet that killed Bunk Trevelyan, and who feels remorse at the death of Benton Todd, is
hunted now for a murder he did not commit. He flees and
hides out at the Proudfit farm, where he is visited by Lucille
Christian, who tells him of Senator Tolliver's advances toward
her. Her twice repeated "He's nothing" defines the emptiness
and the coldness of Munn himself, his betrayal of his own
nature in favor of "events" and abstract ideas. And it plants in
Munn the desire for final venegeance on Tolliver.

It takes Munn two days and two nights to reach the miser-
able house where the once lofty Senator now lies dying. Munn
enters the bedroom and stares across the footboard at his enemy.
Then he levels his revolver. But Tolliver's calm courage is

unnerving. Munn's words, "If I didn't kill you, you'd lie here, in this house, and be nothing . . . you were always nothing," bring the one reply from Tolliver that echoes Munn's subconscious knowledge. " 'Nothing,' the voice echoed questioningly. 'A man never knows what he is, Perse. You don't know what you are, Perse' " (p. 456).

Munn's resolve is gone. He sees now that to murder Tolliver would be a final act of self-destruction as well. The emptiness is in himself. The revolver slowly drops to his side, and Tolliver asks for a drink of water. Munn pours the water from a pitcher and hands the Senator the glass, but at this very moment the posse hunting for Munn approaches the house. Munn escapes out the rear door and heads for the woods, falling twice as he runs in the dark. He sees the form of a man "against the field and paler sky" and aims his revolver. But before shooting "he lifted his arm a little toward the paleness of the sky" (p. 460), and within this moment of hesitation and with this signal the shot is fired that kills him.

This final scene of the novel has been interpreted as suggesting that to the end Mr. Munn is without self-knowledge, that he remains a rider, as Eric Bentley has put it, "in the night of the spirit." Perhaps so. Yet if we return to the final paragraph of Chapter I, we see Warren using a device that Conrad uses in *Typhoon*, and that is the placing at the end of the initial chapter of a passage central to the entire theme. For the paradoxical relation between communion and isolation seems to me to be this theme. In the final scene of the opening chapter Munn stands at the window of his hotel room, looking down at the crowd milling around in the street near midnight. He remembers how he had spoken to them in the afternoon, and in retrospect the poise and exaltation he had felt now makes him feel cheated and betrayed. But then:

He recalled that that afternoon he had said something about what one man owed to another. One man was very much like another. He was like those men, one of them. Unbidden, warm and pulsing, that exaltation returned to him, more perfect than under the brilliant sun. . . . Involuntarily, he raised his arm as though to address a great multitude and tell them what he knew to be the truth." (p. 30)

One is tempted to say that this truth is the sense of communion, the sense of what one man owes another, but the very tone in which it is conveyed in this earlier passage of the novel shows that Munn does not really possess such a truth; rather, he knows it only in a confused and emotional way, and only momentarily. Throughout the novel this dimly recognized sense of true solidarity, while it troubles both Munn's proud isolation and his capitulations to a false solidarity, is always defeated. Yet in the final scene with Tolliver he recovers it, though the recovery comes too late. He realizes that to kill Tolliver would not make him "something," as he thought. He knows now that what he hates in Tolliver, his duplicity, his dependence on others for his existence, have their seeds in himself, and that in himself he must destroy them. Hence the importance of the single gesture of Munn's when he hands Tolliver the glass of water. It is significant, too, as indicating a momentary though unclear recognition of "solidarity," that the final gesture of the novel parallels the gesture in the passage just quoted from the first chapter. "But without thought—he did not know why—at the long instant before his finger drew the trigger to the guard and the blunt, frayed flame leaped from the muzzle, he had lifted his arm a little toward the paleness of the sky" (p. 460).

I interpret this gesture as symbolizing Munn's imperfect awareness of his predicament, not as an affirmative recognition. Returning to Zabel's comment on The Nigger of the "Narcissus," it is clear that in Night Rider there is no movement from "the nihilism of the isolated temperament" toward such a sense of solidarity as is expressed in the narrator's words of his shipmates on the "Narcissus"; "Haven't we, together and upon the immortal sea, wrung out a meaning from our sinful lives?" This is exactly what Munn has been unable to do. Nor does Munn, night rider that he is, ever win from his journey into the heart of darkness, or from his confrontation of his alter ego, the recognition and self-knowledge that Marlow returns with. It is rather the Jack Burden of All the King's Men who finally emerges from nihilism and isolation, to see the spider web image of Cass Mastern's diary as a symbol of what Conrad calls "the solidarity in mysterious origin, in toil, in joy, in hope, in uncertain fate, which binds men to each other and all mankind to the visible world." Yet *Night Rider* is a powerful dramatization of the efforts of a man deficient in self-knowledge to emerge from isolation into solidarity. His failure is that the solidarity he embraces is at its roots immoral and absolutist, a travesty of the true solidarity that begins with "the deep, inner certainty of self."

# 4·Self-Knowledge, The Pearl of Pus, and the Seventh Circle:

## *The Major Themes in* At Heaven's Gate

EVERY SOUL is valuable in God's sight, and the story of every soul is the story of its self-definition for good or evil, salvation or damnation. . . .

Each of us longs for full balance and responsibility in self-knowledge, in a recognition and harmonious acceptance of our destiny. Saints and sages may achieve that harmonious sense of destiny. . . . But we lesser and more fumbling mortals may find at least some intimation of it in the unfolding patterns, however modest, of our own effort toward knowledge.[1]

. . . the clammy, sad little foetus which is you way down in the dark which is you too lifts up its sad little face and its eyes are blind, and it shivers cold inside you for it doesn't want to know. . . . It wants to lie in the dark and not know, and be warm in its not-knowing. The end of man is knowledge, but there is one thing he can't know. He can't know whether knowledge will save him or kill him. . . .[2]

*At Heaven's Gate* is a major novel, and after *All the King's Men* is almost certainly Robert Penn Warren's most important work of fiction. Yet it has remained unknown and unexamined, even by those critics who are primarily interested in modern fiction. In part, this neglect can be traced to the unfortunate publishing history of the novel—until very recently, the uncut text was simply not available. Aside from its importance as a work of art, the novel is essential to any understanding of the total Warren canon. All the themes which appear in the

1 Robert Penn Warren, "Knowledge and the Image of Man." *Sewanee Review* LXII (Winter, 1955), pp. 182, 189–190.
2 Robert Penn Warren, *All the King's Men* (New York, 1946), pp. 11–12.

early work, and which reach their fullest treatment in *All the King's Men, World Enough and Time, Brother to Dragons,* and *Promises* can be found here in a fully developed, comprehensible form. The themes are various, and the approaches differ, but the focus is always the same: Man in relation to his cosmos, to good and evil, and to God.

In attempting to get at the major significance of the novel, we have the work of the pioneer critics, several crucial hints from Mr. Warren, and the benefit of Slim Sarrett's essay on tragedy which occurs in the text of the novel. In this essay are stated explicitly several of the themes and ideas which are of major importance: the "pearl of pus" is the metaphor for the inherent imperfection of any merely human achievement. This pus is secreted, or rather excreted, by the agony of human effort and striving, which must by the nature of things be imperfect when opposed to impossibly idealistic standards of perfection. Here too it is stated that the tragic flaw of the classic tragic hero is always defective or inadequate self-knowledge. In his own Introduction to the Modern Library edition of *All the King's Men,* Mr. Warren remarked that all the characters in *At Heaven's Gate* ". . . with some liberties of interpretation and extension, are violators of nature . . ." (iii); inhabitants of Dante's Seventh Circle. It will be remembered that in the same general classification with this circle are lumped together a grouping of sinners which seems heterogeneous and nonsystematic to the modern mind: suicides, usurers, sodomists, soothsayers, magicians, and diviners. Under the system of theology in Dante's own time, however, this grouping was entirely logical: all these sins are sins of violence: violence against man, against nature, or against God. Thus, all the characters in *At Heaven's Gate,* except for the two or three who represent the wholeness and harmonious development of humanity, are violators of nature.

*At Heaven's Gate* is a novel about monsters.

This is true because all the characters who are violators of nature have grown grotesquely overdeveloped and lopsided in some aspect of their humanity, and maimed and shrunken in others. The concept of evil that Mr. Warren is using is the medieval one of Dante's era: evil exists in the warping or excessiveness of something which under ordinary circumstances is good. One major means of progression in the novel is to show the struggle of the individual character to throw off his monstrosity and achieve wholeness, or in other cases to struggle consistently to become more of a monster. Bogan Murdock, the businessman hero, is the greatest monster in his absolute indifference to any human emotion and his total inability to live in any conceivable human relationship without perverting it and bending it to his own lust for power. His outward appearance is rich and gracious, almost like that of a Renaissance nobleman, but this glittering façade only conceals the emptiness within. It should be remembered that the source of Bogan's wealth and power is usury. In Dante's time, usury was considered a violation of the natural order of things. Man was ordained to earn his bread by the production of food or useful articles, or the performance of some real service. Allowing money (an abstraction) to propagate more money was monstrous, unnatural, and a very great sin entailing the gravest punishment both in this life and the next (*Inferno*, XI).

If, like Bogan, the various characters of the novel are violators of nature, then there must be some concept of nature for them to be in violation of. The subject matter of the novel being as realistic and frank as it is, some care must be taken to point out that Mr. Warren's concept of nature is not at all that of standard literary naturalism. While never disguising the apocalyptic horror of his scene, he is using the method, materials, and some of the techniques of naturalism while being concerned with something quite different. If naturalism were his point of view, his characters would be in violation of nothing, but would be rather in triumphant accord with deterministic-animalistic conceptions of behavior. Charles R. Anderson has stated that much of the power and tension of Mr. Warren's novels grows out of the opposition of two polar concepts: order and violence. Whenever the natural order of things is defied, destroyed, or ignored, violence has occurred, whatever form it may clothe itself in. The heavy concentration of violence in the work of Mr. Warren does not mean that he is creating the violence for its own sake. This merely reflects the extent to which order and decorum have been overturned in the disordered age we live in. Of course, the notion that violence is a bad procedure was not invented by Mr. Warren, but then no one ever supposed he was anything other than the most severe and rigid kind of classicist.

Thus, in the system of order which is implied and understood in Mr. Warren's writing, man knows to some extent what he is and what he must do. With this realization comes responsibility, the one factor which defines his humanity and thus requires him to become something more than an animal. Human beings have always known this; for twenty-five centuries or so they have been saying glibly "know thyself" and "nothing to excess." The sad part is that they so steadfastly refuse to act on such a basis. While still giving lip-service to such concepts, man is busily engaged in just those violations of nature which bring tragedy to himself, individually and to all. Mr. Warren's method in the novel is to set up major and minor examples of these violations and thus create the tensions which develop between the violations and their implied opposites. In the failure of human man, either individually or as symbolic of all men, to achieve these standards, we have the situation of genuine tragedy. In no era would the meeting of such imperatives be easy. In our own time, to save his own self, his own soul, Mr. Warren seems to be saying, mankind must steer a tortuous course beset with difficulties and traps on every side. ("Salvation has laid hid behind a dark bush," said Ashby Wyndham, "like a enemy man up to meanness and waitin for him was coming . . . Hit holds out hit's hand, and there ain't no saying what is in hit. A stickin-knife or a five-dollar bill.") Even as most of his fellow-creatures are falling with loud shrieks of joy into the pit of animalism on one side, the individual must himself avoid the airless vacuum of optimistic idealism on the other. The truth is that tragedy grows as often out of our own inordinate idealism as from the grasping intentional evil of others. We want so much to be more than we are (the sin of Lucifer), and we want to drag others upward with us. Perhaps the greatest sin is to insist that we already have perfection—surely this is the most certain form of the violation of nature.

So there is really only one great theme of discourse in the novel: the struggle of the individual soul to discover and establish who and what it is; to fix a definition that will stand up under any and all circumstances. All the other themes are minor ones that complement and help to state the major one. Man's particular problem in the major theme is the one that informs so much of great literature and philosophy, never better put than in the three words of Conrad's Stein: "How to be . . . How to be." Mankind has wrestled with this problem in various ways in various ages and cultures. In an age where Original Sin has been abolished by the unanimous vote of the community, the true artist is more or less compelled to work in parables and to use negative examples: to say what he can about "how to be" and what mankind should be largely by spelling out what his characters, who must be like ourselves and typical of the age, fail to become or do or live up to.

To have enough self-knowledge to know "how to be," the individual must know where he came from, why he is here, and have some idea where he is going. Most of the characters in *At Heaven's Gate* are violently wrong about where they want to go, violently evil in what they are doing, and violently trying to forget where they came from. Bogan Murdock is the center, the focal point around which the others attempt to define themselves. Like Oepidus, Macbeth, or Willie Stark, Bogan set out to claw his way to the top, to achieve Being in terms of pure power. Like Richard III, he began to use the emotions and feelings of others as levers to achieve his ends, and like Richard, acquired a taste for the gratifications to be found in the pure exercise of domination over the emotions of others. Like drunkenness or drugs, vicarious domination of others may be exhilarating for a time, but considered as an exercise of power, it produces no concrete accomplishment, but rather the opposite, a draining or weakening of the self. Greater and greater dosages are required to produce the effect. For all his glittering exterior, Bogan is one of Eliot's hollow men. On the surface he seems to embody every ideal of a vanished and more gracious age. Jerry Calhoun, on one occasion, muses on ". . . Bogan Murdock's face, strong, swarthy, shrewdly molded, blue-

eyed, aquiline, smiling with closely set white teeth. . . ." [3]
Rich, landed, influential; Bogan manipulates politics, finance,
and people. The symbol of this manipulation is his skillful
horsemanship, and a discussion of horsemanship as a means
of vicarious domination occurs on the first page of the book.
Unfailingly courteous, he is invariably polite to everyone: his
friends, his inferiors, Negroes, his seamier associates, and his
family. At one point, Sue Murdock is thinking: "'. . . He is
so polite; he is the politest man in the world. . . . it's just a
way of making people do things'" (p. 6).

This is his method of fulfilling himself. Only by bending
the will of others can he feel himself to be alive at all. With
certain exceptions, everyone is pulled by it: his wife, his daughter Sue, Jerry Calhoun, Private Porsum, business and political
cronies; thousands of stockholders. Only a few, for their own
reasons, do not allow themselves to be affected. Slim Sarrett,
the self-made intellectual, diagnoses the situation precisely:

"Insolence? . . . To a man like you, Mr. Murdock, accus-
tomed to the exercise of large and small tyrannies and gifted with
an extraordinary talent for self-deception, any truth comes as an
impertinence. You . . . represent to me the special disease of our
time, the abstract passion for power, a vanity springing from an
awareness of the emptiness and unreality of the self which can
only attempt to become real and human by the oppression of
people who manage to retain some shreds of reality and humanity."
(p. 250)

Murdock's violence is always within the sphere of the
spiritual; he never descends to physical violence. In a climactic
scene, when Private Porsum comes to Murdock's home to say
he is going to make public his own part in the criminal transactions of Bogan's financial and political empire, Bogan is
very angry. Mrs. Murdock seizes this opportunity to attempt to
force Bogan to commit an act of physical violence by falsely
accusing Porsum of having seduced her, and urging Bogan to
shoot him, saying she will lie to get Bogan off. But Bogan will
not pull the trigger, and his defeated wife retires again into her
hollow shell.

[3] Robert Penn Warren, *At Heaven's Gate* (New York: Harcourt, Brace,
1943), p. 22. All quotations in this paper are from this edition.

Not merely his marriage but every human relationship is corrupted to the furtherance of his financial manipulations. Even the land he donates to the state for a park to be named after his father is turned to advantage. He encourages the engagement of Sue to Jerry to further his own ends. He destroys the honesty of Private Porsum, the mountaineer war-hero; makes him a bank president and uses him to break a strike. As the book ends, government has been subverted; Porsum is dead; Jerry, who wanted Bogan as a father substitute, is in jail as a scapegoat for Bogan's crimes; and Bogan, who is exploiting the death of the murdered Sue to gain "a million dollars' worth of free publicity," cynically has himself photographed with the remaining members of his family in front of a large portrait of Andrew Jackson, meanwhile piously calling on the people of the state to have "courage."

It is Duckfoot Blake who has the ultimate comment. He has come to the jail to arrange bail for Jerry.

"God," Jerry uttered, "if they get him, if I could just see Bogan Murdock here."
Duckfoot shook his head. "No, it wouldn't mean much. Because Bogan Murdock ain't real. Bogan is a solar myth, he is a pixy, he is a poltergeist. Bogan Murdock is just a dream Bogan Murdock had, a great big wonderful dream. . . . When Bogan Murdock looks in the mirror, he don't see a thing." (p. 373)

It will be recalled that vampires and certain types of diabolical beings are unable to cast reflections in a mirror. To expand on the meaning of this symbolic emptiness, it is significant that in his status as usurer, an inhabitant of the Seventh Circle, Bogan's financial empire is largely a paper creation, feeding on timber, quarries, coal mines, and land. These are parts of nature itself, and thus symbolically more appropriate for him to prey on than, for instance, railroads or factories. He may be the hero of the novel after all. It may be that Mr. Warren has depicted full-blown the hero figure of the managerial age: the completely fulfilled nihilist consciously posing as the last Renaissance man.

Jerry Calhoun is the character most fundamentally seduced by Bogan. Like all forms of evil or nature violation, his fragmentation and lack of wholeness can grow only because that is what he wants most; because he does not want to cure himself. Using the various devices of time shift, Warren plots the career of Jerry Calhoun in great detail. He too is struggling very hard for self-definition, but in a totally mistaken direction. At every important crisis of his life he tries to communicate the way he feels to someone, but can only repeat to himself "I'm Jerry Calhoun . . . I'm Jerry Calhoun." Motherless from birth, all his life he has more or less despised his family: his vicious, snarling, crippled Uncle Lew, his blind and paralyzed great-aunt Ursula, and his decent but inept dirt-farmer father. An early governor of the state, a great-uncle of Jerry's, had built the large but now tumble-down old house Jerry had grown up in, but he does not want to define himself in terms of that past. He visualizes himself rather as the man who does not need the heritage of any past, not even the recent past; who is instead successful in worldly affairs, who uses the ancestral mansion, now beautifully repainted and improved, of course, but only as a backdrop to graceful living. Working his way through the university, he plays football well enough to be named All-American in his senior year. His first corruption occurs when he is willing to let a wealthy alumnus pay his expenses in joining a fraternity. Offered the alternative career of a shabby-genteel academic geologist, he does not hesitate to abandon it to join Murdock (the abandonment of nature for the world of paper finance).

Human enough to feel guilt, he is always planning to "do something" about the old home place and his father, but somehow it is never quite convenient. His attempt to define himself leads to a complete remolding in Bogan's image: in clothes, in speech, in attitudes. Even in becoming engaged to Sue (the major competitive activity among the junior members of Bogan's organization), he is able to congratulate himself that he did it without falling in love with her (noninvolvement in human emotion). Throughout the length of their tortured relationship, Sue realizes intuitively his unconscious drive toward noninvolvement. She sees this in his distaste for his Uncle Lew, Aunt Ursula, his father, Rosemary (a crippled university student), or anyone not "normal": that is, normal enough to want to be like Bogan Murdock, not too abnormal to realize that the ends of life lie in money, clothes, a powerful car, and an estate in the country. Sue tells him: " 'You'll die rich, Jerry. You've got what it takes.' 'But', she resumed, 'You're a cripple too. You're an emotional cripple' " (p. 99).

Subdued but constant throughout the book is the minor theme of contrast between the emptiness of Jerry and the humanity of the father he is trying to reject; between Mr. Calhoun's loving care of the crippled and helpless people who are his responsibility only by marriage, and Jerry's shuddering rejection of them.

Only at the end, in the shock of finding Sue murdered and himself in jail charged with crimes Bogan had assured him had never been committed, does he begin to wake to life again. Temporarily out on bail, brought home by his father, Jerry lies in his old bed in the cold night reviewing his life, fumbling, probing for the meaning, striving blindly toward self-analysis, self-definition. His hate has been turned toward Bogan, but his contempt for his father has not lessened. It will be a long process.

Sue Murdock is the Iphigenia of the story, in that she is murdered in the working out of her father's schemes for his own success. She also completely lacks self-definition, but where Jerry is struggling to avoid the painful process of defining himself, she is struggling to achieve it. Both fail. her method is intuitive rather than systematic, and inherently inadequate. She proceeds in the only way she knows: attempting to define herself in relation to others. Basically ignorant of the world, not exceptionally intelligent, largely the product of her father's money and influence, sought after by many for her money and her family's position, she is almost totally other-directed, but manages to hold on to a kind of basic honesty. Sometimes this honesty bursts out into disorder, as when she realizes Jerry fears her father more than he loves her, and she tries to force him to commit some action of defiance.

Her career is traced in terms of her relationship to four men, her attempts to define herself in the relationship and her eventual rejection, in turn, of all four. In order, they are her father, Jerry, Slim Sarrett, and Sweetie Sweetwater. Without resources to define or verbalize the feeling, she senses the ultimate evil in her father and decides that whatever else, she will refuse to remain a pawn for him. She leaves home. Realizing that Jerry is a pale carbon copy of her father and nothing more, she rejects him also, although she feels lost without him. Always intrigued by the self-sufficiency of Slim, she turns to him, because at the moment, he seems to have the most to tell her.

Walking beside her, speaking in his low, sure, vibrant voice, he told her she had to learn to be alone. . . . He told her she had to learn never to make up a picture of herself, never, never to do that, but to be what she was, that it was hard to do but she had to do it. and she thought wildly, *oh what am I?* (p. 155)

But she does not turn to Slim completely until after his encounter with her father. No one else had ever had the self-sufficiency to tell Bogan off before, and Slim expresses exactly what she had felt was evil about her father. She becomes Slim's mistress.

But Slim as an aid to self-definition is less than complete. Sue drifts in a kind of haze of nonanimation in the circle of persons around Slim, taking completely for granted Slim's own estimate of himself. That haze is shattered when Mr. Billie Constantidopeles appears on the scene. Within minutes it is demonstrated that Slim is an old friend of Billie's, a homosexual, and a complete and cosmic liar about himself and his past. Sue leaves the apartment with Sweetie Sweetwater.

Time is running out for Sue. The doctrine of self-knowledge that Sweetwater preaches is little different from that of Slim. She finds she is pregnant by Sweetwater. He wants the child but will not marry her. In an effort to force his hand she has an abortion, thus symbolically rejecting her last human relationship. While she is alone, recovering from the abortion, Slim Sarrett returns and strangles her. Warren's method of tension is powerfully demonstrated in this scene when Sue, sick and semidelirious, cannot drive out of her mind those images of the time when she was a very little girl, and had lost something or was lost herself, still loved her father, and had run to him. Just as this happens, her father slips his last letter to her under the door, urging her to go away. She has lost something, and she is lost herself, and she knows very well she is going

away: "Her mind slid slowly, then swoopingly, off into blackness, and she did not think or feel anything. Then she felt
that she was rising slowly to a surface, like a diver who has
gone down deep" (p 359).

In one of the key scenes in *All the King's Men*, Jack Burden
dives deep underwater to kiss Anne Stanton. He feels he would
like to stay there forever, if only he could. This represents the
wish to remain submerged below the level of conscious life,
to avoid everything unpleasant and difficult in human existence.
At this moment, on the borderline of consciousness in a far
more perilous situation, even in her violation of nature, Sue
achieves at last her self-definition by willing a return to conscious life.

Slim Sarrett and Sweetie Sweetwater are both idealists and
both are monsters. Slim's essay on tragedy defines a major
tension of the book, but he is a monster nevertheless. We see
him first in the holy poverty of scholarship. Like Sue's, our
first impression of him is that of complete honesty, an absolute
control of the self and the shaping of personal destiny. "One
thing for certain," thinks Sue, "he never claimed to do anything
he couldn't do" (p. 4). This impression deepens as he shows
his absolute disregard for Bogan Murdock. Then the fantastic
entity pops like a soap bubble. The perfected self of Slim
Sarrett is perfect not because it ever existed, but because it was
created by an act of will. Not content with the historical self
he had, Slim invented one more to his own liking. So long as
the world does not know this self is synthetic, the invented self
exists in its many-sided perfection. When that perfection is
exploded, Slim can respond only with violence; ultimately, by
murdering Sue and taking her money.

Sweetwater denies the past also, but in ways which, if less
illusory, lead just as certainly to violence and fatality. Scion
of a 300-year-old tidewater family, he has totally rejected every
association with his family and the past. He knew very well
who he was, but he knew, as Slim and Jerry did, that his past
history was what he wanted to get rid of. He gets rid of the
past not by pretending it never existed, but by constantly allud-
ing to it in order to repudiate it. In violence, in the war, in
his self-chosen status as underdog, he insists that he has earned

the right to his new freedom and self-definition. He has learned, as his father knew before him, that a man must believe in something beyond himself in order to believe in himself. He sees in his one belief, his Marxism, the answer to every problem. From this there follows the classic Marxist contention: he therefore has the right to remake the world. By this chain of reasoning he convinces himself he cannot marry Sue when he has made her pregnant. Marriage is a bourgeois trap, and would get in the way of his program for changing the world; it would flaw his image of himself. Sue might try to manage him, to run his life. "God, you're wonderful," Sue tells him . . . "you're just like my father, you want to run everybody and you dont give a damn for anybody, not anybody in the world, just yourself, just yourself" (p. 320). It is a terrible judgment, but a perfectly just one. In the purity of his devotion to a theoretical ideal, he has denied the one person in the world to whom he owes anything. He is a monster as lopsided as the rest.

The most purely abstract idealist in the novel is Ashby Wyndham, the Godstruck mountaineer. His story forms the alternate half of the diptychal arrangement of the chapters. By casting this part in the form of a dictated statement to the police, Mr. Warren is able to place it in the first person, giving it a kind of immediacy and force it would gain no other way. In tone and diction it is very different from the other chapters.

If there is a single figure who achieves a classic heroic stature in the novel, that figure is Ashby. His sin is pride, and his pride destroys one by one those he cares for: mother, brother, child, wife, friends, and disciples. In the beginning, his pride leads him into blasphemy, greed, lust, and physical violence. After his religious conversion, his spiritual pride, which he cannot realize *is* pride, leads him into consequences even more disastrous. When his infant son dies, Ashby has a vision in which the child explains that he died because he could not live on food bought with money Ashby took from his brother by violence. Determined now to do no other work except to speak God's word, Ashby drags his wife and an assortment of disciples with him down the river on a houseboat, until they come to the city which is the principal locale of the novel. Standing on street corners to preach the word of God, they

are often told by the police to move on. Eventually their
Christian resignation wears out, and in a scuffle with a policeman, the policeman is killed. Ashby is held as an accessory to
the crime. When Private Porsum, who is Ashby's cousin, comes
to get him out of jail, he will not go; he has just found some
sort of final self-definition which he must hold on to.

Read in isolation, as it can be in *Spearhead*, the New Directions anthology for 1947, the "Statement of Ashby Wyndham"
has a power and sweep in its own right as great as anything
Warren has ever done. It counterpoints and restates all the
themes of the book: the struggle of the individual soul to reach
a final understanding, to rid itself of the pus of impurity; the
damaging and destroying of human beings in the pure pursuit of the ideal; the abandonment of nature for the paper
symbols of usury, and violence against one's own family.

Ashby violates nature when he strikes his brother and
forces him to sell the mountain farm for paper money. It is
significant that he then goes to work for Murdock's timber
company, wastefully cutting and destroying nature for ma-
terialistic purposes. After his conversion, so long as he and
the others are on the houseboat in the middle of the river,
isolated from the world, their attempt to live by the purest
tenets of Christianity holds up very well; as soon as they descend
the gangplank into the Babylonic city they are arrested in a
public marketplace by the agents of Caesar (the police), and
the pure attempt fails. The policeman is actually shot by Pearl,
the ex-madam of a whorehouse, whom Ashby has converted.
In his essay on self-knowledge, Slim Sarrett spoke of the
"pearl of pus," the imperfection secreted by the efforts of humanity. Pearl is of course the human imperfection that Ashby
had not made allowance for.

Ashby is authentically tragic. Recognizing fully his own
responsibility for his sins, the full-blooded sins of a youthful
and vigorous man, he attempts to amend his life. Convinced of
the error of his ways, he takes others into the new way with
him, only to lead them to destruction in the end. His fall is
brought on by an excess of virtue too far pursued, yet that fall
is just, and obvious in its cause and effect. Like Private Porsum,
Ashby sees the pattern whole at the end and accepts it, achiev-

ing complete self-knowledge and self-revelation. To repeat Mr. Warren's words at the symposium:

the story of every soul is the story of its self-definition for good or evil, salvation or damnation. . . . Each of us longs for full balance and responsibility in self-knowledge, in a recognition and harmonious acceptance of our destiny. Saints and sages may achieve that harmonious sense of destiny. . . .

We lesser and more fumbling mortals, he went on to say, may have to settle for something less. "But a man don't know, nor was made to," says Ashby early in his statement. Saints will achieve the union with Godhead, but nowhere in his agonized journey does Ashby (or the author) seem to think that the effort, the attempt, the quest, should not have been made. This is the point. We cannot remain asleep or refuse to make the effort.

So far, this account of the moral message the novel has to offer has been summarized in almost purely negative terms. Flippantly stated, this account might be summed up as a series of magnificent examples of how to avoid self-knowledge. But the positive examples are there. Only two, perhaps, stand out: Mr. Calhoun and Duckfoot Blake. Mr. Calhoun does not have to think about self-definition because he has always had it, and never had any reason to reshape his pattern for a new one. He is complete in his humaneness, and his bumbling awkwardness and provincialism serve perhaps only to define that humanity.

Duckfoot represents the contemplative life as opposed to the life of moral action. He has achieved self-definition, at least to his own satisfaction, because he has already explored most of the avenues to it and out of his rich and varied experience had learned what to ignore. He is the comic hero of the novel, hiding his quixotic standards of courage and concern under a veneer of cynicism and world-weariness. He serves as chorus, commentator, definer, and yardstick of humanity. He clearly adumbrates the character of Jack Burden, and the great lesson that Jack had to learn: that the wish not to be involved, to remain submerged forever beneath the surface of conscious life is a form of spiritual death.

Duckfoot is content to warm himself in the gentle round of

his petty pleasures and minor vices; to revel a bit in the fullness of his freedom from folly and illusion, and to enjoy the pleasant experience of watching the folly of others from a safe distance. Under the pressures of the explosive climax of the novel: Sue murdered, Jerry in jail for Bogan's crimes, and the lynch mob clamoring for Bogan's Negro houseboy, who has been conveniently blamed for the murder, Duckfoot is shaken roughly into the wakefulness of moral commitment and action. He is with Jerry to arrange bail, and they are waiting for the bondsman to show up.

Unmoved, Jerry Calhoun said, in bitter satisfaction: "Well it don't matter."

"The hell it don't!" Duckfoot retorted ferociously, his voice rising and cracking like a boy's, his paper-thin, white nostrils twitching; "everything matters, and don't you say it don't! . . . you say it don't and I'll slap you, you fool. I'll slap the pee out of you . . . it matters you're a complete damned fool, a complete, thumb-sucking, self-pitying fool, and it matters you're here and that bastard Murdock is enjoying his bereavement in comfort. . . ." . . . he stood in the middle of the cell and the nostrils of his pointed nose worked in the middle of his high white slick face and he stretched his arm out toward the noise outside, which was terrifying now, and the coat sleeve slipped back off his long white blue-veined bony wrist and he shook his fist at whatever was out there beyond the walls, filling the square, coiling and curdling and swelling blackly under the buildings and the sky . . .

He knew that it mattered. Duckfoot Blake knew that everything mattered. He knew that everything he had ever done or said or thought mattered. He knew that all those years which had been full of his goings and comings and his loneliness and his pride and his pitiful pleasures mattered. He had never known it before, but he knew it now. (p. 372)

Like Jack Burden, Duckfoot has found the final piece in the jigsaw puzzle which is his knowledge of himself. Like Jack, he is at last prepared to "go into the convulsion of the world, out of history into history and the awful responsibility of Time."

# 5·All the King's Men:

## The Matrix of Experience

WHEN I AM ASKED how much *All the King's Men* owes to the actual politics of Louisiana in the '30's, I can only be sure that if I had never gone to live in Louisiana and if Huey Long had not existed, the novel would never have been written. But this is far from saying that my "state" in *All the King's Men* is Louisiana (or any of the other forty-nine stars in our flag), or that my Willie Stark is the late Senator. What Louisiana and Senator Long gave me was a line of thinking and feeling that did eventuate in the novel.

In the summer of 1934 I was offered a job—a much-needed job—as assistant professor at the Louisiana State University, in Baton Rouge. It was "Huey Long's University," and definitely on the make—with a sensational football team and with money to spend even for assistant professors at a time when assistant professors were being fired, not hired—as I knew all too well. It was Huey's University, but he, I was assured, would never mess with my classroom. That was to prove true; he was far too adept in the arts of power to care what an assistant professor might have to say. The only time that his presence was ever felt in my classroom was when, in my Shakespeare course, I gave my little annual lecture on the political background of *Julius Caesar*; and then, for the two weeks we spent on the play, backs grew straighter, eyes grew brighter, notes were taken, and the girls stopped knitting in class, or repairing their faces.

In September, 1934, I left Tennessee, where I had been living on a farm near Nashville, drove down across Mississippi, crossed the river by ferry (where I can't be sure—was it at Greenville?) and was in North Louisiana. Along the way I picked up a hitchhiker—a country man, the kind you call a red-neck or a wool-hat, aging, aimless, nondescript, beat up by life and hard times and bad luck, clearly tooth-broke and probably gut-shot, standing beside the road in an attitude that spoke of infinite patience and considerable fortitude, holding a parcel in his hand, wrapped in old newspaper and tied with binder twine, waiting for some car to come along. He was, though at the moment I did not sense it, a mythological figure.

He was the god on the battlement, dimly perceived above the darkling tumult and the steaming carnage of the political struggle. He was a voice, a portent, and a natural force like the Mississippi River getting set to bust a levee. Long before the Fascist March on Rome, Norman Douglas, meditating on Naples, had predicted that the fetid slums of Europe would make possible the "inspired idiot." His predictive diagnosis of the origins of fascism—and of communism—may be incomplete, but it is certain that the rutted back roads and slab-side shacks that had spawned my nameless old hitchhiker, with the twine-tied paper parcel in his hand, had, by that fall of 1934, made possible the rise of "Huey." My nameless hitchhiker was, mythologically speaking, Long's *sine qua non*.

So it was appropriate that he should tell me the first episode of the many I had to hear of the myth that was "Huey." The roads, he said, was shore better now. A man could git to market, he said. A man could jist git up and git, if'n a notion come on him. Did'n have to pay no toll at no toll bridge neither. Fer Huey was a free-bridge man. So he went on and told me how, standing on the river bank by a toll bridge (by what river and what bridge was never clear), Huey had made the president of the company that owned the bridge a good, fair cash offer, and the man laughed at him. But, the old hitchhiker said, Huey did'n do nothing but lean over and pick him up a chunk of rock and throwed it off a-ways, and asked did that president-feller see whar the rock hit. The feller said yeah, he seen. Wal, Huey said, the next thing you see is gonna be a big new free bridge right whar that rock hit, and you, you son-of-a-bitch, are goen bankrupt a-ready and doan even know it.

There were a thousand tales, over the years, and some of them were, no doubt, literally and factually true. But they were all true in the world of "Huey"—that world of myth, folklore, poetry, deprivation, rancor, and dimly envisaged hopes. That world had a strange, shifting, often ironical and sometimes irrelevant relation to the factual world of Senator Huey P. Long and his cold manipulation of the calculus of power. The two worlds, we may hazard, merged only at the moment when in September, 1935, in the corridor of the Capitol, the little .32 slug bit meanly into the senatorial vitals.

There was another world—this a factual world—made possible by the factual Long, though not inhabited by him. It was a world that I, as an assistant professor, was to catch fleeting glimpses of, and ponder. It was the world of the parasites of power, a world that Long was, apparently, contemptuous of, but knew how to use, as he knew how to use other things of which he was, perhaps, contemptuous. This was a world of a sick yearning for elegance and the sight of one's name on the society page of a New Orleans paper; it was the world of the electric moon devised, it was alleged, to cast a romantic glow over the garden when the president of the university and his wife entertained their politicos and pseudosocialites; it was a world of pretentiousness, of bloodcurdling struggles for academic preferment, of drool-jawed grab and arrogant criminality. It was a world all too suggestive, in its small-bore, provincial way, of the airs and aspirations that the newspapers attributed to that ex-champagne salesman Von Ribbentrop and to the inner circle of Edda Ciano's friends.

For in Louisiana, in the 1930's, you felt somehow that you were living in the great world, or at least in a microcosm with all the forces and fatalities faithfully, if sometimes comically, drawn to scale. And the little Baton Rouge world of campus and governor's mansion and capitol and the gold bathroom fixtures reported to be in the house of the university contractor was, once the weight of Long's contempt and political savvy had been removed by the bullet of the young Brutus in the Capitol, to plunge idiotically rampant to an end almost as dramatic as the scenes in the last bunkers of Berlin or at the filling station on the outskirts of Milan. The headlines advertised the suicides, and the population of penitentiaries, both federal and state, received some distinguished additions.

But this is getting ahead of the story. Meanwhile, there was, besides the lurid worlds, the world of ordinary life to look at. There were the people who ran stores or sold insurance or had a farm and tried to survive and pay their debts. There were —visible even from the new concrete speedway that Huey had slashed through the cypress swamps toward New Orleans—the palmetto-leaf and sheet-iron hovels of the moss pickers, rising like some fungoid growth from a hummock under the great cypress knees, surrounded by scum-green water that never felt sunlight, back in that Freudianly contorted cypress gloom of cottonmouth moccasins big as the biceps of a prizefighter, and owl calls, and the murderous metallic grind of insect life, and the smudge fire at the hovel door, that door being nothing but a hole in a hovel wall, with a piece of croker sack hung over it. There were, a few miles off at the university, your colleagues, some as torpid as a gorged alligator in the cold mud of January and some avid to lick the spit of an indifferent or corrupt administration, but many able and gifted and fired by a will to create, out of the seething stew and heaving magma, a distinguished university.

And there were, of course, the students, like students anywhere in the country in the big state universities, except for the extraordinary number of pretty girls and the preternatural blankness of the gladiators who were housed beneath the stadium to have their reflexes honed, their diet supervised, and—through the efforts of tutors—their heads crammed with just enough of whatever mash was required (I never found out) to get them past their minimal examinations. Among the students there sometimes appeared, too, that awkward boy from the depth of the 'Cajun country or from some scrabblefarm in North Louisiana, with burning ambition and frightening energy and a thirst for learning; and his presence there, you reminded yourself, with whatever complication of irony seemed necessary at the moment, was due to Huey, and to Huey alone. For the "better element" had done next to nothing in fifty years to get that boy out of the grim despair of his ignorance.

Yes, there was the world of the "good families," most of

whom hated Huey Long—except, of course, for that percentage who, for one reason or another, had reached an accommodation. They hated him sometimes for good reasons and sometimes for bad, and sometimes for no reason at all, as a mere revulsion of taste; but they never seemed to reflect on what I took to be the obvious fact that if the government of the state had not previously been marked by various combinations of sloth, complacency, incompetence, corruption, and a profound lack of political imagination, there would never have been a Senator Huey P. Long, and my old hitchhiker by the roadside would, in September, 1934, have had no tale to tell me.

Conversation in Louisiana always came back to the tales, to the myth, to politics; and to talk politics is to talk about power. So conversation turned, by implication at least, on the question of power and ethics, of power and justification, of means and ends, of "historical costs." The big words were not often used, certainly not by the tellers of tales, but the concepts lurked even behind the most ungrammatical folktale. The tales were shot through with philosophy.

The tales were shot through, too, with folk humor, and the ethical ambiguity of folk humor. And the tales, like the political conversations, were shot through, too, with violence—or rather, with hints of the possibility of violence. There was a hint of revolutionary desperation—often synthetically induced. In Louisiana, in '34 and '35, it took nothing to start a rumor of violence. There had been, you might hear, a "battle" at the airport of Baton Rouge. A young filling station operator would proudly display his sawed-off automatic shotgun—I forget which "side" he was on, but I remember his fingers caressing the polished walnut of the stock. Or you might hear that there was going to be a "march" on the Capitol—but not hear by whom or for what.

Melodrama was the breath of life. There had been melodrama in the life I had known in Tennessee, but with a difference: in Tennessee the melodrama seemed to be different from the stuff of life, something superimposed upon life, but in Louisiana people lived melodrama, seemed to live, in fact, for it, for this strange combination of philosophy, humor, and violence. Life was a tale that you happened to be living—and that "Huey" happened to be living before your eyes. And all the while I was reading Elizabethan tragedy, Machiavelli, William James, and American history—and all that I was reading seemed to come alive, in shadowy distortions and sudden clarities, in what I saw around me.

How directly did I try to transpose into fiction Huey P. Long and the tone of that world? The question answers itself in a single fact. The first version of my story was a verse drama; and the actual writing began, in 1938, in the shade of an olive tree by a wheat field near Perugia. In other words, if you are sitting under an olive tree in Umbria and are writing a verse drama, the chances are that you are concerned more with the myth than with the fact, more with the symbolic than with the actual. And so it was. It could not, after all, have been otherwise, for in the strict, literal sense, I had no idea what the now deceased Huey P. Long had been. What I knew was the "Huey" of the myth, and that was what I had taken with me to Mussolini's Italy, where the bully boys wore black shirts and gave a funny salute.

I had no way of knowing what went on in the privacy of the heart of Senator Long. Now I could only hope, ambitiously, to know something of the heart of the Governor Talos of my play *Proud Flesh*. For Talos was the first avatar of my Willie Stark, and the fact that I drew that name from the "iron groom" who, in murderous blankness, serves Justice in Spenser's *Faerie Queen* should indicate something of the line of thought and feeling that led up to that version and persisted, with modulations, into the novel.

Talos was to become Stark, and *Proud Flesh* was to become *All the King's Men*. Many things, some merely technical, led to this transformation, but one may have some bearing on the question of the ratio of fact and fiction. In 1942 I left Louisiana for good, and when in 1943 I began the version that is more realistic, discursive, and documentary in method (though not in spirit) than the play, I was doing so after I had definitely left Louisiana and the world in which the story had its roots. By now the literal, factual world was only a memory, and therefore was ready to be absorbed freely into the act of imagination. Even the old man by the roadside—the hitchhiker

I had picked up on the way down to take my job—was ready to enter the story: he became, it would seem, the old hitchhiker whom Jack Burden picks up returning from Long Beach, California, the old man with the twitch in the face that gives Jack the idea for the Great Twitch. But my old hitchhiker had had no twitch in his face. Nor had I been Jack Burden.

I had not been Jack Burden except insofar as you have to try to "be" whatever you are trying to create. And in that sense I was also Adam Stanton, and Willie Stark, and Sadie Burke, and Sugar Boy, and all the rest. And this brings me to my last notion. However important for my novel was the protracted dialectic between "Huey" on the one side, and me on the other, it was far less important, in the end, than that deeper and darker dialectic for which the images and actions of a novel are the only language. And however important was my acquaintance with Louisiana, that was far less important than my acquaintance with another country: for any novel, good or bad, must report, willy-nilly, the history, sociology, and politics of a country even more fantastic than was Louisiana under the consulship of Huey.

# 6·Melpomene as Wallflower; or, the Reading of Tragedy

EVERYBODY KNOWS that the eighteenth century marked, in English literature, the disappearance of tragedy and the rise of the novel. As neoclassicism set in, something happened to the tragic sense, a something which included the growth of the scientific attitude and the subtle adulteration of the Christian view of experience—in, for instance, the pressure of prudential upon transcendental values. There is a weakening of the grasp of man's inner contradictions and complexities upon which tragedy, and for that matter the highest comedy, depends. In its direction the novel was social, even sociological; its concern was less the troubled man than troubles between men—if it rose to a consideration of troubles at all—and between men who were whole and easily catalogued: Joneses, Allworthys, Brambles, Evelinas, Elizabeth Bennetts, Micawbers, Beckys, Grantleys, Patternes. For literature, the content of experience became stabilized at that level, and on that level some men of letters are still content to remain. But tragic experience, however much enlightenment we have, keeps stabbing at our imaginations: the novel, irregularly, tentatively, and yet with a kind of determination, has kept probing and thrusting toward the tragic awareness of life which drama has never recovered: half the history of English fiction is the quest for tragedy. George Eliot, overly condescended to now, begins to cut back into the inner man; the older Hardy goes further; James, Conrad, and Joyce lay hold of inner obscurities, parts that do not match; Faulkner seizes upon disruptive urgencies and intensities. Robert Penn Warren's *All the King's Men* adds a chapter to the history of the recovery of tragedy.

"Recovery" is probably the right word, for Elizabethan, and

possibly Greek, tragedy has made a mark on *All the King's Men*. Shakespeare won the pit, and this novel is a best seller, which is to say that there is a level of dramatic tension more widely accessible than one expects in the philosophic novel. The plot involves public figures, but the record is finally of the private agony (as with Macbeth and Oedipus). The author begins with history and politics, but the real subject is the nature of them: Warren is no more discussing American politics than *Hamlet* is discussing Danish politics. Then there are the chronic intra-family confrontations and injuries, the repercussions of genera-tion upon generation, as with Hamlet and Orestes—a type of situation which, it may be observed in passing, Aristotle praises. As with the older tragedy, all this can look like steaming melo-drama if one wants to stop at the deed as deed and simply forget about meanings. But as in the older poetic tragedy there is, beneath all the explicitnesses, a core of obscure conflicts, of motives partly clouded, of calculations beset by the uncalculated, of moral impasses in which both action and inaction may damn, and Oresteian duty be Oresteian guilt.

*All the King's Men* is the tragedy of incomplete personali-ties whose interrelationship is rooted, in part, in the impulse to completeness—in the "agony of will." Anne Stanton cannot find it in the uncertain, unfocused young Jack Burden, sardonic in a detachment closer to alienation than objectivity; by contrast the rude, better-directioned power of Willie Stark acts compel-lingly upon her. Dr. Adam Stanton, the man of idea, cut off, driving himself with ascetic, self-destructive violence, seeks, though apparently acting unwillingly, a liberating public deed which allies him with Willie Stark, the man of fact—the split between whom and himself, as symbolic modern characters, provides the explicit philosophic groundwork of the story. Jack Burden, the narrator, rootless, shrewd, speculative, but unin-tegrated, lacking, so to speak, a personality, gives his life an ap-pearance of personal form by his close attachment to Willie, who has cohesion and aim and a genius for the action that or-ganizes and excites—and that still calls up slow questions, ques-tions which Jack, in evidence of his never quite blotted out iota of grace, always keeps asking. Everybody's needs are ironically summed up in the grotesque gunman, Sugar Boy, the stutterer who loves Willie because Willie "can talk so good." Willie completes the others, whose need is a centering and a commitment; but Willie cannot complete himself. In a complex of polarities that are structurally important throughout the novel, Willie also seeks completion in them—an identification with idea and tradition, and with the asker of questions in whom he senses an entryway into a realm beyond facts. For in Willie, the man of fact, there is the paradox of action; action completes and yet is incomplete; action is necessary but is never pure; action begs to be undertaken but imposes its conditions. Adam cannot sufficiently accept the conditions of action, and Willie cannot sufficiently escape them. But if Willie cannot save himself from his gift, he can, as is needful in tragedy, understand himself; the man of action becomes the self-critic in action when, in every phase of the hospital drama, he actually, if not overtly, repudiates his working half-truths.

A plurality of heroes is one symbol of a riven world. There are in Warren's novel other partial men; there is especially Jack, whose story, he says, is Willie's story: he is the riven world which produces Willie and serves him and yet always keeps a last thin aloofness from him, and which through him comes to a possibly saving understanding—the note of hope, of spiritual discovery, which completes tragedy. Jack is a scarred Ancient Mariner telling what happened and what he learned; he stubbornly tells it in a style which recreates things as they were to him, without benefit of the exceptions he might not make in his maturity.

I have stressed Mr. Warren's belonging to the tragic tradition because his book has brought into focus a very distrubing situation—our sheer incompetence to read tragedy. A large number of critics have beaten Mr. Warren around the ears and cried that he should have written a political melodrama. He woos a long-neglected Melpomene, and is told he should be doing a carmagnole with an up-to-date Clio. He tries to give his readers the universal in the unique form which is the individual work of art, and they bawl at him for not sticking to social platitudes. He gives them metaphysics, and they call pettishly for sociology. Well, he does give them some social documentation, all right, but he gives it to them the hard way:

he pictures for them the spiritual condition—the decline of tradition, the loss of an integrating force, the kind of split—which results in Willie-as-hero; he makes it still harder for them by pointing out the kind of greatness Willie had to have to be to a society what he was. Warren says, I take it, that a universal complement has to be a little more than a melodrama villain. But they do not want understanding—because it involves the pain of self-scrutiny? They know in advance that Willie, insofar as he is Humpty, is a bad egg who ought to have had a fall; we should simply and happily hoot him. And feel ever so warm a glow inside. But we can get a warm glow from liquor or likker, and some prefer chemical analysis.

Most of the daily and weekly reviewers who tell America what to read still have the simplified view of *belles lettres* deriving from the eighteenth century. Of some two score of them whose reviews of *All the King's Men* I have been able to see, precisely two have a complete grasp of the work as tragedy: Henry Rago in *Commonweal* and Brainard Cheney in the Nashville *Banner*, both of whom do brilliant analyses. Four others come close: Victor Hamm in the Milwaukee *Journal*, Paul Engle in the Chicago *Tribune*, Granville Hicks in the *American Mercury*, and Lee Casey in the *Rocky Mountain News*. Surely these publication would not come to mind as the first six most likely sources of critical light in America. But by their diversity and distribution they establish the public intelligibility of Mr. Warren's novel; it is clearly not a work for club members only. Besides these six, about fourteen—in all, a little less than half of those I have seen—recognize that the novel is of philosophic dimensions. George Mayberry of the *New Republic* and James Wood of the *Saturday Review* read the book very intelligently; but the philosophic insight of others is often neither large nor secure. Most reviews are laudatory, some of them grudgingly, and others clearly uncertain why. The *Daily Oklahoman* headlines its review, "Nothing To Do But Like This Gay Old Cuss." From such a journalistic cradle, presumably typical, it is, paradoxically, not too far to the mature journeyman critics, a dozen or so of them, who provide the real problem for discussion. They are the ones who fear that Mr. Warren fails to show the dangers of dictatorship, or who outright accuse him of defending or aiding fascism. If these were all journalistic hillbillies, one could shed a tear for the darkness of the underbrush and forget it; but they furnish part of the candlepower of some of the stronger fluorescent lights in Megalopolis—the New York *Times, PM,* the *Nation,* and the papers that subscribe to John Cournos and Sterling North. Further, Fred Marsh of the *Herald Tribune* fails so completely to understand the book that he finally hypothesizes that it may be "intended only as melodrama in modern prose."

It would be easy to compile a florilegium of critical quaintnesses. Only two reviewers, for instance, indicate awareness that the management of the religious theme at the end is more than a pious postlude. The *New Yorker* and the Chicago *Sun* both regard Jack Burden as an interloper; *PM* and Sterling North regard the Cass Mastern episode, which is of high structural importance as an intrusion. Most of the commentators on style should go to Henry Rago of *Commonweal* for a lesson on the quality and functional role of the style. Of three reviewers who use the word *slick,* only Robert Gorham Davis of the *Times* adduces evidence—two sentences, both of which, he fails to realize, are indications of the attitude of Jack Burden; the second he particularly mistreats by lifting it, without explanation, from a bitterly ironic context. But what is one to think of reviewers' sense of style in general when he can find applied to Mr. Warren's writing two such beautifully irreconcilable judgments as those of Fred Marsh in the *Herald Tribune* and Laban C. Smith in the Chicago *Sun?* The former's words: "elaborately stylized prose (since nobody ever either talks or writes like this)." Mr. Smith's comment on figures of speech: "most of them very familiar if not trite, and the full development of these figures and their repetition frequently corrupts . . . a strong and intelligent style."

But the heart of the matter is this: why can so few critics read tragedy, and what are the implications of this disability of theirs? In the muddling over *All the King's Men* we can see several main tendencies, overlapping and not always properly distinguishable; perhaps they are all facets of a central cultural phenomenon. As a group the reviewers exhibit certain habits of mind that have been familiar since the eighteenth century—

habits which appeared as tragedy began to disappear and which, as long as they are general and uncorrected, are, without necessarily intending to be so, hostile to tragedy and to the insights made possible by the tragic sense. Perhaps the presence of these habits means simply the absence of the tragic habit of mind. Then the novelist faces the hard task of creating it for himself. The habits against which he will have to contend are the Puritanical, the sentimental, the scientific, the social-topical, and the lotos-eating or slothful.

The Puritanism that one finds in the reviews of *All the King's Men* is of the pale, literal, unhand-me-sir kind that, when Troy is falling, complains of, or even rises to a certain vice-squad petulance against, naughty words on the wall. Eunice Ross Perkins grieves, in the Macon *Telegraph*, that there is "no really fine" woman in the book and that Mr. Warren has not caught sight of the really very nice things in the South. The same obtuseness appears in two ecclesiastical organs, with which *Commonweal* is in encouraging contrast: Harold C. Gardiner in *America* abuses the book as blasphemous and immoral, and Daniel Poling in the *Christian Herald* regrets that Mr. Warren "goes into the gutter." Mr. Warren is trying to tell them about Troy, and they look for The Story of the Good Little Boy. A man's search for truth is too tough substance for these sentimental hand-me-downs from a simpler day. A cousin of theirs, Ethel Dexter of the Springfield *Republican*, wonders how women can really fall in love with such a fellow as Willie. These are familiar cries for familiar pluckings of the heartstrings. Give the cries a political twist, and they become demands for praise of reigning dogmas, and caveats against inquiry into underlying truths.

The scientific mind turns from esthetic problems to the provenience of the book, the man behind the book, the book's effect on society, etc.: a perverse factuality trespasses on the domain of the imagination. Certain reviewers cannot separate Willie Stark from Huey Long; some actually fear that Mr. Warren is not *biographically* accurate. Such minds cannot distinguish fact and fiction, the point of departure and the imaginative journey; they cannot realize that a few biographical facts are merely, and can be no more than, an alterable design for a mold into which the artist pours such dramatic body and such values as his insight permits. How can these people read Shakespeare? Some of them, self-consciously sharp, scream "special pleading"; Sterling North and Robert Davis consider the novel a personal apologia, an apologia, Davis says outright, for having edited *The Southern Review* at Louisiana State University. It may be remarked parenthetically that Mr. Davis's criterion, if applied with any sort of consistency at all, will deprive most universities of their faculties and most money-making periodicals of their reviewers. What is of critical interest, however, is not Mr. Davis's squinting detectivism, but the pseudoscientific, psychology-ridden cast of mind, with which he is obviously well satisfied, that makes it literally impossible for him to read and understand the literary evidence. He cannot tell what the story says; he simply cannot grasp the author's detachment and integrity.

This category of incompetence overlaps the next, where we find the science-and-society frame of mind. Historically, this kind of reader represents the main tradition of the English novel, which finds its tensions in social patterns, in problems of relationship in society rather than in the individual. But societies change, and with the evolutionary friction the social becomes the topical. To us, in our day, the social appears as the real, and atmospheric pressures tend to convince the writer that literature ought to be an adjunct of societal reordering. Now this concept, if taken as profoundly as possible, could accommodate high literature; Mr. Warren is concerned with society: his very subject is the split personality of an age. But the self-conscious practitioner of social consciousness does not want such radical investigations; he has already done the diagnosis, and all he wants is a literary pharmacist to make up the prescribed vitamin and sulfa pills.

The social-topical critics, bound by their inflexibly applied theory of literature, cannot read the individual work. But there are degrees of subtlety among them. Granville Hicks, as I have already said, gives so sensitive an account of *All the King's Men* that he does not belong with the table pounders at all—except for one small point: he notes Shaw's and Steffens' insistence on changing a corrupt society, and adds that Mr. Warren says nothing of socialism. That is all; yet it suggests that Mr. Hicks wants the novel to do something which is hardly in its province. But he holds to his dogma with such tact that he is not blinded to the goodness of what has been done. It is quite a step down, therefore, to Saxe Commins, who in the Cleveland *News* pays formal tribute to Mr. Warren's various skills but goes on to express regret for Mr. Warren's indifference to Negroes and "the people who should be the concern of the state." Mr. Commins' social concern is familiar: he wants a conventional conflict developed by standardized dramatic symbols; he wants the novelist to be a one-man pressure group instead of a man of tragic vision. So, dogma-bound, he gravely warns that the novel serves to glamorize the man in the "bullet-proof limousine" and thus to "invite disaster." Diana Trilling of the *Nation* imagines that Mr. Warren is defaming Hegel's relativism and hence gets things so out of focus that she perpetrates an extraordinary series of misreadings. She calls Jack Burden's Twitch theory "embarrassingly maudlin"—and completely misses Jack's repudiation of the theory. She says that Jack's "moral awareness" is of "low quality" and that he has a fine eye but "no equivalent gift of inward vision." She utterly misses his long search for truth, his reflectiveness, his later understanding of Cass Mastern, his insight into the Adam-Willie cleavage. What must a man do to exhibit vision? Declaim the Bill of Rights? Mrs. Trilling thinks the hospital is meant to establish Willie as a benefactor and that Mr. Warren approves of Willie because Willie is Jack's "hero." Even a strong commitment to liberal dogma seems hardly sufficient to explain, in a justly distinguished professional critic of fiction, such gross oversimplification of what a book says.

Dawn Powell gives the readers of *PM* little more than flippancies; but she closes with the warning that increasing regard for the strongman legend may be paving the way "for a really successful Willie Stark." Sterling North's purely literary comments are too geuinely stupid to warrent mention; what he lacks in insight he makes up in insolence and malevolence. But is he, in his political and moral judgments, really the honest barbarian he looks? Beats there a heart of gold below the red neck? Or is he the slicker in the backroom who knows what the customers want? Are there pleasant little pills in the innocent, downturned palm?

Diana Trilling, Dawn Powell, and Sterling North—a pretty bedful. And when we find the somewhat primly schoolmasterish Robert Davis's head on the same pillow—he assures us that Warren is playing Parson Weems to Huey's Washington—the picture has a wonderfully satisfying completeness. For what do they all do but pull the covers up over their heads and refuse to listen to the real warnings about the society they are so preciously and loudly concerned about? They have taken the symptom for the disease, and they want the symptom denounced; out, out, dark pimple. When an artist takes the symptom and traces it to radical causes—and when he even shows the kind of consciousness that nourishes the causes and with a severely disciplined hopefulness shows a possibly saving alteration in that consciousness—they mistake him for a germ carrier. The artist proceeds from the region to the civilization, and from the civilization to the dangers of disintegration implicit in human life; this is tragedy; but they cannot read it, and in their confusion they are as complacent as if they were protecting Humpty down there under the covers.

Before we turn out the light and tiptoe away from this dormitory and its fantasies, we need to note that, aside from missing what is in the book, Mr. Davis prescribes a formula for contemporary fiction: that "we fight men like Long with the utmost resolution . . . to preserve . . . free, open, pluralistic societies. . . ." One may doubt whether *Macbeth* would have been improved if it had been conceived as a recipe for the curtailment of royal abuses. Mr. Davis makes the old confusion of citizen and artist; but, what is far worse, he is apparently bent on imposing upon the artist a topicality, and a predetermined point of view, which must dull and destroy his insight. It is dangerous to read badly; but it is a terribly serious matter when an élite itself—I refer to most of the critics I have quoted—when this élite, as if moved by a devastating self-distrust, calls for easy propaganda in place of the difficulties of tragedy. It is easy to hate a villain; and it is usually the groundlings who want life reduced to a manageable melodrama. What if all artists give in?

In many of these readers of *All the King's Men* there is plain slothfulness—not as a personal vice but as public habit which appears to have grown since the eighteenth century, to have been nourished upon and in turn to have insisted upon, a relatively simple, one-dimensional literature. Not that there has not been difficult, complex, poetic writing; but it has been exceptional, and, until lately, rather much neglected. It is obviously not quite fair to pick Leo Kirschbaum of *Commentary* as the sole exemplar of the well-intentioned, easygoing readerhood, for he has tried not to be careless or casual, and has indeed worked hard at his assignment. But in him the moral becomes beautifully clear: as a sharp reader of Elizabethan tragedy, and as one who understands poetic values, he is precisely the person who ought to read *All the King's Men* with especial discernment. Yet his trouble is that, as a man of the long post-1700 age of prose, he somehow approaches the novel with a totally different set of assumptions—an approach which is tantamount to an abdication of his critical powers. As a modern work, the novel is going to be explicit, straightforward, resonantly in favor of the accepted goods, adapted to intelligent upper-middle-class sentiments, not too poetic, and with the philosophy, if any, prompting pretty audibly from the wings; and if the work draws its skeletal materials from modern history, it must stick faithfully to what we all know to be the truth about those materials. Now Dr. Kirschbaum would never read Shakespeare or Sophocles like that. He would unconsciously junk all these preconceptions and start with the text. But in his modern *acedia*—and perhaps it is the literary *acedia* of any age—he starts, alas without knowing it, with something else that the text is supposed to fit into. So he misses entirely the central theme—the split in modern consciousness; in Jack's unrelenting philosophical inquiry he finds only callow, even pathological insufficiency; and the complex attitude of Jack to Willie, which involves not only his being hypnotized by the genius of action, but also his sense of guilt and his paradoxical detachment and critical distance from Willie, Kirschbaum takes to be an "amoral and mystical approval of the American fascist Willie Stark."

It may be worth repeating, as we leave the reviewers, that

enough of them glimpse the novelist's intention to establish his
power of communication. Those who miss it are, in the main,
not at all dull; but by some habit of thought, some cast of
mind, which seems to come from the mental sets of the civilization, they are blocked off from seeing how the novel, as tragedy,
works. Mr. Warren treats them as independent minds, able to
slip away from societal apron strings. In fact, he never condescends to his readers; those who would read him aright will
have to work out careful patterns. It would have been easy to
supply a chorus indentifying Willie's half-truths as half-truths;
but Warren does it indirectly by having Willie in effect repudiate—his attitude to the hospital denies his formal relativism
—his own announced positions, and by having the implicit repudiation seen through the awareness of a Jack Burden who is
himself experimenting with concepts. Jack could have under-
lined his reservations about Willie, but we only see those reservations nibbling at the edges of an apparently whole-souled commitment. In the midst of strenuous muckraking Jack tells
Willie, "I'm not one of your scum, and I'm still grinning when
I please," and thus we see both the split in Jack and the withheld area of self which differentiates him from the Duffeys and
Larsons. The split in Jack—that is, the split in an age—finds a
symbol in half-truths, with which the difficulty is precisely that
are partly true. While striving toward a whole, Jack veers from
half to half. In early years he is inactive, his personality is dif-
fuse and amorphous. There is no imperative in either tradition
or work; as a lover he ends—this is one of the most delicately
managed episodes—in a hesitation which is in origin an echo of
an old honor, thinned out now into a wavering sentiment, and
which is in effect a negation. What Anne does not find in
Jack she finds in Willie; what Jack does not find in himself he
finds in Willie—resolution. But, riding on another man's activeness, Jack the doer is never free of Jack the self-critic; he
justifies by half-truths, but: he also accepts half-truths uttered
in judgment. The photographer says, ". . . you work for Stark
and you call somebody a son-of-a-bitch." He is half right, half
wrong, Jack thinks, "and in the end that is what paralyzes
you." Now the sense of paralysis is ironically a symbol of re-
orientation: Jack is trying to make his action and his idea cohere

—a private parallel to his outward act of bringing Adam and Willie together. But the still more embracing irony, the irony which is all the preachment for which anybody could wish lies in Willie's relation to his half-truth world. For his dubiety of his official philosophy is activated too late. For him the half-truth of acting according to the facts has been a whole truth; of the paralysis of others he is born; from the start he is always shown acting; and in turn all the spirit, the essence of action has somehow formed young Tom Stark. What is the end of Tom Stark? In the hospital bed he lies *paralyzed*—a fine climax to the counterpoint of kinesis and paralysis and a symbol of Willie's real failure. Willie, as Jack says, "could not tell his greatness from ungreatness and so mixed them together that what was adulterated was lost."

Who would read the book aright, we have said, must find the patterns. Jack, searching for a past, kills his father; Willie, searching for a future, may be said to kill his son. What Willie learns, there is not enough life left to define wholly; it is Lucy who seizes, in a quiet irony, the instrument of continuity into the future. Jack finds a truth, a basis for values, a faith. All this is part of a very complex theme of past-and-future, a theme which is really another way of presenting the split in the world. Here the split is defined chronologically; the separation of fact and idea is also man's separation from his roots, a separation which appeared extensively in *At Heaven's Gate* and which appears intensively here. Jack's separation from the past is so extreme that at first he cannot understand Cass Mastern's acute sense of moral responsibility; the essence of his inner development in his coming to terms with the past, knowing the reality of guilt, and learning, with Cass, that "the world is all of one piece." There is a skillfully managed irony in the ambivalence of the past: when it is no longer a nourishing tradition, it is a terrifying skeleton: *the* past is gone, and each man has only *a* past that he can be coerced with. The skeleton, the sterilizing past, is all that Willie professes to believe in (even while being drawn to the Burdens, who represent traditions, the fertilizing past): Jack digs up each man's past and discovers *the* past; from case histories he progresses to the meaning of history. He moves away from his old misvaluation of the past, of which the two faces are cynicism and sentimentality. ". . . we can keep the past only by having the future, for they are forever tied together." ". . . only out of the past can you make the future." Faith is proved by deed, and fruitful deed comes only out of the long wisdom. He is, at last, prepared to face history, to enter "the awful responsibilty of Time."

Shift a few pieces on the board, and the history theme becomes the knowledge theme, which can be traced from episode to episode and from reflection to reflection. "Life is Motion toward Knowledge," Jack argues. Willie's career is a progression in self-knowledge, and Jack's is a passion for knowledge that leads from factual to moral awareness. ". . . all knowledge that is worth anything is maybe paid for by blood." Jack's self-criticism is important here—the innumerable passages in which he catches himself at lying, or self-deception, or histrionics; or understands his feeling that Duffy "had . . . like a brother winked at me. . . ." Or shift a few pieces again, and the action theme becomes a study of participation and withdrawal, with its echoes in Jack and Adam and Hugh Miller, and the conclusion to which it leads, that there are no perfect choices: ". . . there is always a price to make a choice." In one sense the body of the work is the regeneration theme: the variations range from a prefrontal-lobotomy to the Scholarly Attorney's efforts with "unfortunates" to the acquisition of new insights by Cass Mastern and Jack Burden.

As the consciousness of an age, Jack also embodies its philosophic searchings. Jack appears first as an idealist, and there is a nice implied contrast between his version of Platonism, which rationalizes away responsibility, and Adam's, which takes insufficient account of the facts. Then Jack plunges into pragmatism, but it is a drug and never a very efficient one; under the pressure of pain he falls into mechanism—the Twitch theory. But eventually he rejects the world as idea, the world as act, and the world as mechanism; these are the half-truths of a disintegrating order. What he envisages is a saving union of the idealist and pragmatist impulses of modern man; while the brillance of Willie is his executive mastery of fact, his greatness, in which the others "must" believe—the margin between him and the ordinary political operator—in his emergent awareness of the inadequacy of fact. If they cannot believe in that, there is nothing left; but they can believe, for tragedy reaffirms the whole truth which measures the failure of the incomplete man. Humpty is Willie and he is also Jack—that is, the man who has broken into parts. Nor will men and horses, human intention and mere animal strength, reunify man. That is, reintegration transcends the secular; Jack moves, at the end, toward the deepest possible grounding of his world view, a grounding in theological terms. He assents, "in his own way," quasicommittally, to a metaphysic which accommodates evil, not to despair, but to define salvation. The reader recalls the earlier words of the Scholarly Attorney, "God is Fullness by Being." Humpty is partialness. The fall in the old rhyme becomes a version of his Fall.

Some such matters the critics may reasonably be expected to see. Let it be said, if it need be said, that no one expects them to see more than the evidence. They need not like the evidence—a situation which as we all know, *non est disputandum*; they need not consider the evidence sufficient to prove what the author wants proved. For various reasons they may not like the author's looks. If they think him unhandsome, that's their privilege; but, it may be repeated, they are wholly obliged to take a good, long, direct look at him instead of using one of those hasty city-street snapshots at twenty-five cents a peep. What contests he will win will appear in time. But those who have looked close enough to realize the intellectual and imaginative richness will know that they have been at least in the neighborhood of greatness. There is room, perhaps, for further coalescence of the gifts that appear brilliantly in, for instance, the vitality of Willie, the ironic commentary of Jack, the Jack-Anne idyl and the weak spot where it is breached, the bursting fullness of image, the reflective probing. For the present reader there is room, still, for some reproportioning and for some filling out, with the logic of feeling and motive and the immediate concretenesses of man in action, of the immensely moving symbolic paradigms whose rightness carries one into wholeness of admiration and into all but wholeness of assent.

# 7 · Tangled Web

IN *World Enough and Time* Robert Penn Warren again tackles the theme which was the core of *All the King's Men*—the failure of a private, subjective "ideal" realm to come to terms with, to be integrated with, to be married to a realm of public life and activity, the realm of politics and society and group action, of law and justice. Warren's fourth novel is less neat than his third (not that neatness was a prime virtue of it), in the sense that *Hamlet* is less neat than *Othello*: it is longer, and its length springs from a mind that overflows with its observings and recordings, and is relentless in its questionings and questings; the seams are strained by a redundance of plot; by the piercing, tireless images of outer and inner life; by the figures that qualify and communicate so substantially as to belie the initial innocence, or justify the initial shock, of the words; by the bursting intellectual action, the tracking down of motives, the search through the labyrinth of personality, the formulation and reformulation of meaning, the alternate embrace and rejection of theory which are the coordinates of moral and philosophic growth. Here is enfolded enough of the world and of time— enough for the young protagonists to come to the borders of self-knowledge, enough for the reader who would fix a little more clearly the outlines of the world and of self, enough to make an adequate definition of this work depend upon a great deal of studious re-reading by many critical readers.

The immediate world is Kentucky and the time is the first quarter of the nineteenth century: Warren sticks to the central method of his other three novels, digging up a pretty well-preserved skeleton of action from recent history, covering it with the flesh of imaginatively conceived story, and giving it the life of human (suprahistorical) meaning. Such a literary anthropologist always runs the risk of a tap on the head from some errand boy of science whose chief punch is: has he tampered with the facts? Of course he has. And only by doing so does he extend his anthropology beyond a museum operation and make it a proper study of man for mankind. Literary anthropologists have for a number of years been very active in Americana, and their recreation and transmutation of various American pasts may be understood as an aspect of the development of an imaginative self-consciousness, of a feeling and yet critical awareness, the achievement of which might well let the artist reflect on his share in the forging of the uncreated conscience of his race. This throwing of a certain coloring of the imagination over the ordinary—and extraordinary—things of the past, however, may minister to different kinds of consciousness. The past itself may be used only as a new veneer for stock literary sideshows ("entertainment literature"). The past may be used merely to create a sense of the past (the standard "historical novel"). The past may be used only to create a sense of the present (the historical allegory). Or the past may be used to create a sense of both past and present, or of realities that are neither past nor present because they are both. This is the field in which Warren works brilliantly, though to the puzzlement and disappointment of all those whose expectancies have been nourished in fields one, two, or three. (Even among the professionals: read a review by an established historical novelist, and see the anguish seeping through; or one by a semiliterary slickster, and see what he sees—only an I-push-over-easy wink to Hollywood.) But if Warren's past is Everytime, there is no woozy timelessness or lack of ubiety in the drama; documentation is heavy. The dates are all there and can be checked in the record; the geography is meticulous, and can be checked on driving maps; many characters are given full biographies, and at least some may be checked in *DAB*. But calendars, court transcripts, diaries, maps, *DAB*, and all that take us only to the threshold of the work.

The narrative organization of the theme, despite the

kinship between the two books, is quite different from that of
*All the King's Men;* the earlier book uses a narrator, Jack
Burden, who tells of tragically separated men of ideas and men
of action and of his involvement with both, who duplicates
within himself the split in society, and whose failure of understanding, until almost the end, is a major source of tension.
In *World Enough and Time* the author tells directly the story
of the conflict between Jeremiah Beaumont and the world in
which he lives (his friend Wilkie Barron; his once-mentor,
Cassius Fort, whom he murders; and all the private interests
and social and legal forces arrayed against him); then he uses
Jeremiah's journal as a means of comment on Jerry's intentions
and actions; and finally comments himself on both action and
journal. Thus we have not only a level of action, which itself
is very complicated but two levels of comment. Since Jeremiah
is made not only as articulate as Jack Burden but also, if no
more wise, at least a more conscious searcher of motives and
meanings, the element of reflection and inquiry is larger in the
present novel. Jerry's frantic philosophic quest, which ranges
from self-deception through various tentatively held views to
new insight, rarely ceases. Yet at times it covers pretty well-worn
ground so that, despite its intensity, it can let the story down
into a stasis; and the tireless repetition of questions can become
actually nagging. But the total effect is one of a manically
exhaustive ripping apart of excuses, justifications, defenses, ruses,
consolations; of a furious burrowing into ever-deeper layers of
self-understanding until almost every clarity becomes a puzzle
and every dependability a delusion. Characters who end their
search for an author in Mr. Warren's fold come under a hard-
bitten taskmaster, who has an indefatigable eye for subterfuge,
for the empty heroic, the phony benevolence, the slippery
self-seeking, the concealed or direct malignity, the impulse
to wound or sell or kill. Yet it is important to distinguish this
deep-lying suspicion, this embracing skepticism, from a me-
chanically, doctrinally hard-boiled way of looking at things; it is
the difference between the maturely sensitive and the half-
grown sentimental. Wisdom has its affirmations and its nega-
tions; here is the negative side of wisdom. The flaws and failures
of men are wonderfully dramatized, and they are in every sense

right; but the small acquisitions of joy or honor skim by thinly. Let us by no means undervalue the awareness of Lilliputian chicanery and Yahoo savagery; without them, narrative can't get beyond polite reassurance and good clean fun. And let us also keep in mind that, if affirmations are of the threshold, tentative, acquiring somewhat less of dramatic conviction than the weaknesses, trickeries, malevolences so watchfully described, in our day the wisdom of negation seems almost the limit of the possible, at least for the man in the world who will not live by cliché and slogan.

Self-discovery is not an autonomous process, with the materials yielding up their own prinicples of definition; rather it is the application to the self of the best available categories of meaning and value. The basic categories in *World Enough and Time* are "world" and "idea," which, as we have said, are clearly related to the governing concepts of *All the King's Men* but which certainly aim at a larger inclusiveness and are intended to put a finger on basic human motives. Viewed neutrally, "the world" is simply the forum, the marketplace, the scene of public activity; viewed ideally, it is the realm of the cooperative search for justice; viewed in terms of the dominant facts, it is expediency, opportunism, flux-worship, deriving principles from polls (private, unwritten, but none the less taken), spotting the winner. This is the inevitable degenerate form of the cooperative principle: cooperation unideally—without the "idea"—is getting on with, and getting on with easily sinks into getting on, and getting on into getting. Warren gives due play to all the potentialities of the world: at his trial for murder, Jerry is defended by two attorneys of radically opposed political parties, emblems respectively of "worldly decency" and "unworldly truth"; and Cassius Fort, Jerry's victim, who like the lawyers lives and acts in the world and who has a due share of "human weakness," is apparently actuated by political conviction. But the chief figure in the world is Wilkie Barron (of whom we have already seen something in Bogan Murdock of *At Heaven's Gate*), Jerry's friend and his Iago, the Mr. Worldly Wiseman of the tale, who never backs the wrong horse, fails to make the proper gesture, or falls into an unprofitable passion (like the too-successful sea captain in *Lord Jim*, he finally commits suicide in midcareer). Among the men of the world, he must be the principal actor for us of the twentieth century, whose "every effort is to live in the world, to accept its explanations, to do nothing gratuitously." Finally, beyond club-man-competitor Wilkie in the range of worldlings are the lesser and leaner fry of vote sellers, perjurors, and cutthroats—the success-boys with the make-up rubbed off.

Since for a novelist of Warren's stature the world is not big enough game, the book naturally belongs to Jerry Beaumont —to "idea." If one were a good positivist, he would scorn the idea; if one were a sentimentalist, he might present it as high nobility in itself; if a Platonist, he would define it as reality. Instead of doing any of these things. Warren is writing a tragedy of the idea—to paraphrase Hardy, "a tragedy of the unfulfilled idea." Jerry early discovered, he thought, "the vanity of the world" and yearned to "live in the pure idea." This was enough; he could renounce the world—retire from a legal career and create a private idyl (by taking up the cause of, and eventually falling in love with, a girl he doesn't know, Rachel Jordan—so excellent a symbol of both capacity for devotion and a fanciful separation from reality that one is loathe to question the event and the way of its being brought about). But the idyl itself led back to the world, and Jerry found his unworldly motives mixed with worldly; so we find him trying to compel the world to "redeem" the idea (murdering Rachel's seducer, Cassius Fort, whom he had made into a symbol of the world; and by deceit striving to have the world, through its courts, declare him "not guilty" and therefore acknowledge the innocence of his idea turned into act). After the inevitable failure of this project, Jerry falls entirely into the world, accepting both a jailbreak appropriately engineered by Wilkie (for his own purposes) and a drunken and lecherous sanctuary among Yahoos in a wretched junk-strewn swamp controlled by an aged scoundrel whose last vocation in treachery was piracy on the rivers ("the blank cup of nature," Jerry calls it. Murder, said the pirate, c'est naturel—that happy phrase by which today we beatify so many cravings and indolences. There is a reminiscence of Edmund's appeal to nature in *Lear*. The episode is a biting parody of romantic naturalism, of innocence secured in

Arcadia). In Jerry's view there has been a necessary evolution from the first of these stages to the third.

The story has another representative of the "dialectic" of the idea—Percival Skrogg, a tubercular father hater who pursues "the Justice in my own mind" by various means from demagogic journalism to political trickery and inordinately successful dueling—a killer who is eventually assassinated. But for years he had lived in fear, which in part superseded the "idea" and allied him to the "world."

What, then, is the "idea"? If I read the novel aright, Warren accords to the idea the same breadth of treatment which he gives to the world. In one light it is aspiration, the sought nobility, the good dreamed of, the felt ideal of justice, the uncontaminated and holy thing. Rachel and Jerry read Plato, and Jerry once (from his accomplished murder) rides home in the style of a knight of chivalry. But the idea is held in the private mind, and it can become a purely private reality; yet it seems, in virtue of its withdrawn purity, able to claim general fealty and public obeisance. The idea becomes the *idée fixe*, the love of right the sense of rightness. Impulse and uncriticized motive creep into the idea. It becomes will, drive, the compulsive personality, the doctrine without deviation or qualification, the end which claims all means. It becomes mania. It tries to compel history. Opposite, the Wilkie Barrons are only trying to ride history's coattails. One gives too little (to time, to humanity, to the world), the other too much.

If this sounds pretty simple, the narrative mass from which it is extracted is not simple. There are all the inner complications of Rachel and Jerry, in whom the author has discovered an extraordinary range of impulses; there are the fairly complete histories of various supporting characters (Jerry's and Rachel's parents, various politicians, the crooked lawyer Suggs Lancaster, Cadeau the pirate): there is the incalculable interweaving of private life with the public issue of Relief vs. Anti-Relief, New Court vs. Old Court; the immense detail of plotting and executing murder, of a trial in which state witnesses cross up each other and the prosecutor, and the defendant tries by suborning perjury to outsmart both the false witnesses and his devoted attorneys; of the slow unraveling of machinations and mixed

motives and psychological and political maneuverings (a mass
of ingredients best held together in the second half of the
book, where the movement is far more sure and the action
yields less to the impedimenta of explanation and discussion
which have not fully surrendered to, or been forced into, the
narrative stream). But above all this, the interrelationship of
the parts is such as to yield an immense suggestivity of meaning;
there is a confluence of diverse motifs and patterns; there are
imaginative extensions, constant examples of what Richards
calls felt depth and recession. The story can be read in the
light of various ways of organizing experience. Cut out enough,
and the rest goes neatly in psychoanalytic terms: the condi-
tioning "trauma" in the lives of Jerry, Rachel, and Skrogg (only
in Wilkie the worldling is adjustment hereditary, so to speak),
the religion-sex short-circuit in Jerry's life, the father-murder
pattern in Jerry and Skrogg, the various scenes in Jerry's life
where the return-to-the-womb is hinted (a tip to the alphabetic
analyst: look at the series of demonic and questing characters
in Warren's books—Jasper Beaumont, Jerry Beaumont, Jack
Burden, John Brown. Surely, by a brief flight at anagrams, that
obsessive *JB* must be convertible into something or someone).
Cut out enough other parts, and the rest can go as a study of
the relationship between a man and a woman, especially of the
man's unwittingly forcing upon the woman a role which min-
isters to needs of his not clearly understood; a kind of study
which makes possible the author's most complex and most
generally successful portrayal of a woman. A more inclusive
approach: through the traditional situations into which the
story falls. For instance, the tragic mechanism of the family
curse operates for both Jerry and Rachel, each of whom in
some way duplicates a parental bias or flaw and so increases his
burden of self-discovery. Again, Jerry plays Othello to Wilkie's
Iago, in a variety of situations. More markedly, Jerry is Hamlet,
the student, the questioner, plotting a revenge (in discoursing
on which the author uses as his text "What's he to Hecuba?"),
using a literary mousetrap to secure the admission of what he
already knows to be a fact, thinking that "nothing could repair
the twisted time," refusing to kill Fort when the act would seem
morally incomplete (Claudius at prayer), abusing his sweet-

heart and driving her mad, literally comparing a hoodwinked plotter to Rosencrantz and Guildenstern, near the end even listening to quips from a gravedigger. In Jerry is focused the action-contamination theme so frequent in Shakespeare: how mediate between a fugitive and cloistered virtue and the contamination inherent in the work that must be done (a theme of interest to Warren since *Night Rider*)? The juxtaposition of sex and death, in both act and reflection, recalls both a traditional association and the specific Elizabethan ambiguity in the use of *die*. The idea that hardens into will is a favorite George Eliot theme, and Jerry's attempted flight and unforeseen involvement may be set against the roughly comparable experience of Heyst in *Victory*. It of course does Warren no service if these comparisons are taken to imply that his work somehow includes all these others; all the analogies should suggest is the breadth of *World Enough and Time*. At the same time there is a general Elizabethanness of cast—in the combination of full and violent action (including a kind of helter-skelter finishing-off of physical lives) with rich rhetoric and overt philosophical investigation—that defines an important influence on Warren's imagination.

Or the story can be read as a myth of America. *World Enough and Time* is, like Warren's other novels, with their Kentucky, Tennessee, and Louisiana backgrounds, southern only in the surface facts; yet it comprises more than the others of the American story and temper. Half the characters are self-made men, with the animus and drive generated on the other side of the tracks. Their stories are success stories seen in tragic perspective. They have dreams—a word used just often enough to comment lightly on the "American dream." In the contest of Reliefers and Anti-Reliefers, both with clearcut twentieth-century analogs, we see the archetypal standpat and reformist tendencies (since Warren contemplates neither side through rose-colored glasses, we may soon have a communique from Northampton, Massachusetts, pointing out that his treatment of Relief is not in accord with the most enlightened political thought of our day and is therefore deplorable esthetically as well as morally). One characteristic passage neatly debunks a modernist-positivist debunking of dueling; any fight for an unseen, intangible, but felt value—a war for instance—is a duel. Most of all we sense the two "streams of American thought," the "idealist" and the "practical," with their contradictions and overlappings and ways of becoming corrupt. Jerry is obviously not written as a national archetype, nor does he accidentally become one, but in him there is much that we can see in ourselves: the turning "from the victor to the victim," the conviction of inner rightness, the inconsistent dreams, the quickness to anger, the sense of injury, the accidental involvement, the self-deception, the contradictory impulses to withdraw and to dictate to others, the confusion about means, the desire to live by the private view and yet to have public justification, the passion and the calculation side by side.

There are other themes: the elusiveness of truth, however fanatically pursued; the enigma of self; the "paradox and doubleness of life" (the enemy as friend, the coexistence of incompatible motives, all the lies against Jerry combining to tell the truth); the seat of justice—in the heart or in the law? (Jerry wavers between the two positions.) There are the subtle comments of figure after figure: the pirate who betrayed the Cherokees had foreseen their end and "had cashed in on his investment while the market was still good." The rich dark-light imagery is a system of meaning in itself. Recurrency is structurally important, notably in the recollections of scenes and sensations—the picture of the martyr, the first sex experience, the enchanting music from the keelboat, the sense of oneness with nature—which establish links among different episodes in Jerry's life. There is a recurrence of the lives of the fathers in the lives of the children; there are a half-dozen versions of the go West young man dogma, most of them commenting ironically on the dream. All these kinds of communication will have to be taken into account in a final assessment of this book; nor is it an abjuring of the critical function to insist that the definition of a complex work of art depends upon a continued collective experiencing of it.

The book is all these things, but it is one book, and the author has indicated how he wants us to see its oneness. When we first glimpse "A Romantic Novel" on the bang-bang jacket, we automatically assume that Random House is bravely dreaming of some deception in the drugstore. But "A Romantic Novel" is also a subtitle, so that it is official as well as promotional. It seems to me that there are three ways in which "romantic" may be taken. At is simplest there is the "romance of adventure"—the almost perfect crime, the pursuit of the suspect, the deviousness of the trial, the jailbreak, the love story, the attempted suicide, the quick gunplay and fistplay, the bravado and battles of wit. At this level it might all be out of Scott, and from Scott might have come a workable title—"The Tangled Web," which, despite the heavy moralism of the context, would pretty well describe the complication of physical and moral action. Yet all this apparatus of romantic melodrama, when qualified by a central tragic awareness, yields something more serious than a romantic-melodramatic effect. Again, "romantic" describes the kind of personality the book deals with: Jerry as Byronic hero is intimated by his and Rachel's and Fort's devotion to Byron. Indeed, *Childe Harold* is an arsenal of mottoes and epithets for Jerry: "self-torturing sophist," "I have not loved the world, nor the world me," "I have thought too long and darkly," "Wrung with the wounds which kill not, but ne'er heal." Jerry is hardly so self-contained as Byron-Harold imagined himself to be, but he is impulsive, suspicious, bitter, melancholy, devoted to an ideal, in search of the fine and noble, hoping for too much, disillusioned, attitudinizing, demonic, exacerbatedly sensitive, self-questioning, self-tormenting, self-deceiving, self-detecting, self-pitying, with all the anguish and despair and nostalgia for a happiness not accessible to the "dark" personality. (He even employs "romantic irony" in commenting on his venereal sore.) In "pure" romance he would be merely a suffering victim of the world, and indeed Jerry has a neurotically active sense of betrayal by the world; but this romantic hero is seen in perspective. Compared with Wilkie's entire devotion to self-advancement, Jerry's dedication to the gratuitous act is impressive, but all his dedication does not dissolve the corruption which encrusts the act itself. The second and final stage in the tragic transformation of romance is Jerry's coming to understand and to reject his earlier self. At the end he does not stand off and gesticulate. He judges himself.

At the third level, then, the book is a study of a basic kind of impulse to action. Jerry calls himself guilty of "the crime of self"; he speaks of having acted from "a black need within me." We have already spoken of the tendency of the "idea" to become "uncriticized motive" and "compulsive personality." The kind of human motivation defined in Jerry is suggested by such terms as the self, the personality, the subjective; here we find the private sureness, the inner insistence, the confidence in the rightness of the heart (as in Hitler), the intransigence of the will, the flight from discipline, indeed the very summation of individualist pride. This "kind of impulse" may lead to both scorn of the world (which may range from simple retreat to challenge and defilement) and effort to subjugate the world: Jerry ultimately comes to see what Rachel had seen earlier, that he had "tortured" her into crying for Fort's blood and thus providing a factitious moral imperative as veneer for an almost instinctive drive.

The human pattern exhibited in Jerry, and with variations in Rachel and Skrogg, is universal. If I am right in judging the ultimate applicability of "romantic" to be the "kind of impulse" which moves Jerry, then the author is describing the timeless by a time word, using a term of specific historical relevance as a means of concretizing the issue. Time and the timeless meet when, in the failure of an ideal tension among impulses, one or another enjoys a temporary historical dominance, as did the Jerry-impulse—the basis, really, of the cult of the individual— in the "Romantic" period and indeed in most of subsequent American history. Whatever name one might give to the antithetical and equally timeless impulse—the Wilkie-impulse— it is clear that its period of dominance was another one; Wilkie has affiliations both with Lord Chesterfield and with the president of the junior chamber of commerce to whom the author refers in a double-voiced choral comment near the end. The problem of these contending impulses, which provides the intellectual framework for the drama of Jerry, really finds its analogy in Coleridge's epistemological doctrine of the subjective and the objective, which in perception reciprocally modify each other. So in moral life a "subjective" and an "objective" view of reality, of innocence, of justice—intention and deed—must interpenetrate, lest the idea or the world run mad. This is not the "practical" principle of compromise—the doctrine that *the* truth is the sum of many half-truths, or the political expedient of the committee swollen into a metaphysic —but the insistence upon a recognition of all the impulses and and of the problem of finding a unity. (Extremes can compromise and even cooperate in a remarkable way; mania and success can sleep together comfortably. Skrogg as idea and Wilkie as world always collaborate politically. And Skrogg—the idea as gangsterism—has a couple of thug bodyguards, a fine concession to the way of the world.)

The conception of the romantic here advanced in the name of the author may grieve professional pedlars of romanticism, at least those whose style is that of a stockholder with an investment to protect. But in many ways it need not do so. Warren has written a study, not a tract. Jerry always aspires; he has the Ulyssean character—to strive, to seek, to find. He is always played off against the positivists; his chief error is to try to be positive—to guarantee the future. He comes to grieve at, not to rejoice in, the "cold exile from mankind" which results from an attempt at a purely private ordering of life. The theme of alienation—that seclusion which emerges from and punishes the crime of self—is always present and is explicitly central in Jerry's final self-analysis. Whether this be regarded as the summit of the dialectical progression of a romantic, or the saving modification of a romantic credo, Jerry puts it this way:

There must be a way whereby the word becomes flesh. There must be a way whereby the flesh becomes word. Whereby loneliness becomes communion without contamination. Whereby contamina-becomes purity without exile.

In these words of longing for what is impossible in life yet must always be sought if life is to have order, Jerry speaks a religious, in part even a Biblical, language. This way of speech, which is natural in the character that Jerry has been shown to be, serves not only to communicate the meaning of the moment but also to pull together strands of suggestion that have run throughout the story. Early in life Jerry had been under the influence of one of those evangelists "who got their hot prides

and cold lusts short-circuited into obsessed hosannas and a fe-
rocious striving for God's sake," and for years he was obsessed by
a remembered picture of a female martyr in flames whom he
could imagine himself either rescuing or helping to destroy. He
declares himself an unbeliever but tends always toward a religious comprehension of experience. He thinks of his campaign
against Fort as a "mission"; he thinks first that his idea will
"redeem" the world, later that the world must "redeem" the
idea. Honest trial witnesses make him "as reborn." He is passionate about his "innocence." He seeks "peace" by confession.
He is agonized by Munn Short's story of his spiritual death and
his recovery by faith. In fact, with his early conversion establishing the pattern, Jerry has always led a kind of pseudoreligious
life: he needs an all-embracing, peremptory spiritual command,
but his way of finding it is to universalize an unidentified cry
from within. Nowhere is the falseness of his devotion more
apparent than when he finds "peace" and "grace" in the ex-
pirate's stinking sanctuary. He is aware that it is a horrible parody of grace and innocence, but he clings to his raw Eden. He
reads the New Testament in Greek and falls into drunkenness
and debauchery. With a dirty slut he finds "peace" and "communion."

But Jerry cannot rest in irony. Like Everyman, and like the
traditional tragic protagonist, he comes to knowledge, not by
magic illumination, but as the outcome of prolonged searching.
Then he no longer seeks revenge, or pardon, or justification; he
knows that "I may not have redemption." He must "flee from
innocence and toward my guilt"; he seeks suffering and expiation. This is his ultimate renunciation of the doctrine of self,
of the private determination of value; it is the acknowledgment
of spiritual reality, the bowing to cosmic discipline.

Jerry is killed before he can complete action in the light
of his new knowledge, but not before he can close his journal
with a question: "Oh, was I worth nothing, and my agony? Was
all for naught?" And the author closes the novel by repeating,
"Was all for naught?" At first glimpse this may seem a kind of
lady-or-tiger coyness, or an emcee's request for audience participation, or even a romantic preference for the incomplete. Rather,
I think, the rhetorical question does two things: it is a kind of

*de te, fabula,* and it raises the issue of whether such a tragic fable can be meaningful now. The book does not raise a finger to make the answer easy: the excellence of *World Enough and Time* is precisely its difficulty. The dramatic and intellectual texture is dense; nothing is given away. Which is as it should be. The acknowledgment of the crime of self and the acceptance of guilt are hardly likely to seem pleasantly familiar to us unskilled in tragic perception. Which is as it must be. Our bent is to look for causes, and to find something, or someone, to blame.

*Frederick P. W. McDowell*

# *8* · The Romantic Tragedy of Self in
## *World Enough and Time*

MORE FULLY THAN in his other works, Robert Penn Warren in *World Enough and Time* elaborates the tragedy of a man betrayed by inner insufficiency. This insufficiency takes the form of a tempermental romanticism which transforms things from what they are into what they are not. So deep-seated is this uncontrolled romanticism and its correlative—the abnegation of the critical intellect—that self-knowledge comes too late to retrieve the disaster springing from the "inward sore / Of self that cankers at the bone." Jeremiah Beaumont's promising life has been thrown away in following will-of-the-wisps which had originally promised to be embodiments of the "noble idea." All Warren's novels, in fact, chronicle the tragic wasting of human resources through a continuing failure by their protagonists, even when essentially admirable, to attain wholeness of vision. The presence, in varying degrees, of a naïve and uncritical idealism and a naïve and uncritical intellectuality constitutes the tragic flaw in Warren's heroes. They alternately take themselves too seriously or not seriously enough: they too intensely feel their own tempermental uniqueness and importance, while they fail to comprehend fully the moral and philosophical implications of what they do. Thus in *All the King's Men* Jack Burden can neither fathom the riddle of Willie Stark nor determine his own place in the scheme of things until his pride is shattered; in *At Heaven's Gate*, Jerry Calhoun is powerless to circumvent the influence of Bogan Murdock which he comes to recognize as malign; and in *Night Rider*, Mr. Munn cannot make effectual his ideals because of his pride and political ignorance.

In *World Enough and Time*, Warren uses the frame of history to isolate spiritual misadventure. History provides an implicit commentary upon the tragedy of misguided aspiration. It enhances at once the value of the aspiration, since too few in any era are capable of emotional intensities, and the poignancy of its futility, since any one person's conflicts, no matter how absorbing to him, become relatively insignificant in the historic process. Jeremiah Beaumont is assimilated to his own era; his guilt, futility, and redemption are, therefore, implicit in the philosophical premises of nineteenth-century romanticism. Certain aspects of romanticism undermine his character before some of them, at least, can be redirected to work his salvation. Dynamic qualities in Beaumont, traceable to an unreflective immersion in environmental romanticism, are a self-conscious innocence, an obsessive individualism, self-deception, an aggressive self-aggrandizement, an infinite longing for a disembodied ecstasy or a merging with the "Absolute," an impatience with limitation, a need for a single-minded purity in psychology, a histrionic pretentiousness, an idyllic optimism alternating with a posturing despair, a sadistic gusto, a pantheistic exaltation, a blunting of moral distinctions, and a disregard of social obligations. In short, his intensity of wayward vision envelops others to their destruction: he extinguishes Rachel's strength of mind and eventually her body, and he kills, for the loftiest reasons, Colonel Fort, potentially the wisest man of his day. Jeremiah is truly "une âme maudite," spoiling his own life, and involving others in disaster, simply by virtue of his being an innocent.

Unable to modify his inflexible prejudices, Jeremiah continually deceives himself. As a young man he first had felt the disparity between the illusion and the reality, but was powerless to dispel its disruptive force. He had become aware of the great gulf between his longings—the "idea" of glory—and the actualities of life: his quest for spiritual beatitude had ended in a sordid sexual act, and his quest for earthly security had ended in a quarrel with his grandfather. The romantic aspiration for an infinite ecstasy takes more thorough hold of him later; yet continued disappointment of these ideal expectations does nothing to modify their fervor and their unreason. Romanticism, recognizing man in T. E. Hulme's phrase as "an infinite reservoir of possibilities," inspires in Jeremiah this quest for the infinite and this impatience with limitation. His romantic bent is so strong that he willfully disregards all realities that would cause him to revise his prejudices; his deliberate, if unconscious choice, therefore, is to live in a world of false illusion. He lives too much in the world of dreams or the world of romance, and cannot separate the fancied from the actual, the conventions of literature from the realities of life. Jeremiah wishes to belong to the world but finds he cannot; at the local tavern after his marriage, he almost becomes a part of the world but he cannot discard his self-induced alienation. When challenged by others about his motives for marrying Rachel, he evades the positive effort necessary to extinguish the unworthy doubts which follow. He prefers to think of Fort as the sacrificial scapegoat whose blood will wash away this alleged stain to his honor. It is easier to externalize one's conflicts into an enthusiastic, all-enveloping crusade than it is to resolve them intellectually. Jeremiah is always too concerned with how he will appear in other people's eyes to be resolutely true to how he will appear in his own eyes.

His imperfect realism brings calamity, because it encourages a disordered life and a high-flown contempt of the actual in a continued pursuit of the impossible abstract ideal of remolding the world nearer the heart's desire. "Nothing was wrong with him which he could properly explain, even to himself. Nothing was wrong except that the world was the way it was." A sense of mundane reality—

the satisfactions of work and the turn of the seasons to show the fruit of his labor . . . the labor for a general good and the justice of Relief, his joy in the love of Rachel, his hope for the future and the child [1]

—he rejects because it cannot be reconciled to the abstractions by which he governs himself. He does not realize that the Idea must be brought to the test of the world, and achieve thereby a more than bloodless existence if it is to redeem rather than to destroy. Only at the very end when he emerges from the chrysalis of self does he have an urgent sense of this when he feels,

[1] Robert Penn Warren, *World Enough and Time* (New York: 1950). All quotations in this essay are from this edition.

"There must be a way whereby the word becomes flesh. There must be a way whereby the flesh becomes word."

Despite his ingrained emotionalism and his impossible aspirations, he feels the need for a coherent explanation of an intrinsically incoherent world. This coherence, at the explicit level he desires it, he will not recognize as impossible through the nature of things. From his early days he had had in his religious moments the feeling that he was "the victim of some gigantic joke or conspiracy," which he was unable to understand or to cope with. "The blindness of man's fate" distresses him unduly since there is nothing in his philosophy to account for the irrational nature of reality. He always tries to order reality, not to understand the conditions under which it can be ordered.

Taking a creator's pride in fashioning a grandiose drama from his life, Jeremiah delights in the ingenuity with which he attempts to make the actuality conform to his exalted illusions. He always dramatizes self instead of trying to understand it; he must become the "transcendental ego" and be spectator to the pageant of his own life—a reductive and pretentious self-scrutiny which Irving Babbitt called "romantic irony"—even when, as at his trial for murder, he is fighting for his life. His previous attempt to play knight-errant has failed—he had worn a red ribbon, the color of blood, as his lady's favor when he had set out to murder Fort. When one theatrical action fails, he thinks of another inflatedly dramatic scene to play out. He confesses to his mentor, Burnham, that all his tragedy began when Burnham taught him "the nobleness of life." Since he is, he feels, doomed, he would not now die "less than Roman" and he commissions Burnham to get him laudanum. Jeremiah had planned a truly magnificent end for himself and Rachel, a double suicide complete with exotic trappings. The emetic effect of the laudanum mixture, however, Jeremiah had not counted on. Instead of an exalted end in their subterranean fastness, the lovers retch. Instead of glorious death, there is physical prostration: this abortive "Liebestod" emphasized symbolically the falsity of a too enthusiastically embraced subjective ideal. It is not so much Jeremiah's instincts and ideas that are wrong but their fatal exaggeration when he objectifies them in action. As Warren contends, it may be impossible for a man to live "unless he prepares a drama" to shore up his human identity "against the ruck of the world." But Beaumont's drama is too grandiloquent and humorless. His obsession with his own uniqueness places him, to his undoing, too squarely beyond merely human good and evil.

Prior to the end of the novel, Jeremiah Beaumont is too consciously lofty to be morally great, too proud of ordering his own destiny to achieve greatness of destiny, too attitudinizing for the selflessness and the humane equability indispensable to a true, as opposed to a romantically inflated, nobility. Fort has, however, humility and a knowledge of his own insufficiency. Paradoxically, Fort reaches a modicum of greatness through a minimizing of his powers. Fort is human in his frailty and does not, like Jeremiah Beaumont, pretend to be above frailty. Fort, a fallen human being, is not beyond sin but is not proud of it. Fort is in his way great because he is "not embarrassed by the accent of greatness," because he does not seek greatness, because his humanity is spontaneous, because his suffering and knowledge of men induces a haunting tragic sense.

Beaumont's destructive pride, the form his misapplied creative energy assumes, contrasts with Fort's creative humility. Like the Ancient Mariner's crime as Warren describes it, Jeremiah's is also that of pride, of the will conceived in abstraction, existing outside of time and the chain of cause and effect, unchastened by any human motive or feeling. Jeremiah, like the Ancient Mariner (and all mankind), is conceived in "original sin,"—"from our mothers' wombs our understandings are darkened," says Coleridge—but he comes only to a slow realization of this. Like the Mariner and his comrades, the unregenerate Jeremiah judges the morality of an act in terms of its personal advantage rather than in terms of its originating spiritual source, the condition of the will.

The disappointment of Jeremiah's hopes for peace in the West is ironic. Like other improvident dreamers who never find rest within, Jeremiah always hopes for beatitude in new surroundings. He seeks for peace outside himself because his inner life is too disjointed for wholeness to irradiate from within: he is incapable of the detachment which would give his energies

direction, though he is capable of the objectivity of an ener-
vating, self-scrutinizing irony. He seeks escape in a new land,
escape from a self that will never give him rest, for "Innocence
is Motion, Innocence is Time, Innocence is West." Jeremiah's
nostalgia is that of the romantic temperament for some place
of ideal peace and loneliness, where the self-tortured soul can
find sympathy and healing for the coldness of this world.

The ideal Eden of Beaumont's fancy had always been the
Far West—beyond the reaches of the civilized. Now that he is
about to attain his fancied Eldorado as a refugee from justice,
he suspects, with sickening dread, that his illusions have been
extravagant. His brutal guides, Moe Sullins and Jenkins, the
grayness of the land overhung with rain and mist, the physical
exhaustion of Rachel on the trip, and Jenkin's description of
the place they go to as one where "nobody keers what yore
name is or what you have done" increases his apprehension.
This has been a pilgrimage to a land of degredation to parallel
the inner degredation—unconscious as yet to him in his pride—
that Jeremiah Beaumont has undergone. This brutalized pilgrimage to the Far West is ironically at variance with Jeremiah's
still continuing quest for a disembodied nobility. His first impression of the settlement brings back the memory of his visit
as a youth to his Grandfather Marcher's "where all seemed
sodden and bemused past the human hope"; he is thus over-
powered by the realization "that a man might live his years
and end but where he began," an implied parody upon the
romantic notion of the glorious eternal return. Instead of the
brilliant land of his imagination, there is a squalid settlement
ruled by the sensualist river pirate, La Grand' Bosse. Even
Rachel's beauty fades here. Jeremiah's revulsion at her ugliness,
when he finds they are prisoners, is as overcharged as the force
of his passion which had, in the first place, broken down
Rachel's resistance to him. He now looks at her countenance
and finds a pronounced brown blotch on it—a blemish to her
beauty and a symbol of spiritual decay like Jeremiah's sub-
sequently acquired venereal sore. As he gazes on her faded
countenance, he asks in anguish, "Was it all for this, was it all
for this?" He is even tortured by the fact that La Grand'
Bosse has rejected Rachel as concubine, despite his knowledge

that, had Bosse taken her, his own life would have been torment. The only peace he can now find is in the "single, separate, dark massive moment that swells up flatly like a bubble from the deep mud." He is overwhelmed by his discovery that "in the beginning there was the Word and the Word was with God, but in the end there is the mud and the mud is with me." The mindlessness of this hopeless abandonment to natural force recalls his frenetic abdication to sensual passion in his prison cell.

Disappointed at the sordidness of his life in exile, Jeremiah takes to drink; at Rachel's mild remonstrance, he is confirmed in his debauchery, and becomes increasingly cruel and abstracted toward the person who had inspired his spiritual quest. Through her greater realism and honesty, Rachel could have helped Jeremiah had he been able to learn from her:

I had never entered into that region where her soul abode and kept its house, Oh, might I have done so! And had I done so, I might have followed her glimmering as through the maze of a dark forest and come upon her at last in some sunlit glade and sat with her calmly there upon the grass, holding her hand. Then all might have been different.

He could not learn from Rachel, however, because he has intellectualized away all spontaneity from his passion, with the result that he can no longer feel "the holiness of the heart's affections" and be instructed spiritually by them. Rachel is, moreover, "sunk in her own darkness," and he could not now get to enter her soul even if he wanted to.

In purposeless fashion, he turns from her to pursue knowledge in the abstract, "lapped in the arrogant chastity" of this desire, reading the Testament in the original Greek. This becomes as blind and insatiable a passion as that for drink; the Faust-like pursuit of knowledge divorced from the spirit is an unpardonable sin, and more reprehensible, if anything, than Jeremiah's previous aspiration after pure spirit divorced from knowledge. Arrested in his preoccupation with self by a realization that Rachel is losing her reason, he finds to his dismay that he has no other resource. Though Jeremiah pretends to be a law unto himself, he is unable to withstand adversity with patience. He actually lacks the self-reliance and independence he has romantically flaunted at other times. His is an individualism without stabilizing doctrine or intellectuality to give it base. He is proto-Nietzschean in most of his attitudes save that he lacks redeeming moral strength. Like the Martin Decoud Warren depicts in his essay on *Nostromo,* Jeremiah Beaumont cannot endure when thrown back upon himself.

As measure of his customary impassioned belief in self, there is Jeremiah's naive elation in the murder of Fort. He had keenly anticipated this exaltation ever since he first took Rachel in his arms—a decadent fusion of ecstatic love with an ecstatic fixation upon the shedding of blood, a sadism Jeremiah conveniently rationalizes as the claim of honor upon him:

The moment when he should strike Fort and the moment when he should at last take her into his arms fused into one moment, the two acts became one act, the secret of life, and all that lay between him and the act was ugly and meaningless.

Jeremiah Beaumont has the superb conviction in the rightness of his act that an innocent child would feel in having carried out the command of its parent. To Jeremiah the act of revenge is simple and God-appointed; the goodness of his intentions in his eyes precludes the need for exhaustive scrutiny of his behavior; little does he realize that duty, rigidly conceived, may be entirely pernicious. At the time of his trial for Fort's murder, in the midst of the blood he had shed and the lies which hem him in, he holds fast to his preconceived ideal of innocence, until Munn Short, his jailer, makes him uncomfortably aware that a true innocence is heart-felt and outgoing rather than intellectual and ingrown, "innocent only is the heart music . . ." As Warren implies in the poem, "Love's Parable," the only valuable innocence is earned through spiritual travail, and transcends the evil it cannot ignore. Any other kind— especially the abstracted sort which fails to ensure its integrity through a recognition of the Evil which threatens it—is purely an accident and has but a fortuitous relevance to the real truth, as Hilton Hawgood claims:

"For innocence—it is an accident. It is always an accident. We did not do it for accidental innocence. No—we did it for—for truth. For truth, Beaumont. . . . What else is there to do for? That's all there is, and nothing can hurt it. Not our lies or guilts, for it is

bigger. It is higher. And we know it is there. Even if we cannot
see it. Nothing can hurt it. Not even our innocence can hurt it!"

An inward innocence does not demand, in Jeremiah's philosophy, an innocence in fact; innocence in his view is personally
predetermined and bears little relationship to ultimate truth. He
can readily rationalize, therefore, any degree of guilt in the
actual world of men.

He also feels at one with nature, and his emotional exaltation soon assumes mystical overtones. In a lilac thicket just
before the murder he rests his cheek on a twig outside the
window of Fort's home and feels suffusing through his veins a
pantheist glow—reminiscent of an experience he had had in
youth  when he touched a snow-laden beech. The intensity of
the emotion he now focuses upon his project makes him at
one with nature and with God. Like other romantics, as Paul
Elmer More described them, Jeremiah succumbs to "the illusion
of beholding the infinite within the stream of nature, instead
of apart from that stream." He feels that "all had moved to
this moment"; his criminal purpose now has an apparent
transcendental sanction, precisely because he adjudges it noble.
What amounts to lynch law has now its ideal justification in
the appeal Jeremiah makes through Nature to a divine benevolence. Again Jeremiah oversimplifies experience in his innocence,
failing to realize that in nature creative primitive energies and
stark evil are both present and that the exaltation nature inspires
cannot altogether be acknowledged divine. Unless we are lacking in spiritual humility, our fallen condition, our common guilt,
our beclouded perceptions cannot permit us the presumption
of accepting at its apparent mystical value such an externalized
source for emotional intoxication. Granted that God reveals his
sacramental presence to man through nature, that nature is
ultimately spiritual in essence, and that Jeremiah has an intuition of this, he immerses himself too headlong in it. Such
naturalistic fervor without the infusion of human sympathy
leads to spiritual paralysis, despite the overflow of spirit in its
communion with nature or despite the intellectual conviction
that through such mysticism we become divine. A subjective
sympathy with nature has to be supplemented, therefore, with
a more objective range of values. Nature or the wilderness in

the novel becomes, in part, an emblem of original sin, since it holds in solution both the destructive and the spiritual. These contradictory forces are also to be found in precarious balance in the soul of man.

The quest for the Absolute, divorced from all contingencies in actuality, can never be satisfied, and its aching persistence brings calamity: witness the fates of characters in works so diverse as *Faust, Manfred,* Hawthorne's *The Birthmark,* and Balzac's *The Devil of the Absolute.* Jeremiah's intuition into the absolute order of the world is too easily achieved, it is too little earned by personal suffering or by intellectual effort, and it represents a too expeditious victory of unity over diversity. It follows from the tendency in romanticism to confuse the human realm with the Absolute or religious realm. His super-human aspiration carries within it the seeds of havoc as we find them also in romantic heroes like Werther, Julien Sorel, or Heathcliff. At all costs, Jeremiah wishes for that delusive peace described in Warren's poem "Crime" as "past despair and past the uncouth isolation." Actually, Jeremiah's apprehension of the absolute truth, which, according to him, can alone justify a man's pretensions, is too shadowy to be meaningful. He is so in love with the one that he forgets the many; when he courts Rachel he is carried away, as he reads to her from "The Symposium," by Socrates' vision of the idea of absolute beauty as the highest beatitude. Abstract Platonic essences appeal to the romantic who wishes to despise the inconvenient facts.

Jeremiah learns slowly that spiritual truth is not only instinctive and self-regarding, a matter of inner conviction, but something which transcends the self and comprehends it in relation to other men. Until too late, he does not understand Fort's dictum that "it is iniquity for any man to forget he is not alone and that the good of other men is his duty, and that the state is our life." Jeremiah lacks the sense of the human community because he is devoted to abstractions and dazzled by a bizarre conception of his self-importance. He has moral fervor but it is turned inward to satisfy his intense soul, so that other individuals in his eyes lose intrinsic value. At the trial, he has "some air of self-complaisance which wins regard but not hearts." Like Conrad's Kurtz or Decoud as Warren has described them, Jeremiah is "the sinner against human solidarity and the human mission." He does not realize soon enough how self-centered he has always been, how ruinous natural grandeur in human nature unrelieved by love of mankind can be. Having rejected society after his crime for the promise of peace in the wilderness, Jeremiah finally sees that his life as outcast is a veritable death-in-life, and as a means to his own salvation, he again tries to establish his connection with humanity by going back to Frankfurt to deliver himself over to the law. He can now understand at last the Kantian injunction to use men as ends rather than as means; he had even used his wife Rachel to gratify his romantic predilections instead of forgetting self in affection for her. The need Jeremiah feels to participate in the community when his resources of self fail is a sense of responsibility which his libertarian nature had previously scorned.

At the end, the facts and the moral order they support can be denied no longer. Because its objective existence could not be demonstrated to the earlier Beaumont, he had rejected its provenance; his conversion convinces him of the impossibility of living either in intellect or emotion alone, without a positive ethic. Only after his noble purpose in killing Fort boomerangs and blots out all possibilities of earthly glory does he realize that the task of the intellect is not to prove the existence of the moral world, but to accept and explore it. He then rejects the romantic ideal of aggrandizement of self in acknowledging moral limitations upon the expansive ego. Realizing, too, the universal presence of evil in man and nature and the need for spiritual grace to be delivered from it, he passes from a dangerous innocence to spiritual sophistication.

As Warren states in his essay on *Nostromo*, it is "man's fate and his only triumph" to serve an idea of some sort. All along, Jeremiah had realized that men need philosophical sanctions to order their lives; until too late, he has embraced the wrong ones. His quest, though arduous and potentially worthwhile, has all but been wasted. There are, ironically, depths in Beaumont, but he shies away at first from exploring them fully because their honest recognition then would entail a moral consistency at variance with his quixotic idealism. With respect to Jeremiah's insistent question, "Was all for naught?"—the last words, too, in the book—we are to infer that his life had value. For he has reached inward to the vital forces lying deep within personality and he wishes to capitalize upon them. He has a sense, too, of the constricting influence of an unimaginatively embraced tradition and respectability. Better than these are the violence and contamination that fall to Jeremiah Beaumont, Warren would imply, for he at least is not complacent. Sensitive enough to realize the barrenness of "the terrorless intellect," Jeremiah is one of those tortured souls whose ability to experience life and to gain from it inner light distinguishes him from men like Wilkie, the Parhams, La Grand' Bosse, and the Jenkins brothers, whose hollowness is complete. Their naturalism deifies the empiric fact, while Jeremiah's aspires after the spiritual principle behind the facts.

Warren's focus, however, is in large part ironic, since he refuses to sentimentalize the traditional attributes of the "romantic hero" Jeremiah represents. Throughout the novel Warren subjects Jeremiah's motives to rigid scrutiny and establishes the fallibility of heroic strength when it scorns mere human weakness. Despite all its inner intensities, the self-sufficient heroism which Jeremiah consistently emulates inhibits inner development and encourages no valid knowledge of intrinsic values. When it turns outward for external confirmation of alleged greatness, it finds, in reality, only what it delusively seeks for. For most of the novel, therefore, Jeremiah Beaumont is its hero in name only, if a hero is one with whom we are to share the fullest sympathy. Because of his excesses, Jeremiah actually becomes its villian, while the villain in his fancy, Colonel Fort, despite his patent imperfections, becomes its informing center.

Yet Jeremiah has a largeness of soul which never quite induces our alienation, even when he is most sanctimoniously self-righteous and evil. In his non-resistance to Jeremiah, Fort has some sense, too, of Jeremiah's worth, maniacal as he has become in his obsession with revenge. Jeremiah as generalized symbol for fallen man, guilty of the original sin of self-sufficient pride, incites also that concern we feel for our own guilt.

When Jeremiah at last sees himself as he has been, the sincerity of his conversion is in proportion to the evil he has, in some degree unwittingly, generated. To understand the novel aright, we must therefore be aware in its last pages of Warren's inversion of its inversion, his negation of its negation. The personality of Jeremiah then becomes more than satiric commentary upon romantic excess, it becomes the positive impulsion in the book. Beaumont is no longer the "hero" of romantic travesty; he becomes the indisputable tragic protagonist who not only triumphs over forces that defeated him but who uses them to attain Grace. In its intensity, his tempermental romanticism is no longer a liability, but provides the radical energy accessory to his conversion. In showing that rebirth is possible only to those who feel deeply, his sympathies are romantic.

The impulse of revolt is paradoxically both spiritual and anarchic. Though Warren stresses Beamount's anarchy, he also is sharply conscious of his restless aspiration. If moral anarchy leads to murder, emotional responsiveness leads to remorse and regeneration. Jeremiah's quest for psychic illumination is ultimately rewarded, irrespective of its calamitous results to himself and to Fort—though Warren never lets us forget that incursion of spiritual power at so great a price is tragic, if not nefarious. While nothing can excuse his crime, Jeremiah has at least a soul to be humanized.

The romantic was ever on the alert for the transcendent, the ineffable, which would pierce beyond the spiritless actuality, and he was always concerned with what man may become. Though Jeremiah willfully disregards the facts in his mania for becoming, this desire for becoming is positive as well as negative. A man may aspire towards the angelic as well as the demonic, towards Baudelairean transcendence as well as Baudelairean degredation. The demonic and the angelic both transcend the limits of the natural and the rational, and are the opposite poles toward which fervent souls can aspire. If subjective impulsions, directed inward to the self, give us the DeSades of actuality and the D'Annunzian heroes of fiction, these same impulsions, directed outward, give rise to the ethic intelligence of Goethe and Wordsworth, of those who use inner purity in the service of God and man. Trapped by his fervent personality, Jeremiah becomes a criminal in trying to exemplify his own cencept of nobility, but he is also, by the magnetic affinity between polar opposites and by his very preoccupation with nobility, a potential saint. In its aggressive denial of the divine, the demonic, one pole in romanticism, has within it the seeds of its opposite. The situation is tragic, when, as with Beaumont, negative impulsions immobilize until too late potentially stronger motivations of a positive kind. When intermittent sincerity and intensity like Jeremiah's are present, egocentric flamboyance of personality can yield to fullness of soul —both are equivocally included within the complex of attitudes called romanticism. One way, Jeremiah Beaumont represents the dissolution of personality as it is absorbed into the directionless flux of the external world without the counter-balance of inner standards for control. Another way his restless questing embodies a craving for spiritual irradiation, and a thirst for a regenerative influx to transform his vision and revitalize the vision of others. If, through his initial lack of discipline, he is delayed in attaining wholeness, he has had even then its germs to contrast with the caricatures respectively of idealism and worldliness, Skrogg and Wilkie.

The book relies too greatly upon travesty and irony in defining Baumont's character, so that its discussion of ultimate issues is too intellectual and abstract. The novel is at times deficient in emotional force, with the result that we are too far removed from Jeremiah Beaumont's difficulties despite our implication in them. Lacking universally respected spiritual authority, the modern age demands that its artists also be philosophers, so that in Warren's metaphysical type of fiction, it is natural for the intellectual to predominate over the emotional. Consequently, the symbolic lines of Warren's characters are often more striking than their individualities. To compensate for this discursiveness and diminished impact is Warren's urgent sense of mission, the instilling in modern man an awareness of his religious heritage and the need for spiritual restoration. In the best sense an eclectic and a truth-seeker, Warren

juxtaposes through a conscious effort of the intellect the in-
congruities of existence to arrive at uniquely sharp insights into
reality. Haunted by the depth and complexity of life, Warren
in a naturalistic age has reasserted the provenance of the spirit,
and has enriched our experience by encompassing both the
dangers and the glories of the subjective life.

# 9·Mr. Warren and the Reviewers

OH, WHO AM I?—these, the first words of Amantha Starr, heroine of Mr. Robert Penn Warren's *Band of Angels,* are also the first words of the novel which records her own recital of her search for an answer. The same question ought to be posed, but too seldom is, by everyone who sets up as a critic. Not asked continuously; the result of that would be the submergence of another Amiel in the quicksands of another *Journal* (Amiel's is far from being all in print *yet*). But often enough to make of the occasion a sort of yearly Day of Atonement.

It is a platitude to say that we judge as we see, and we see what we expect to see. Put into the best jargonese, this becomes "Our valuations are not independent of our explications." Almost any critic can point out this fact about the other fellow's criticism—which is precisely what I am about to do. And no doubt this shaping of preferences by expectations is not only inevitable, but desirable. It is on account of it that criticism remains an art, that is to say, an activity that can be applied over and over again to much the same materials with the production of ever new and unforeseeably interesting results. But the critic must strive to maintain a flexibility of approach, a generosity of stance—which is not the same thing as a sentimental final score. The best critic does not forget—though he need not waste time worrying about—the fact that he is himself a datum in every criticism he writes.

Before I look briefly at several reviews of Mr. Warren's book, let us run over briefly those events of Amantha's story which the "candid camera," had one been following her about, could have recorded. Born about 1843, daughter of the slave-holding owner of a not specially prosperous Kentucky plantation, her childhood years were motherless; for her mother died before Amantha's recollections began. When nine years old, she was sent North to be educated at the academy and college at Oberlin (the Collegiate Institute had been rechristened College only two years before, in 1850). "Those whey-faces and knob-heads of Oberlin," as the luxury-loving "Miss Idell" of Cincinnati (actually Mrs. Herman Muller, and Starr's mistress) termed them, were ultra-Evangelicals and ardent Abolitionists; and Amantha was imbued with a tinge of Oberlin attitudes, if not entirely of Oberlin convictions. All the greater was the shock to her, then, on being summoned home to Kentucky by her father's death after some seven years of schooling, when she found herself seized as a chattel, to be sold to satisfy claims of creditors against her father's estate. Her mother had been neither white nor free; and her father had never made out the "papers" that would have conferred freedom on her.

From 1859 through 1866, Amantha's story shifted to New Orleans and the river country near it. Only sixteen when she was taken downriver to be sold, she was bought by Hamish Bond, a well-to-do plantation owner whose "kindness is like a disease." He was kind to "poor little Manty"—a phrase which indicates her destiny as both she and those around her saw it; but his kindness disabled her from repelling advances which made her his mistress. Now the mounting national tension and finally the oncoming of strife around and in New Orleans itself share the scene with Manty's own fortunes, though the larger currents of action are kept subordinate in her narrative. Set adrift by Bond for her own safety, she was rescued from an awkward street encounter by Tobias Sears, of Litchfield, Massachusetts, who, she was later to learn, "had nobility like a disease"—an infection he seems to have acquired in part from reading Emerson's essays. In the autumn of 1866 Amantha Starr became his wife.

From this point onward, much of the novel concerns Amantha's attempts to discover whether nobility and the kind of love that springs from nobility can release her from the conflicts and repressions which the phrase "poor little Manty" connotes. Her huband's military service in command of Negro troops was succeeded by almost fruitlessly idealistic efforts as an official of the Freedmen's Bureau. From St. Louis on westward through a series of ever smaller communities, the novel follows the two, until finally, about the year 1889, in the prairie community of Halesburg, Kansas, a last encounter between black and white—a grotesquely comic encounter this time—reaffirms what there is of worth in Tobias' character, and sets Amantha free from the oppression of her quest.

So much for Amantha's own story; now for the critics' comments. But I must confess that from this point onward, I shall become quite unabashedly hypothetical. Among the critics I have read, several are completely unknown to me. Others are gentlemen well known and esteemed, who have published much. Far too much, usually, for me to range over their output in order to prop the assertions of so modest a piece of writing as this. I shall therefore in each case do no more than to suggest several presuppositions which, had they been held by the critic, would in my opinion have led him to write pretty much what he did write. In many sorts of investigation, a first step toward accounting for given phenomena is the construction of hypotheses *sufficient* to account for the phenomena. A choice among these hypotheses—for often, several will fulfill the conditions— is a later stage which I do not aspire to reach. It is enough for my purposes if I can confer plausibility on the propositions set forth in my opening paragraphs. And since I am ascribing preconceptions to critics on no better warrant than supposition, I may not ascribe them *tout court* to the authors of the reviews I shall cite. I shall append an X by means of a hyphen to the name of the author, to denote the imagined critic who, operating from the preconceptions I assign, would have written the review being cited. This Mr. Critic X may or may not have any close affinity with the critic who *did* write the review.

First, then, for Mr. John F. Sullivan in *The Commonweal*.[1] He describes *Band of Angels* as "this combination of Gothic form and the theme of sin against the Negro," and neither de-

[1] November 4, 1955, p. 1478.

votes much space to nor thinks very highly of the result. Yet
the quoted phrase is fair enough as the beginning of a description of this novel, though it is not, as Mr. Sullivan seems to
suppose, the whole description. Until the casual reader runs over
in his mind some of the great names in American letters—Poe,
Hawthorne, Melville, Twain even (in some passages), E. A.
Robinson, Hemingway, Faulkner—he may not realize how
nearly central in American literature the Gothic tradition, which
can be succinctly characterized as "a literary eploration of the
avenues to death," has been. Yet it is a commonplace to remark that American literature in the eyes of foreigners is in
large part a literature recording violence. This record ranges all
the way from the physical and physiological simplicities of
thrillers to the subleties of writers who dissect Freudian depths
with a finesse emulous of Henry James. Mr. Faulkner is obviously our outstanding contemporary "Gothicist." But it does
not follow, as Mr. Sullivan alleges, that Mr. Warren is nothing
more than Faulkner's talented disciple.

"The sin against the Negro" is another good start, but Mr.
Sullivan does not carry the idea far enough. For that sin is
represented not solely on the story level, in the violence committed by an inhuman legality against the self-respect of the
heroine, as well as in all the manifold other brutalities incident
to slavery which come within the compass of Amantha's recollections. The "sin against the Negro" is not only enacted by
characters; it is symbolized by them. Hamish Bond, we learn
from his autobiographical confession to Amantha—a bravura
sample of Mr. Warren's stylistic powers, unforgettably vivid—
began his career as a captain in the African slave trade, and wit-
nessed and profited by—though he did not himself commit—
inhuman horrors. He now seeks to expiate, by benevolence to individual victims of the situation from which he has profited,
his share in creating that situation. But the name he now goes
under—Hamish Bond (his real name is Alec Hinks)—is Warren's way of intimating that the benevolences of a man and of
a civilization do not cancel complicity in sin. Nor does nobility, so long as it condescends from the lofty rostrum of a
conscious relish of its own motives. Witness the career of Tobias
Sears.

Indeed, the motif of slavery transcends even the ethical and social issues generated by Negro slavery in the United States, crucial as these have been and continue to be in our national scene. The second paragraph of the novel, immediately after the paragraph which opened with "Oh, who am I?" declares Amantha's other consuming preoccupation: "If I could only be free, I used to think, free from the lonely nothingness of being only yourself when the world flees away, and free from the closing walls that would crush you to nothingness." The placing of this passage, and its status as the whole of a paragraph, indicate clearly the connection between one's achievement of freedom and one's recognition of one's own identity. The conflict within Amantha Star—a conflict sometimes evident only in unpremeditated utterances and actions that operate to betray others—is continuously represented as a struggle between what in her nature she shares with the whites, and what she shares with the blacks. But the struggle is not only that. Were it no more, human beings might discover some fine day that they had risen clear of the "human situation"—*la condition humaine*. "Oh, who am I?" is the cry of the human soul, flung into "a teeming darkness, straining soundlessly with forms struggling for recognition, for release from that dark realm of undifferentiated possibility." One of those forms, but half-emerged from the darkness, is the questioner himself.

And now, back to the predisposing biases of the critic whom I have agreed to call Mr. Sullivan X. But in this case, since I really know nothing whatever about Mr. Sullivan, and do have some acquaintance with *The Commonweal*—as what person interested in a worthy American culture shouldn't—I shall call my suppositional critic Mr. Commonweal X. For *The Commonweal* is the organ of certain cultured, progressive elements within the Roman Church in this country. And the whole impact of that church on its members is such that any enterprise, however unofficial, influenced by it is likely to manifest a more than ordinary degree of ideological cohesion. Hence, Mr. Commonweal X.

What Mr. Commonweal X said—and did not say—in reviewing *Band of Angels* is very much what I would have predicted. The review totally ignored the philosophical dimensions of the book, and implied that Mr. Warren had sold out to Hollywood. (The story of Amantha Starr is, to be sure, a "natural" for Hollywood; what Hollywood can make of her story concerns, however, an artistic construct other than the one I am discussing.) The representations of the physical aspects of sex relationships conducted without benefit of matrimony did not directly draw the reviewer's fire. As much can probably be found in the pages of accepted Catholic novelists. Why, then, would Mr. Commonweal X bestow at least a qualified lay benediction on the latest Mauriac or Graham Greene, and yet set Mr. Warren beyond the pale with a firm if polite anathema? Because, I surmise, Mr. Warren's characters, when they sin, do not sin with an explicit theological awareness. Souls sin; and enlightened Catholic opinion does not object to artistic representations—even powerfully moving representations—of that fact. What the church cannot condone is any obscuring of the theological explanations of sin. If the soul strays, it strays from God; if the soul is tempted, it is tempted by the Devil. Fate will not do; chance will not do; no philosophically expressed interpretation will do, unless that interpretation be firmly anchored to the terms of the Christian revelation.

Now, it is notable that Mr. Warren's book, though pervaded by a sense of national and personal destiny deeply infected with sin, makes no essential use of any theological scheme of salvation. The pietistic theology of Oberlin is presented in several of its varieties; but it is the moral atmosphere of Oberlin which affects Amantha. She never shows any sign of turning, in her difficulties, to the Christian promise. The only important character who does seek to ground his life on the Christian gospel, albeit a contortedly scrupulous version of it—Seth Parton —receives for his reward a fortune gained as a wheat speculator in Chicago. This is almost too pat an irony; but it is the only effect credited to theology in the lives of those who matter in Amantha's story. Hence Mr. Commonweal X is in duty bound to disprize Mr. Warren's book. The church can more readily forgive those who rebel against it than those who ignore it. The former at least testify to its importance.

From a quite opposite point of view, Mr. Warren has been

scolded by Mr. Maxwell Geismar in *The Nation*, who among
other things says:

> Mr. Warren has never been a primary fiction writer; that is to
> say, either a writer whose primary source is life experience or a
> writer whose work is of major importance. His talent is literary
> and derivative; it is often only a bright mirror of the fashionable
> influences of his period. He is a formalist and conceptualist—the
> perfect example of the dry mind—who writes very well indeed,
> but who views life in terms of abstractions. . . . The core of Mr.
> Warren's work has never been the search for, or inquiry into, any
> kind of social or human liberation; but rather a kind of corrosive
> cynicism and despair about all forms of freedom. This sense of
> self-imprisonment is never really related to the present heroine,
> who has no heart to begin with, but it is the one genuine thing in
> the book. . . . Since the people are puppets, the historical back-
> ground, of the story becomes its single virtue. But since Mr.
> Warren's basic sympathies lie with a literary legend of the Old
> South, it is difficult for him to describe the real issues of the Civil
> War in an intelligent light. That this picture of a fratricidal
> conflict should be called a product of a brilliant historical imagi-
> nation as it has been, seems to me a measure of an epoch which
> is busily revising the whole meaning of our national heritage. . . .
> At best it is a sophisticated revival of the Southern romances of
> the 1900's. . . . What Mr. Warren creates here is practically an
> idyll of slavery in the Old South, and it certainly seems so when
> the war does break out.[2]

To indicate the presuppositions of many sorts—economic,
social, and occasionally artistic—which foreordained Mr. Geismar X to come to the conclusions announced in the sentences
quoted is almost too easy. Indeed, my fiction of a Mr. Geismar
X wears a bit thin, for Mr. Geismar, who did write these sentences, so ingenuously displays his prejudices. One feels almost
embarrassed to comment, as one might in walking behind a
self-assured lady at a garden party when a generous amount of
her slip was showing. But let us preserve the amenities: it is
Mr. Geismar X who could not help writing as this reviewer has
written.

Note, first, that "Mr. Warren writes very well indeed."
Nothing further is said by way of explanation or illustration of

2 October 1, 1955, p. 287.

this statement. Yet one might suppose that an entire book review could be devoted—and most profitably—to just the elucidation of this judgment. Perhaps Mr. Geismar X is not interested in writing? But the pursuit of this inquiry might lead us into a cul-de-sac; let us fare forward: "Mr. Warren's work has never been the search for . . . any kind of social or human liberation. . . ." Weigh that phrase in the mind: "social or human liberation." Then try it the other way round: "human or social liberation." Perhaps I refine excessively; but in Mr. Geismar X's way of putting it, I cannot dispel an implication that human liberation is consequent upon and possibly a by-product of social liberation; and that social liberation might conceivably be achieved by (or imposed by well-wishers on?) a humanity, none of whom as individuals had previously in any valid sense experienced liberation. Anyone who feels this way about the relative importance of social trends and individual efforts will most likely not be much interested by individuals, unless these are consciously allied with some social trend. Mr. Warren's characters are caught up in social trends, and have attitudes toward and opinions about these; but a major element in Mr. Warren's total vision is an awareness of the disparity between these attitudes and opinions, and the realities which have evoked them. Hence Mr. Geismar X finds Mr. Warren's people to be mere "puppets" and is interested only in the "historical background" of Mr. Warren's novel. (Would not a Mr. Geismar X be likely to object to any work of fiction in which the "background"—historical or other—was not the foreground?) But Mr. Warren cannot "describe the real issues of the Civil War"—at least, "not in an intelligent light." What were these "real issues"? We are not told. Perhaps the reviewer assumed that knowledge of them is so general as to make any reminder superfluous. But Mr. Warren is not stupid (I hope our Mr. Geismar X would concede this much), and he seems not to know them. So perhaps a reminder would *not* have been superfluous after all. But now the truth—not about the Civil War, but about Mr. Warren's book—comes out: "it is a sophisticated revival of the southern romances of the 1900's"—though, somewhat oddly (a kind of ambidexterity in time), it manages to be a "measure of an epoch which is busily revising the whole meaning of our

national heritage." I cannot see anything portentous about "revising the whole meaning of our national heritage"; I had supposed this, or something like it, would be the sustained and sus-
taining intention of all historians, of whatever species, who deal
with the history of our nation. For to understand anything more
fully is to "revise" a "meaning." I had not thought, however,
that the meaning of America is being revised back toward the
1900's. I might not object; for the world of the 1900's was the
world in which I was young, and it wore a vernal bloom. *Eheu,
fugaces!* Which is a curious way an old Latin writer had of
doubting, somewhat emotionally, that the meaning of anything
can be revised *backwards*. The hydrogen bomb does not permit.
Not even if Mr. Warren tries to seduce us thither by the en-
chantments of "an idyll of slavery in the Old South."

With this last phrase, perhaps the most "simplistic" (to
avoid uncomplimentary terminology) of Mr. Geismar X's biases
comes to a climax. Not only is he a sociological abstractifier of
the human scene, but he is an ethical rigorist. We *know* that
Negro slavery was (and is) a sin against humanity. We *know*
that the South wished to perpetuate this system. We *know* that
the victory of the North resulted in some kind of freeing of the
slaves. Therefore anybody who intimates that some northerners
not only were not saviors of the Negro, but even behaved to
him with a treachery worse than the brutalities of the South, in-
asmuch as it struck at its victims from the very quarter to which
they looked for help, must of course be an ethically obtuse sentimentalist. As must also be anyone who represents any Southerner as in any respect exemplary in his dealings with the Negro.
Mr. Geismar X thinks Mr. Warren a falsifier because Hamish
Bond is kind to his slaves. In the eyes of a critic with Mr. Geismar X's preconceptions, Hamish Bond is simply a social datum
who is being employed to obfuscate an ethical issue. That
Hamish Bond is a symbol on a more philosophical level of
meaning is, for Mr. Geismar X, simply an example of what in
this review is slightingly referred to as "rhetorical eloquence and
. . . philosophical disquisitions." "Disquisitions," I have noticed,
is a word almost invariably used by persons who dislike the
topic to which they are referring: in this case, philosophy. It is
strange, by the by, that a critic so sure of the identity of Right

and Wrong should be so little impressed by philosophy. Does
he suppose that a Right and Wrong worth the while of any
civilization are likely to emerge in the absence of any philosophy? Automatically perhaps, as the last and best fruit of
modern technology, or of the Union for the Social Control of
Democratic Freedom? I cannot here speak for another. But were
I to adopt the preconceptions which seem to me evident in a
Mr. Geismar X, I should find myself viewing not Mr. Warren's
novel alone, but the whole tale of human history, with a continuous sense of sorrowful frustration, overlaid at moments by
impulses toward rage.

A singularly noxious, because potentially most unfair
species of critic is the critic-who-runs-to-post-his-reviews-before-
he-has-read. As a specimen of this critic I may adduce Mr. Anthony West X, who seems to have written a review labeled
"Science Fiction" in the *New Yorker*.[3] (Mr. West X is not
necessarily to be identified with the Mr. Anthony West who is
a regular reviewer for that journal.) At the end of this review,
mostly occupied with Aldous Huxley's *The Genius and the
Goddess*, Mr. West X found that he still had a scant column at
his disposal. He seems also to have heard that a gaggle of pesti-
lent loiterers called New Critics have been seen infesting street-
corners, and might be an annoyance to even the fleetest of
reviewers on the shortest of runs. So Mr. West X resolved not
only to polish off Mr. Warren's novel, but to finish off these
hindrances to rapid traffic. This last he achieved by the irony
of an annihilating compliment—to *"The Sewanee Review*, the
highest conceivable authority on matters relating to native
culture in general and multilevel writers in particular." Now
the way is clear for the one-yard dash. Mr. West X choses for
particular notice only Manty's connection with Hamish Bond,
as who should say, "The extra-legal *must* be climactic." From
the novel he quotes only a passage recording Manty's awareness
of Hamish's thumb on her belly while she is reflecting on the
way history at any moment interpenetrates the particularities
of individual lives at that moment. Admittedly, this passage is
one of the less happy samples of Mr. Warren's powers. But it
offered Mr. West X a chance—the only chance of any kind that

3 October 15, 1955, pp. 168–73.

he took. He follows the quotation and concludes his review with the comment that "This, as the *Sewanee Review* might say, adds a new dimension to the phrase 'making history.' You, too, can do it."

I trust I am not being exaggeratedly multi-dimensional in saying that the final brief sentence applies beautifully to the entirety of Mr. West X's comment on *Band of Angels*. "You, too, can do it." But who else would wish to?

Let us remove now to pastures more amiable. Mr. Coleman Rosenberger in the New York *Herald Tribune Book Review*,[4] setting out from a recognition of the many-sidedness of the book—"saga and symbol, myth and explication," with somewhat exaggerated comments along the way (the novel is "peopled by characters who are driven and demon-haunted"; Amantha's "perception and understanding are prodigious"; Mr. Warren allows himself scenes which a lesser novelist would find unthinkable"), arrives at the conclusion that *Band of Angels* is "a major work by one of America's finest novelists." Less eulogistically, Mr. Carlos Baker in *The Saturday Review*[5] judges this to be "a good book on a serious and important subject." (I should have supposed, a whole Chinese egg of subjects, each more serious and important than the ones it encloses.) And, to cite but one more witness, Mr. Arthur Mizener in the *New York Times Book Review*,[6] though in part adversely critical, grants Mr. Warren "the most penetrating and most beautifully disciplined historical imagination we have." (Again, I would suggest a qualification. When Mr. Warren's imagination operates in history, it operates through his style. When he interprets, his imagination is metaphysical.)

Since Mr. Rosenberger is most emphatic of the three in his praise, I shall let a Mr. Rosenberger X symbolize reviewers predisposed to applaud; I do not pretend that this symbol is appropriate for either Mr. Baker or Mr. Mizener in particular. The chief defect I find in my Mr. Rosenberger X is a too great readiness to translate complexities into attainments. Rightly perceiving that, *other things being equal*—a qualification likely to

4 August 21, 1955.
5 August 20, 1955, pp. 9–10.
6 August 21, 1955.

slip from one's grasp when one supposes it to be firmly in hand
—other things being equal, then, a complex work is more likely
to embody high artistic merit than a less complex one; the
critic judges favorably the work he is considering, simply because he notices in it evidences of complexity. But a number of
questions remain to be considered. Let us suppose that on one
of its levels a book is notably impressive (and I think nobody
will deny that on the level of narrative adroitness, most of *Band
of Angels* is effective), does this success enter into the success
of the book on other levels? And does it enter as an impediment
or a reinforcement? Is the copresence of diverse significances
achieved with a minimum of sacrifices of the possibilities attainable on each level? And, finally, are the several kinds of significance woven into an all-comprehensive pattern, or merely
braided together into a kind of rope? It is of questions such as
these that I am not certain our Mr. Rosenberger X reminds himself often enough.

I have by no means read all the reviews of *Band of Angels*
which may have appeared in reputable journals; in particular,
I do not know what our English cousins made of the book. But
I can hardly imagine a better review than the one by Mr. Leslie
Fiedler which appeared in the *New Republic*.[7] If I were to
construct a Mr. Fiedler X to serve as a typical figure, that figure
would typify the critic as humane psychologist. I add "humane"
to indicate that in writing of the kind represented by this particular review, the depth attained by the reviewer—and psychologist seem to be aiming at depth nowadays—has not
entailed any loss of balance. The reviewer writes with a clear
sense of the relations of the novelist to his generation, of
the mode of this novel to other kinds of writing, and of the
characters within the novel both to the temperaments the
novelist has created for them, and to the social milieu in which
he has placed them. Nor does Mr. Fiedler, like one of the other
reviewers I have cited, falsify Mr. Warren's presentation of that
milieu by seeing it through warping spectacles of quasi-proletar-
ian clichés.

It is a temptation—which must be resisted—to quote the
whole of Mr. Fiedler's review in order to do justice to its excellence. He first "places" Warren, as an introduction to "placing"

7 Vol. 133, pp. 28–30 (September 26, 1955).

his novel. Mr. Warren, he finds, was neither old enough to belong to the Lost Generation, nor young enough to have been almost compulsorily a 1930-ish Marxist. So much by way of initial advantage. Mr. Fiedler finds Warren nearest akin to Faulkner, being

indeed, the only serious contemporary writer I know able to achieve the typical Faulknerian corkscrew motion of action, that inward and downward circling toward a climax of horror, which makes of plot an outward symbol of our inward flight from and attraction toward the revelation of guilt.

In discussing the mode or genre of Mr. Warren's writing, Mr. Fiedler says,

I have been convinced for a long time that Warren was feeling his way toward a form which would be neither normal prose nor poetry, but I have never been able to find a metaphor to define it. Since reading *Band of Angels,* I have become aware that what he has been approaching for so long is something not very different from nineteenth century Italian Opera. . . .

This suggestion, which Mr. Fiedler develops interestingly, is perhaps rather fanciful; but it is the kind of trial "placing" that might well lead on to a valuable discussion of the status—today and in the foreseeable future—of the historical romance.

It seems to be a professional temptation—to which some reviewers have succumbed—to know all about the South *because* the reviewers are not southerners. This knowledge can then be substituted for any southerner's novel they chance to review. A novelist who, like Mr. Warren, ventures to intimate that the North, as well as the South, exploited the Negro, is accused of being an apologist for the *ancien régime.* Mr. Fiedler is guilty of no such naiveté; he has kept his eyes on this novel. "The final impression is of the Negro staggering from the known horror of his past toward the unknown frightfulness of his future through the special terror of slavery, where his guilt and suffering compound the already intolerable burden of his white masters."

Mr. Fiedler's skill in elucidating literature through psychological analysis comes out in the precision with which he identifies the mainspring—or rather, the *lack* of a mainspring— in the heroine's character:

It is this strange paralysis of Amantha, her inability to walk through unlocked doors, which is the keynote of the book. . . . we are confronted with a passive sufferer, who in the immobility of her self-pity permits man after man to make of her an occasion for self-destruction . . . she chooses only to be nothing. But it is because she is nothing that she destroys: and she must be nothing because she cannot will to say the words "I am a Negro" . . . *Band of Angels* is essentially a book about the disease of pity.

I shall end by noticing one more review, equal in merit to Mr. Fiedler's. The product of Mr. Roderick Craib, it appeared in *The New Leader* for September 26, 1955. Both to record appraisals of Mr. Warren's book which I share, and to illustrate signal adequacy to the task of reviewing, I could not hope to do better than to quote from Mr. Craib's review a series of passages in sum quite extensive:

Manty is immersed in the life around her until she fades away and the people she is telling about become the center of interest. Since there are several dominant characters who occupy her attention by turns, the effect is of a series of third-person narratives . . . *Band of Angels* is so much concerned with Manty's freedom that other aspects of Manty's development are omitted, and the omission makes her seem less than a whole woman. . . . This is the one serious flaw in the book. If Manty, the focus of the book, is incomplete, so is everything else . . . Manty is in the position of the hero of Blake's motto who states, "I must create a system or be enslaved by another man's," but unfortunate Manty fails to create her system; she is enslaved by other men's. Paradoxically Manty, the only continuing character in the book, displays no independent existence. She exists, not because *she* thinks, but because *someone else* thinks her. The literal fact of her slavery is always paralleled by a psychological subjection to one or another of the dominant characters. . . . Still paradoxically, . . . these characters create no lasting systems either. . . . This may well have been what Warren intended: it does make the point clear that Manty cannot solve the problem of her own existence if she looks for the solution outside herself in the forever vanishing realities that surround her. This is a point that could be made in other ways, however, and the question naturally arises whether or not it is worth sacrificing the vitality of the book to make it in just this way . . . Manty, "poor little Manty," as she consistently thinks of herself until she achieves freedom in the end of the book, is . . . looking for the fullness of the world, but rather than attempting to create it out of her own emptiness is seeking it in the emptiness of those around her, and of course does not find it. . . . It is a measure of the book's pretensions to being a major novel that Manty is looking for fullness of the world; it is a measure of the book's uncertain achievement that the reader feels that Warren has rigged the game against Manty.[8]

It is difficult to state—at least, to express fluently—wherein the superiority of this review lies. Flaws are easier to define than merits. I should say that merit here consists first in the critic's keeping his eye steadily on materials furnished by the novel under review: scenes, characters, events, comments; on all of them, not a selection of some of them spotlighted to accord with easily identifiable preconceptions of his own. And, second, to the materials the critic applies, in his job of appraisal, the most broadly human interests and sympathies, brought to a sharpened focus when some matter of literary craftsmanship is at stake. And one whose human interests are broad must write as if aware—must sometimes write as explicitly stressing—the manifoldness of points of view from which a work remains intelligible and justly perceived. It is such qualities as these that I think I find implicit in Mr. Craib's review.

As for myself, I dissent chiefly in that I do not feel Mr. Warren to have rigged fate against Amantha. She encountered great vicissitudes while still very young; while not beyond middle life, she attained what she had desired. A Greek tragedian would have thought her quite well off. My chief reservation about Mr. Warren's book I should focus elsewhere. Although I enjoyed his novel in the reading, and have found it profitable as a subject for reflection afterward, I was at no point—not counting the scene in the African jungle—caught by the living speech, the actual drinking, the veritable presence of a character alien to me and yet as if in the flesh before me and endowed with angelic vision into the soul, in the same way I had been caught in, for instance, *At Heaven's Gate* by the "Statement of Ashby Wyndham." Here was an achievement not unworthy to be mentioned in the same breath as Dickens, or the Shakespeare who created Mistress Quickly. This evidence of the artist at full stretch in every phrase I did not find in *Band of Angels*.

8 Pp. 24–25.

# *10* · Miscegenation as Symbol:
## *Band of Angels*

TRYING TO EXPLAIN changes in images of the Negro from *I'll Take My Stand* to *Band of Angels* and *Segregation*, Robert Penn Warren almost apologetically recalls "the jangle and wrangle" of writing his Agrarian "Briar Patch" essay, drafted at Oxford at the same time as his first novelette. The discomfort of reducing Negroes to the obligatory status of farmhands contrasted with "the holiday sense" of writing *Prime Leaf*. Though convinced that, in 1929, no one—South, North, Negro —was ready to end segregation, he recalls that the world of essays encouraged a rhetorical evasion more so than fiction. A 1957 *Paris Review* interview reports his self-analysis: "In the essay I reckon I was trying to prove something and in the novelette trying to find out something. . . ."

Because the biography of John Brown, somewhat later, was a roundabout defense of the southern temper, its Negroes became "kinky heads" hardly worth civil disorder or disturbance of local practices. Novel after novel, however, made of other Negroes sympathetic though minor figures, proportioned to the theme at hand, ready scapegoats for men deluded by their own righteousness: a Negro is executed for Bunk Trevelyan's crime, and Perse Munn, defender of the guilty man, nearly kills another Negro later, in a panic of flight (*Night Rider*); Anse, Murdock's Negro manservant, is almost lynched after being falsely accused of Sue's murder (*At Heaven's Gate*); Cass Mastern's thoughtless affair with Mrs. Trice ends when his witness, her waiting-maid is sold irretrievably downstream (*All*

*the King's Men*); Jerry Beaumont disguises his face by means
of a black cloth, after killing his surrogate-father Fort (*World
Enough and Time*), so that the slayer will seem to have been
a Negro (a mulatto slave was supposed to have fathered
Rachel's firstborn: Jerry is avenging this defamation which he
believes has originated with Fort). In "Blackberry Winter" and
"Her Own People," the manner of Negro suffering illuminates
the meaning of all mankind's tribulations, sometimes better
than anyone is prepared to realize.

The Negro as symbolic victim first achieves *prominence* in
the character of George, slave boy bullied, quartered and mutilated in *Brother to Dragons*. Unresisting and, at the moment
of execution, almost consenting, George has only three spoken
lines in the whole narrative:

> I was lost in the world, and the trees were tall.
> I was lost in the world, and the dark swale reared.
> I was lost in my anguish and did not know the reason.

Yet these were the first lines of *Brother to Dragons* which
Warren composed; and though mute, George is articulate, living; and dead, his bones speak for him. Not his suffering, nor
the terribleness of the crime, in themselves, is so important as
the before and after of those whose lives interlock with
his.

The characterization of George, for all its fierce impact
on our source of compassion, is not conceived as social protest
for its own sake, which as Warren cautions in his Paris interview

denies the textures of life. The problem is to permit the fullest
range of life into racial awareness. . . . Race isn't an isolated
thing—I mean as it exists in the U. S.—it becomes a total symbolism for every kind of issue.

Thus in *Segregation* he has argued that racism, by the very
act of taking refuge in "antique virtue," denies change which
alone has the capacity to create individual features: so that by
denying the Negro his right to self-definition, southerners have
multiplied divisions which exist in all men and have failed to
achieve their own moral identity. They have sunk back into
the anonymity which accompanies mass reaction and delibera-

tion. Similarly, in *Band of Angels*, the problem of miscegenation is treated in such a way that although it makes direct
comment on the results of classification by race, more impor-
tantly it serves as a symbol for mankind's inner self-divisions,
its angry half-impulsive, half-repelled attempts and failures to
discover identity.

Like George, Manty is a victim—but a highly conscious
one, articulate even in the shuddering reaches of her inward
journey. With extraordinary insight, Warren has made her
rebellion against that growing self-consciousness the source of
her evil season, mirror to the weather of civil war around her.
It is Manty's insistent, self-pitying view of herself as victim
which victimizes her more than society ever could (as *Segregation* contends, the problem is not to learn to live with the
Negro; it is to learn to live with ourselves).

The attempt of a few critics to dismiss *Band of Angels* as
a preconceived Hollywood "mistress-on-the-mattress" farce is
confuted by the actual movie's failure even to approximate the
novel's themes or to suggest the inner contortion of its characters.
What the novel provides, for the first time in the Warren
effort, is a complete context of crediblity, these elements in
which the corkscrew motions of the soul can be described
without exaggeration as progress—world enough and time: duration—what Perse Munn, Jerry Calhoun, Jack Burden, Jerry
Beaumont were all too young to have in sufficiency. *Band of
Angels* gains by being narrated from the point of view of Manty
matured and capable of respecting the anguish of her recollected
earlier self. She demands pity or justice no longer; but—like
Willie Stark in his (as yet unpublished) *Rise and Fall* and
Jerry Beaumont—an understanding that surpasseth peace.

It is herself she has been fleeing. Simply by running no
more, not because exhausted but because disabused, she stifles
the two cries which have shadowed her passage: "Oh, who
am I?"; "If only I could be free. . . ." Refusing to accept the
absolute denial of self imposed by slavery, she retreats in fever
to the other extreme, absolute selfishness, careless of even those
who tried to love her: her father, and Hamish Bond. These
she rejects after having used her sex and youth to incite their
pity. They are her dolls, to whom she gives endearments like

sweets but secretly clings, needing to be needed. They are her victims, along with Rau-Ru and Tobias; but she is theirs, too, for thinking to find herself in them, for expecting to make their strengths hers. The characterization is one of Warren's subtlest and truest, though at first glance most puzzling. Manty is so frail and disordered a young woman, so easily denied person and reduced to body by those routines of subjection, passion and bondage, that she seems to fade in the vicinity of masculine color and mass. Yet this is precisely her most powerful advantage, the trap that literally kills Hamish Bond and Rau-Ru. No one really can be brutal to her. Manty's suffering is psychological, and largely self-inflicted.

She herself is aware, occasionally, of her hold on Bond. When he offers to shoot Charles in a duel for having insulted her, her pride is caressed. In violent need, Bond himself earlier has already raped Manty, as if struggling to repossess his former innocence by violating her; or in a manner of mutual branding, so that she will never be able to leave him again, nor he ever successfully desert her.

Manty welcomes the rape of Bond (the morning sight of his scarred leg turns her terror to tenderness) and seeks out the cuffs of Rau-Ru as a kind of recognition, decorations from fellow-sufferers, to satisfy her own need to be pitiful; and to invest herself with the power of forgiveness. This fault in her, however, defeats itself, almost in mock confirmation of Seth Parton's latter-day edict (years after dispassionately testing his passion by not lusting after her, on the scene of a local seduction) that "only in vileness may man begin to seek." Her very exaggeration of her role as victim finally places her in a position where she has to believe that misfortune has sandpapered her down to less than nothing or that her deepest wounds are of her own making. Rather than deny herself identity, she accepts the burden that goes with it and achieves that wavering balance suspended somewhere between solitary confinement and the status of mere chattel: the absolute self and statism (man as statistic).

Such transformation would seem extreme, had Manty not been equipped with that weakness or strength (even full-grown in wisdom, she is never quite sure which:

Is it our need that makes us lean toward and wish to succor need, or is it our strength? . . . Do we give love in order to receive love, and even in the transport or endearment carry the usurer's tight-lipped and secret calculation, unacknowledged even by ourselves? . . . Or do we simply want a hand, any hand, a human object, to clutch in the dark on the blanket, and fear lies behind everything?) [1]

This passed as love for Bu-Bula, made her feel an accessory to the selling of Shaddy, constructed an image of restored life from a horse's golden apples, helped her to reassure Dollie when the servant felt unloved and to kiss a Negro child who had approached her, let her sustain Tobias when he felt like a pebble in an avalanche and forgive his own nobility turned selfishness. All these prepare for her final quiet and knowledgeable embrace of life. Such rehearsals of grace, intuitive yearnings not however without some inner comprehension, preserve Manty from petrifaction through overself-concern, at its starkest when a son is born to her in Kansas and dies almost unobserved. At times she is even so scrupulous as to feel burdened with not only all past choices but those not chosen as well:

It was, in a way, as though the thing not done—the flight not made—is always done, too, and never releases you from the grip of the old possibility, and you can only escape from the done, never from the not-done, which in its not-doneness is always there being enacted forever.

Furthermore, although she cannot find herself in others, she discovers in their common pattern of illusions why she cannot. Bond, despite repeated references to people's being only what they are and demanding that men face facts, has as much an assumed identity as Manty. In a story as perfectly within the story as a cavity is in a tooth, he is revealed as Alec Hinks, ex-slave trader, driven to his inhumane business by the anonymity of his weakling father and by a desire to demonstrate the absurdity of his mother's false memory of slave servants. Thus he has made her lie come true, "but true in some shocking not respectable way," as Warren says, "that would violate her need for respectability." Bond, in turn, is rejected by his own "son,"

Rau-Ru, his *k'la* and secret self, in an attempted denial of that relation. Rau-Ru puts the noose around Bond's neck, although he is not sure that he would actually have killed Bond had the latter not jumped to make sure. By that time Rau-Ru has an assumed identity of his own: Oliver Cromwell Jones, puritan and protector, zealot of his own interpretation of the law. However, cruelty does not fit him well. He saves Manty from the bushwackers, his motives now obscure even to himself. And it is such fevers of kindness which distinguish Rau-Ru, Bond, and even Tobias (Whose nobility is like a disease) from the more permanent and demoniac hypocritical disguises of Charles, Seth Parton, and Miss Idell.

Captive to his own slave-running days, Bond once excused himself with the words: "I didn't make this world and make 'em drink blood, I didn't make myself and I can't help what I am doing." It is Maule's curse, from *The House of the Seven Gables,* that is summoned by this talk of drinking blood and the relevance of Hawthorne's novel, in which each member in a family line brings death on himself not through the malignancy of some predestining agency but through his own greed, his own recommission of an original sin, is as clear as the epigraph from Housman: "When shall I be dead and rid— Of the wrong my father did?" (Is it coincidental that "Oliver Cromwell Jones" is a near-rhyme for Oliver Wendell Holmes, Bostonian racist who compiled physiological "proofs" for the heredity of evil?) Man inherits the conditions of evil, yet is capable of choosing otherwise. Tobias explains, in words that recall Willie Stark,

"But it's so hard right in the middle of things to remember that the power of soul must work through matter, that even the filthiness of things is part of what Mr. Emerson calls the perennial miracle the soul worketh, that matter often retains something of its original tarnishment . . ."

Without choice there is no identity; talk of human helplessness is self-pity in the extreme—which Bond will not allow himself. And so the example is set Manty, who resents Charles' speaking of Bond as *pauvre vieux.* In exchange, Bond and Rau-Ru sense in Manty's fragile trust the limits of their own willingness to end pretense. Each becomes at first the accomplice of, then the catalyst for, the others.

Because of this elaborate system of facsimile selves which makes truth shiver through the fabric of disguise, the theme of the novel cannot be diminished even when Manty seems to pale in importance. Indirection is the method not only of the novel but presumably of life. Aaron Starr's attempted kindness to his illegitimate daughter is obstructed by society's remission laws; but Manty blames only her father. Service of an abstract good can even be a vice, as it is with Seth Parton and as it threatens to be with Tobias who, however, is rescued by his sense of the incongruous. They are presented as less criminal examples of "northern justice" than those corrupt reformers, heavy-handed General Butler and light-fingered Colonel Morton, for whom fairness is equated with force. Manty's rebellion against her growing consciousness of a self which displeases her devises scapegoats out of those around her, just as the North purged itself of all guilt by transferring the sins of Yankee slave-traders to the southern planters' already burdened conscience. But the novel's countermovement has its own triumphs. Good also works by indirection.

Manty, in reconstructing her past, tries to link her rape with Harper's Ferry and all other simultaneous events of which her own life is the "summing up." In the lives most closely associated with hers, those of lovers and enemies, she discovers the same doubts and delusions, the same struggle against entrapment. The more the wounds are ripped, to exhibit them for sympathy's sake, the less chance is there of healing. But the struggle itself against bondage of whatever kind is sanctified, becomes a bond of glory, provided it is accompanied by recognition that the worst form of human subjugation is self-abasement, assuming the position of pure victim.

Although Manty, in her frailty, sometimes believes herself only "an expression of History" as if a lifetime were one enormous livelong rape ("you do not live your life, but somehow, your life lives you, and you are, therefore, only what History does to you"), she privately admits, in time, that such thoughts are a tactic of evasion. As often as she sidesteps responsibility, to be free of all guilt, she is surrendering her right to herself. The drama enveloping her impersonates and reveals her inner conflict: the Civil War, the whole social fretwork based on the myths of miscengenation—these are projections of her own self-division. The northern reformers, armed with righteousness and bayonets, do not constitute a band of angels. Reform is a matter for the individual soul, whose health or disease society merely reflects; it cannot be imposed, any more than freedom can be absolutely given or denied, or can even be defined absolutely from without.

By indirection, Manty's western flight becomes pursuit: in the image of Halesburg's beggar, and of Old Slop, being embraced by a son to whom self-respect is more important than commonplace pride, she contemplates herself. Her stumbling tremulous progress towards self-realization coincides with the progressive suffrage which Tobias Sears advocates until, rebelling against his father by carrying the old man's beliefs to their absurd conclusion (as Bond had done with his mother's), he demands immediate and full extension of privilege.

In *Segregation* Warren has made the same point, more bluntly: "Gradualism is all you'll get. History, like nature, knows no jumps. Except the jump backward, maybe." In the *Paris Review* he has complained of ineffectual do-gooders and levelers intent on creating a superconformity in the name of equality: "I feel pretty strongly about attempts to legislate *undifference*. That is just as much tyranny as trying to legislate difference. . . . Furthermore, you can't legislate virtue." And in his address on "Knowledge and the Image of Man," Warren has described as a congenital part of the Christian ethic "the right to define oneself," despite a continuous "osmosis of being," to distinguish himself from the world and from other men and to make his very own way towards salvation or damnation. Even well-intentioned common man-ism, that special form of condescension which New Dealers sometimes promoted, is therefore objectionable.

In the crucible of flesh, which a novel such as *Band of Angels* provides, such perceptions are tested under a fire that sets in motion the shuddering ripples of Manty's life, her shriveling contraction and slow magnification. The central figure, usually an executioner, apocalptic knight, now is become victim; but what is revealed to her is not the perfection of her grief nor its legitimacy. Through the long welter of circumstance this outcast learns more than endurance, more than disguise for survival's sake. She learns that only through separateness is identity earned and is permission finally granted to rejoin the body of those equally distinct and, because innocent of self-inflicted error, equally fulfilled. Between two absolutes, rejection and subjection, she achieves her station.

# 11 · Journey to the Interior:

## The Cave

IN THE MIDST of his italicized commentary at the conclusion of *World Enough and Time*, Warren's irony measures modern commercial distraction against the reverence of Indians once afoot in "The Hollow Land," place of great caves, Kentucky. Here the tribes fought and hunted and consulted divine justice but never dared dwell because "It was a holy land, it was a land of mystery . . . the gods lived there." Confronted by the officious disregard of European settlers self-instructed in justice, "the gods fled, either into the upper air or deeper into the dark earth."

Any mythic reference here is too fleeting even to be enigmatic. But the reader who *does* bother to wonder, on the run, can scarcely accommodate those caves sacred to conscience and the novel's earlier womb-tomb imagery of unconcern. There is a uterine remoteness about both Gran Boz' hideaway, his canebrake settlement, and Beaumont's dungeon prison, where, while awaiting execution, he recalls those impulses to hide forever which came to him as a boy secure in secret underground passages. Like recurring submarine images in Warren's canon, these are symbols of a characteristic desire to be unborn or to be among the uncommitted dead, to be relieved of both time *and* eternity; and as such they are contrary to any concept of caves as a place of sanctified encounter. In *World Enough and Time* Warren was unprepared to explore fully the still-buried meaning of his many-chambered symbol. The reference is a memorandum only, a mapping of coordinates for some long day's later search.

Warren, a Vanderbilt student at the time of Floyd Collins' entrapment at Sand Cave, Kentucky, in 1925, refused to take part in the heroic exploitations that followed. Nevertheless, the incident was too revealing of the dark side of man's good intentions to be forgotten. During the last stages of *World Enough and Time* Warren felt those commotions—the collision, interpolation, peremptory fusion, projection—which mark the burdening of simply chronicled character with eventfulness.[1] Four more works were to intervene before, in late summer, 1957, the actual writing of this communal attendance on disaster could begin. However, the minotaur and clutch-doll imagery, respectively, in *Brother to Dragons* and *Band of Angels* were preparations for the work in progress.

The pilgrimage of historic accident through a labyrinth of associations toward personal configuration in fiction marks more than the maturing writer's practice of craft. It becomes a tangible equivalent and demonstration of his own life-web philosophy, the inevitability of revealed interconnections. Through the years an initial insight has grown into a system of correspondences massively engaged, in *The Cave*. No previous work of Warren's has been structured so completely according to apparently discrete but thoroughly parallel multiple points of view. Here, theme is influential in form almost totally. Yet only to the reader is the interpenetration of dreams, both evil and hopeful, visible; and self-admission is withheld from just enough characters, who like Mrs. Bingham resist introspection or take refuge in fabrication, to prevent the over-perfection of a *tour de force*.

While the essential problem of each—reconciliation of any man's many identities—has been a commonplace with Warren ever since "Brother, My Brother" appeared in the June, 1925, issue of *Fugitive* magazine, never has it found such epitome and focal occasion as in the enigma of Jasper Harrick's motives. Jasper is no Floyd Collins in disguise (Ike Sumpter's reference to the original accident establishes it fictively as a much earlier

1 Letter from Robert Penn Warren to Leonard Casper, September 28, 1959.

analog and even as an incentive to his own exploitation); but rather an image only in the moving minds of others. He is opportunity—and his own ambiguity is well commemorated in their uneasy grappling with choice and consequence.

Greater than the temptation to make Jasper a fractional counterpart of Collins, and thereby to burden history with sole responsibility for inferences drawn from its casual facts, must have been the attractiveness of familiar romantic mythology associated with the land. Jasper's half-Indian heritage, together with those affinities already remarked in *World Enough and Time*, suggests an appropriateness available in the character's being sealed up forever enshrined in an earth-chamber, his sacred source. Nevertheless, Warren's intimate connection with the new agrarian philosophy in the 1930's did not leave him susceptible to sentimentality, however engagingly elevated. His repeated indictment of the western dream—that simply by change of place one can restore innocence to full fresh righteousness—reached a climax in *Brother to Dragons*. There he accused Jefferson himself, to some disciples the very prophet of agrarian life, of possessing an overfacile vision of human perfectibility. Nor is he presented as the "buried god" of fertility rites (compare Eliot's "Come in under the shadow of this red rock") whose sacrificial death will redeem the countryside—although his father and Nick Papadoupalous wish for their own sake that he were. His deliberate removal from visible action and the equivocal nature of his own reasons for cave-crawling prevent assignment of any simple meaning to Jasper.

Did Jasper become a caver, in casual "dark-dreaming" completion of himself "with the whole earth tucked in around him," as Monty enviously says; or to escape having to live up to his father's spitting image, as Celia charges? When Jasper prefers the seasonless underground because "a lot of things don't matter down there," is this a death-wish subtly stated, womb-longing, the trap of timelessness as despairing disengagement, a new Great Sleep? Or is it some superior stage in the act of transcendence, relinquishment of the "boot"-body which liberates his spirit for enjoyment of the immutable, timelessness-as-eternity? If his inward journeying earns him the name of new frontiersman, is this a search for sedatives (as it was for western dreamers, fugitive from guilt) or for steadfast truth, some midpoint unmoving? To such riddles there are almost as many answers as there are images of Jasper; for he is no more know-able than the need of others—which expresses him—permits. Does truth change, as Jack Harrick and Mac Sumpter agree; does God? Or only the image of these in the sickly human eye? The heart of each man's mystery lies with Jasper in that weight-less center of the world "where all bargains are debated, and all transactions are made." But who is there unafraid to go, confront himself in loneliness? On different occasions Jack and Nick complain that no man can trace how he came to be him-self (partially because there is a natural repression of certain admissions). How, then, can one expect to pass judgment on another? Yet—Warren argues the dilemma—others are necessary context and cause for individual self-knowledge.

In earlier novels the affected search for identity often was, in fact, a search for impossible innocence. It proceeded vicar-iously, and therefore vainly, through submission to, then venge-ful disavowal of, another's role as projected prototype. Senator Tolliver is Perse Munn's proxy father—and, later, his scapegoat; Murdock is Jerry Calhoun's; Fort is Jeremiah Beaumont's; Bond and Rau-Ru are Manty's; more deviously, Willie Stark is Jack Burden's. In their very frustration a few discover confirmation of that ideal process prescribed by Cass Mastern: "It is human defect—to try to know oneself by the self of another. One can only know oneself in God and in His great eye." Struggling toward this ideal, man's passionate appetite for exaltation may find expression in religious travesties such as those orgies in-spired by evangelist Corinthian McClardy in *World Enough and Time*. The confusion of desires, the violent insistence on self-discovery through exploration of another's body, is a motif current throughout the novels but perhaps epitomized in the tortuous history of Sue Murdock's failure to find fulfillment with any of three lovers; or condemned Beaumont's division of his dungeon hours between minute recording of his motives and lustful use of his wife—both mechanisms for justification.

In *The Cave* selfhood is asserted not through night-riding violence or meat-axe venegeance, but through sexual outrage and quasiviolation. With an impulse largely unconscious (described independently by two characters as the fierce "clawing out" of some inner animal) human need gropes through lust for love, through desire for a reality beyond desire. Rachel's protest—"I'm just not going to let you use me for some kind of Grade-A masturbation"—is descriptive of both Ike's self-glutting and all those substitutes for higher satisfactions generally acceptable to society at large. During intimacies with his wife Nick Papadoupalous keeps his eyes closed, to assist the illusion that platinum-blonde Jean Harlow is the partner of this love act and, consequently, that it is purified. For the same reason—self-assurance: no one even gets Nick's name right—when his wife is sick, he uses Dorothy Cutlick, a near-albino, in the dark of her rented room. Similarly, Isaac, sensing that his father's marriage was prompted by envy of his wife's first lover, feels that he was conceived in the dark, as a kind of accidental by-product of Mac Sumpter's self-gratification. Even Rachel acts most pleased with her lover because "You give me, me, Ikey." She kisses him, eyes closed, remote, withheld. Old Jack Harrick, in a fit of confession, recalls the unnumbered girls, many unnamed as well, "wanting something from him, always a different something, but something, and always something he didn't care whether, in their emptiness, they ever got or not." His enumeration of the ignored and ignorant is counterpart to the mass orgies, appropriately in the dark, committed when word of Jasper's death panics spectators into proof of their own will to survive.

The pattern of sexualism as violation or indifference, as an act of self-assertion only, is most prominent in the first third of the novel. Only gradually, in a kind of inverted Freudianism, does it become clear that far from all acts and objects symbolizing sexual drives, these drives themselves are kinetic accessories or expressions—shadows in a Platonic cave—of even more intangible metaphysical needs. Realization comes at a pace suited to the unsteady struggle of those few for whom the sex act purges physical desire without satisfying some deeper raging claim. In the midst of his resentment of Jo-Lea's cold sufficiency, and with intentions of another sort altogether, Monty finds himself pleading his love, for once, from his very "in-

nards." The same blinding compulsion had once driven his
father to his knees, during a night walk among the dogwood
with Celia. Their bodies were dreaming the same dream, in joy;
when suddenly he felt the terror of not knowing who he was,
and only her hand sustained him; so that he croaked out,
"Marry me . . . !" Years later Nick Papadoupalous as suddenly
senses the decency in his overfed, bedridden wife, an ex-strip-
teaser, as she refuses to earn blackmail for them by performing
an abortion. Holding her cupped hand in his, he examines its
emptiness and recognizes his own. A single touch—instinctive,
not violent—silences the loneliness of people even in the act of
expressing it.

Warren has never failed to find the multitude of voices
required to impersonate his varied characters. Nor has he in-
truded for the first time here, although so much has to be conveyed by a townspeople's impoverished speech, language too
primitive to explore and formulate the subtleties of essential
experience. *This* folk idiom is not illumined with Biblical emblems and God's cryptic similes, as was the sworn statement
of Ashby Wyndham in *At Heaven's Gate*. It is as common as
grits, unvaried as backyard news in a small Tennessee town. Nor
is Nick's raw city talk or Ike's campus-cultured magnifications
less inarticulate, however distinctive. Yet while conceding that
a fabulous spokesman in such company would be unlikely,
Warren does suggest that each voice may be a syllable in some
vast reverberant word; and he achieves this effect by relying on
a rotating, cross-sectional point of view, with credible planes
of analogy implied in the very repetition of certain common-
places which begin to assume consequence and to function as
cunning, though minor, refrains.

Symbols also, in sufficiency to constitute several correlative
motifs, speak for the inexpressible. The cave as human emptiness and as yearning for fulfillment so profound (a chronic
"soul-ache") that it implores the comfort of companionship
finds minute and simultaneous reflections everywhere. Jo-Lea's
heartbeat is like the dark sound down a well; upon first meeting
Celia, Jack Harrick says solemnly, "I bet if I threw a rock down
your well, I'd be listening down in the dark a long time before
it hit water." He resents the cancerous hole right where "a

man's thinking and feeling and living ought to be"; and Celia feels a sense of defraudment, an infinitesimal inner hemorrhage, when her husband denies the power of love to transform the grime of the smithy. Such images of wells and innermost physiology are kindred to those box shapes which signify identity's dual nature—its terrible confinement and its comforting singularity. The most striking are the coffinlike room of Mac Sumpter, Baptist minister who feels overscrupulously guilty because he still longs for his dead wife's fugitive flesh; and the recurring appearance of Jasper's guitar, "His Box," which becomes a communal voice as it inspires folk ballads for this occasion. While expressing all men's hopes in the act of elevating one to the status of legend, it also requires of each player-composer improvisation. The novel begins and ends with "His Box." Because others know it is too precious to have been left intentionally in the overnight dew, they search for the owner: it has spoken for Jasper. At the end it is another's voicebox, intended for a third—symbol of kinship, the weight and consolation thereof. Old Jack Harrick, fiercely independent but on every conspiring occasion forced to admit his need, proclaims at last as he plays the guitar, "Every man's got to make his own kind, his own kind of song."

What is more expressive, however, than all these other symbols is that unself-conscious gesture which joins characters again and again, their simple touching, the gentle laying on of hands in instinctive benediction or entreaty. Touch is witness to the truth of self, lest it be only a dream dreamed from one's own dire weakness. That such gestures are not always agents of grace is apparent in *Band of Angels*, when Manty meditates her own outstretching passion: Is it our need that makes us lean toward and wish to succor need, or is it our strength? . . . Or do we simply want a hand, any hand, a human object, to clutch in the dark on the blanket, and fear lies behind everything?" It *was* fear that made Jack Harrick seize the hand of Celia, that dark night under the dogwoods. But the other instances are less equivocal. Celia is determined to hold Jack's hand in the hour of his dying, and hopes that, waiting, he will place his hand on her head. She regrets not having touched Jasper before he left. Ike, almost reluctant at times to continue

his deception, longs for the hand of his mother who died at
his birth. After Sumpter has protected Ike's lie with a half-truth
of his own, he warns the Greek that he is not worthy of Nick's
touch. Finally, Jack Harrick, remembering that Monty "has
gone in to hold his Big Brother's hand," begins to play his
son's guitar and sing, "I will come under the land. In the dark
take your Pappy's hand." And when his wife comes to him,
lightly he *does* lay his hand on her head.

Symbols and structure, reconciling personal with public
worlds, convey the double meaning of both the world and its
words. "Love is self-betrayal," both terrible and wonderful; for
self-worship and self-worry are mere vanity unless one's dream,
his image of himself, concedes the reality of his need. A man
may even feel urged to kill those he loves—his wife, his son,
his father—because they are other than he and demanding, or
because they threaten to outlive him and to find satisfaction
elsewhere and so destroy old comforting truths by latter-day
denial. But what is man without that larger identity which love
alone permits and extends? He is Isaac Sumpter.

The novel's most lonely figure is Ike, who sees in Jasper's
entrapment a chance to regain the pride lost when Jews at
college mistook him for one of themselves. The tragedy at the
cave becomes his property. Instead of earning his heroism, by
completing the rescue, he capitalizes on what he too quickly
prejudges is disaster. Because his father compounds his lies, Ike
succeeds in becoming the very stereotype that he had pretended
to resent—the stage-Jew, man of profane guile, self-pitying im-
poster, killer-clown—welcome later to an executive suite in some
false-image factory equally dedicated to "putting one over on
the dumb schmucks." The price he pays is that he must always
be "totally himself," only.

Ike is a composite of Warren archetypes: the glittering
Pharisee; the calculating judge who punishes the gross world
by crucifying himself, murdering innocence in their name (they
are largely indifferent; and this he resents most of all) and
conducting ceremonies for his own canonization. He is as much
victor-victim as George, willing martyr to the meat axe in
*Brother to Dragons*; or Manty in *Band of Angels*; or Mrs.
Bingham in *The Cave*. He forces Rachel to reject him because,

failing to understand that only through need is self completed, he considers acceptance on terms other than his own belittling. Similarly he takes almost morbid pleasure from the thought that his father is guilty of his mother's death and, like Abraham of old, is plotting Ike's as well—by implicating him in that childbirth as accomplice. He has no inclination to forgive, lest he lose that role as plaintiff and prosecutor which preserves him from acknowledging imperfections of his own. His self-imposed part requires that he feel betrayed even by his father's kindness. Mac Sumpter's corroborating lie sets the ultimate "knife" to his scarified flesh. Leaving his father for the last time, Ike looks back—an appeal to be stopped, to be touched; but Mac does not appear. Ike has achieved the utter loneliness of those deluded crowds in the woods who have used tears, prayers, booze, and now one another to avoid "the dark mystery which was themselves." So conscious is he of his performance as some sacrificial Isaac never to be rescued that unwittingly he becomes his brother's killer, Cain.

Nevertheless, Warren does not commit the error of his character: he takes no joy in accusations. Rather, he startles by demonstrating how transparently subtle the space is between blindness and vision. Ike's error is not that he is an opportunist, not that he hopes to profit even from catastrophe; but that his profit is commercial, rather than any kind that can alter his values. Mac, Nick, and Jack (not Ike), almost in a paradigm of effort and through cumulative revelation, learn from the death of Jasper the conditions of life. They are witnesses to his common ground. The ambiguity of his motives, the inexactness of his situation, are reminders of their own ambivalence whenever confronted by the same alternatives implicit in the cave: escape or encounter. The duality of life itself, happily, delivers man as often as it snares him. Any fall, certain covenants being fulfilled, can be fortunate. By admitting to the minotaur in their private caves, they are more prepared to be men. The very reaching out, to be touched, to be taken, is the initial gesture in a humble ritual that occasions its own reward.

God is not their scapegoat; that would be supreme self-pity. In order that consequences may remain men's responsibility, they consider the possibility that God adjusts His will to theirs.

Such responsibility is the terrible price of self—since possession of free will without absolute knowledge must sometimes be terrifying. Nevertheless, theirs is a quiescent faith in God's love, because of God's own need.

Their trust in the possibilities of an ever-coming overwhelming love is founded on those momentary proclamations of flesh on flesh, beatitudes by hand. For the first time Warren's truths emerge not as the result of long-suffering introspection, syllogistic convergings in one man's mind; but, more credibly, from implications that leap from the exchanged confessions of two cornered old men stricken wise by realization that the loss of their sons greatly matters. In this act of communion all previous configurations foreshadowing mutual salvation are completed. Prepared to be spat upon, the fathers have never seemed less proud, nor more worthy.

*The Cave* has no exemplum, no play within to compensate for the dumb show without. Articulation of the parts is made both mode of expression and matter expressed. So many times Warren has considered the present contingent on the past, part of one prolonged continuum. Now the present, in turn, becomes point of departure for a future unforeseen, with the same courage of faith risked in *Promises*. Bingham no longer speaks of abortion. And Jack Harrick who, at the instant he feels he can never die, falls into dimensionless dark and reaches for Celia, now touches her again and is told, "Don't ever die!" Having looked into his own eyes in the meantime, he is prepared for death; and ready for life. He strikes his clanging anvil chord, careful however not to damage "His Box" for Monty, who in time must have his own say, his own as well as a family identity, a common sense of self and kind. He strikes his chord. Anyman's moving hand on the moving strings becomes the image of sound becoming light; image of the bardic writer's art.

# 12 · Trial by Wilderness:

## Warren's Exemplum

WILDERNESS IS A NOVEL written by a poet-dramatist, whose selective method attempts "to write the particular story," free from all distraction.[1] As if to avoid the sort of excessive introspection which sometimes clouded such earlier historical fiction as *World Enough and Time* and *Band of Angels*, Robert Penn Warren has chosen a narrator who is only self-conscious and thoughtful, without being capable of either total recall or gratuitously perfected self-knowledge. He has refrained from romantic melodrama of the order which the Civil War readily makes available to the American folk imagination. He has foregone erotic passages such as those in *The Cave* which alienated monocular critics. Although *Wilderness* has somewhat more scope than *The Red Badge of Courage*—primarily because, as Don W. Kleine points out,[2] its antihero is a kind of picaro-pilgrim with a doleful countenance—nevertheless its modest panorama is held deliberately remote from front-line thunder. The poet in Warren does not even resort to lyric streams of consciousness, in order to provide continuity and to compensate by emotional intensity for episodic brevity. Instead, the art of Warren's poetry is perceptible in image becoming motif; and his sense of dramatic investiture, in scenes hieratically conceived. His hope has to be that his philosophical poem becomes a "blooded abstraction" and not transparent allegory or costumed morality play.

The extent of the author's gamble is perhaps most evident

1 Correspondence with the author, March 17, 1962.
2 *Epoch*, XI (Winter 1962), 264.

in his choice of narrators. Adam Rosenzweig is presented from
the first in a typical stance, alone outside the house where his
father lies dead. His role throughout the novel is that of the
outsider, in search of the light of a livable self, resurrection from
the limbo of his inheritance. Despite his deadening Bavarian
ghetto, some dreaming part of himself was liberated and sustained by his father's sacrifices to freedom and justice, on the
barricades of Berlin in 1848 and, for thirteen years, in prison.
But the shared ideal becomes exclusively his own; Adam is born
into nakedness, when his sickly father lets his brother force him
to admit that his life has been blasphemous. He has trusted
man more than he has trusted God; he has not lived resigned to
the Law. And man has betrayed him: the German uprising has
brought some degree of freedom to all but the Semitic peoples.
From that moment, six months before his funeral, Adam's
father was dead: "To be dead, [Adam] thought, that was to
know that nothing would ever be different." Adam looks at his
boot, cunningly designed to disguise his foot's deformity. He
looks up to the splendor of mountain peaks, above the conspiring aloofness of the ruling houses. Assuming the obligation repudiated by his father, he too steps outside the Law (although
accompanied by phylacteries, shaw and prayer book in a bor-
rowed satchel): he enlists as a mercenary, to assist the Union
cause.

    Adam, whose untraditional name suggests his alienation
even from his people, suffers additional exclusion by removal to
foreign shores. When his foot's defect is discovered, he is not
permitted to remain in the hired ranks. Nevertheless, still an
idealist—in the absence of any experience (he is nearly thirty
and yet has never known wealth or a woman, in part because a
German-Jew needs a family-founding permit before marriage is
allowed), he moves like a hermit figure through the American
wasteland. Always he is someone else's shadow—rescued by a
Negro from drowning in a cellar shortly after himself having
helped "Shag them niggers!" in the slums of New York; adopted
by Blaustein, the store prince, to replace a son killed in battle;
reduced to assistant on a sutler's wagon, feeding the mouths of
suffering soldiers, and not their souls. Only by an act of com-

pleted violence, when Adam actually kills a berserk scarecrow trooper and with one shot betrays what was so long chambered in his heart, does he finally achieve some degree of manhood and person.

How is it possible to sustain a novel of *in*experience, told from a nondescript point of view? Can any author make credible the sudden emergence of identity in a *naïf* whose first thirty years were so unremarkable that they seem to constitute a case of arrested development? Apparently Adam lived so much in his father that there is nothing recorded of those long years except Adam's daily labor with timepieces and his lonely nights in the dark, awaiting the broken old man's return. (One would like to believe that Adam's assigned age is not mere convention, designed to abstract him further into a crypto-Christ; but that the space between the related civil wars in Germany and America requires that Adam be older than he seems. In any case, the thirty years are a statistic only; and Adam, before he sees the mutilated Negro hanging like an effigy in the mob-emptied streets, is static, a nonperson.) Is Warren's central character so much an Everyman that he is no-man; so universalized in name and heritage and ritual action that he is never realized in full-blooded particular?

In *Moby Dick* the narrator, Ishmael, is rapidly exchanged for an omniscient point of view and is not recovered until late in the novel. The fact that readers seldom notice this conversion is surely due to the larger-than-personal nature of Ishmael, most evident in the sperm-squeezing scene. Outcast Ishmael is even Ahab written small and humanely. He is so easily absorbed into the communal figure of the crew and, by extension then, of mass mankind that the change in narration is apparent only. In *Wilderness* Adam's role is somewhat analogous. He is so much the uninitiate, the inexperienced idealist, that events impress themselves graphically on him. Because his nature is unformed, Adam does not even exist as some personification; and the subjective readily yields to objective narration. In Chapter IX there is an unequivocal shift in point of view from Adam to Jed the sutler who, behind barred doors in winter quarters, paces the cage of his cabin, trying to fathom his own childhood. Adam could never have had access to such privacies. Yet the shift, since it occurs gratuitously, would seem a matter of indifference even to the author.

Although Adam at first appears disembodied, defined as he is by deformity, by lack, by otherness, by the dream unfulfilled and disregarding, his final emergence is not unprepared for because his sap and substance, his body, is composite of each of those graphic persons he has known. They are stages on the journey across what only seems a wasteland but what is actually a trial by wilderness, to the burning bush of achieved knowledge and to parturition (only a thin "diaphragm of lyric green" separates him from the powerful noon, at first; then his whole world burns) in the last chapters. The novel moves quickly from scene to scene, sometimes with no more transition than continued intensity: like a poem committed to images rather than to grammar or scansion; like a play, willing to foreshorten everything but dramatic truth. It is precisely the absence of distraction—the starkness of Adam's undefended response—which thrusts so many of *Wilderness'* moments forward into memorability.

The mutilated Negro hanged from a lamp post by a northern mob weary of war; the dark rising flood, man-made, in the cellar trap; the aftermath of Gettysburg, the body robbers; Mose at his alphabet; Simms Purdew, battle hero, ramming the heads of tied Negroes into washtubs of flour and buried greenbacks; Adam's bugle-sharp outcry at the heavens, from the animal-pen remains of the broken winter camp; the endless cavalcades "winding into the anonymity of distance"; the homely, maniacal attack of the scarecrows. . . . All these are the fire-seared and sharpened conditions of Adam's birth. On a variety of occasions Adam ponders the *ifs* of his strange passage. If the mountain had not gleamed so white; if the *Elmyra* had not rolled and betrayed him to a fellow-cripple. . . . Each of these and other moments is not a fatal accident enforced on inert man. Warren's canon has never been committed to determinism; but to causality, yes. And at the hour of illumination when Adam, having killed and having thus fulfilled the hate and fear of otherness that masked itself as ideal devotion, admits too the role he played in the murder of Jedeen Hawksworth and the subsequent flight of tortured Mose Talbutt, he takes on himself his share in the moral linkage of events. "He knew that, in the end, he would have to think every *if*—every *if* which was life." Every flaring detail, however detached it seems from Adam, becomes his secret motive, his *if*. Finally he accepts his flaw as his fortune, and moves on—toward the grandeur that the epigraph from Pascal implies: toward an awareness of human misery, without self-pity but with gratitude. Here is Warren's recurring version of *felix culpa*—Abel improved for having been Cain.

The theme of the oneness of man is glossed by this gradual transplanting of flesh onto Adam's archetypal spirit. At intervals the other characters have already shown their solidarity, even in seasons of most grievous mutual revulsion. From the instant that he first conceives of joining the conflict between the States, Adam wants to believe that his purpose is pure—the deliverance of freedom and justice—because he cannot bring himself to confess his innermost motive: the desire to kill a world that is different from himself, and from his dream. Only at the end can he say, " 'I killed him . . . because his foot was not like mine' ": and so the end becomes his beginning. He has become the true proxy son of Blaustein who knew so well that "The hardest thing to remember is that other men are men." There is Herr Zellert who keeps pigs on the streets under the Schloss, so that he will not be mistaken for a Jew; bald Duncan with the stiff knee, wounded when he fled Manassas and bitterly reminded by Adam's supposed mockery aboard ship; Blaustein who unjustly calls the Plattdeutsch rapists and runners, because his son died at Chancellorsville when Stonewall Jackson broke their hired ranks; Jedeen Hawksworth (described as a "centaur," at one point, for his mismatched clothes) who resents his dependence on "Mr. Blow-steim," the rich Jew, and is even more confused about his own motives for having once defended a slave who struck the son of his owner; Mose proves to have once been an army deserter, but defends his action by insisting that Negroes had not been allowed to do anything else except dig privies; Monmorancy Pugh is trapped into killing conscriptors lest they send him to kill in daily combat. All these and others are flawed, like Adam himself (whose name in Hebrew means "man"): but what man who confesses and is contrite cannot be forgiven?

Adam the innocent eats finally from the tree of the knowledge of both good and evil; and is redeemed. He becomes Slew, for Old Slewfoot, and for his climactic performance as slayer-Cain as well. Yet in that supreme act of hate, at last he understands love, the power of forgiveness, and its superiority to self-righteous, untempered crusades in the name of freedom and justice. Having come his long pilgrim's way and having slain in defense of another's life, Adam knows he would do it all again: "But, oh, with a different heart!"—with all the difference that distinguishes conscious from unconscious act.

It is the heart that rescues, the Original Goodness—perhaps more immemorial and ingrained than Original Sin itself. Man's inarticulateness, his failure to find fullness of expression (much less satisfaction) for his deepest needs to know and to be known, finds repeated metaphor here. America, first seen, appears as a green shore on which a dog barks unheard; Maran Meyerhof's imploring O of widowship-to-be remains unvoiced; Mose works his bits of alphabets as if in search of a name that will identify him beyond the brand (W for "Worthless") that he bears; Adam awaits a voice crying in the Wilderness that will set him free:

To shut the eyes—that was a mistake. For immediately the darkness of his head rang with a thousand cries. The cries had the strange, clear, bountiful, vaulted and vaulting hollowness of a cry uttered in the deep woods. . . . The red reflection of the flame glowed on faces from which the eyes distended maniacally, and in which the mouth made the perfectly round O of the scream, the scream he could not, in fact, hear.[3]

There are the cave images too, dark inward places where man confronts some portion of truth's terror—in that nearly fatal New York cellar; in the cavernous dwelling of Monmorancy Pugh, driven underground by the ironies of militant pacifism; in the scrub and blight pine of the Wilderness itself: "going in them woods after Ginnal Lee—it is like crawling in a cave at night to wrassle a bear and it the bear's cave." And there

3 Robert Penn Warren, *Wilderness* (New York: Random House, 1961). All quotations in this essay are from this edition.

are recurring references to the groping combat of civil war as an elephant, unknowable to the blind walking-wounded, trampled by its passage. . . . So dark is human understanding that men scarcely know their own worth. Goodness *has* to be engrained, to advance against such ignorance.

If violence abounds, and rationalized hate, so too does kindness, welling as unexpectedly as grace and revelation from secret springs. A seaman instructs Adam in ways to escape being returned to Europe when his deformity is discovered. In the aftermath of Gettysburg, preacher Mordacai Sulgrave is acknowledged as one who hid from battle beneath a bed; yet once he sucked pus through a tube from a man's swollen throat. On the same occasion, Jed Hawksworth who has long dreamed vengeance on the North Carolinians who ostracized him protects the corpses of the brave Carolinian dead. Beneath the vile face of Simms Purdew, Adam sees the simple trustful boy Simms must have been. Adam is able to move Millie the Mutton, to expose the upward gaze in the camp follower's roving eye. Pugh's wife finds it in her heart to forgive her husband's failure to weep when their son dies during their doomed running feud with the conscriptors. Pugh himself, recalling the recoverable good days of his marriage, lets Adam escape him alive.

Charity such as this vindicates human yearning for faith and hope. It is the other half of Blaustein's warning: the hardest thing to remember is that other men are men (the problem, in its fullness, of man as Negro). It is in Original Goodness, which conjugates God and man, that Adam finally discovers an end to the division which had torn his spirit at the beginning of his pilgrimage. Against his uncle's injunction that wisdom is total resignation to the Law, he had weighed the advice of Jacob the cobbler that life robbed of ambition—the right to dream, to choose—is trivial. The uncle's satchel, the cobbler's boots Adam has carried all the way, into the brightening knowledge of his mystery. Because there is love, the Law itself requires something far more difficult than resignation: will, action; and responsibility for consequences. Not will unbounded, but will limited by and attracted to that example of love. To wear the boot as disguise is to risk messianic vanity. Adam, pure idealist, longs to be heroic sacrifice, to suffer in public splendor; but

finally knows that of him a more heroic decision is demanded—
to be unheroic; to be like all others, in a way unforeseen, de-
formed, and nameless; in humility, to be worthy "of what they
as men and in their error, had endured." They are all parts of
an alphabet constantly reshaping itself into a single run-on expression of human mingling and meaning. If Mose and Jed and
kindred figures are the body of Adam, he is their conscience—a
ritual of expiation in search of a guilty act to atone; he is their
intelligence, capable of seeing their sameness.

Adam is capable, therefore, of realizing what so many of
these other blind men measuring the elephant could not realize,
the extent and meaning of their goodness which justifies forgiveness. And he is capable of altering his heart in accord with this
knowledge. As in Warren's earliest novels, in *Wilderness* we do
not see the last stage of revelation tested. Nevertheless, that
stage has been attained creditably, without the fullness of its
philosophical burden's having to be borne by one young and
average man. Every occasion confirms every other, and informs
on Adam. If he still seems undersized at novel's end, the cause
may be that the book is not Adam's, but he is the book's.

*Wilderness* is, in one sense, the fictional counterpart of
Warren's other 1961 volume, *The Legacy of the Civil War;
Meditations on the Centennial.* Modestly avoiding any delusions of definitiveness while massive commemorative histories
and commentaries are being published, *Legacy* is as finite in
scale as *Wilderness* is and as subject therefore to the charge of
slightness and abstraction. It is content to summarize without
preference the moral positions of North and South in the 1860's
and to establish similarities in the apparant extremes of the "ir-
reconcilables." The Abolitionists, appealing to an absolutist
"higher law" (Garrison was prepared to burn the Constitution),
reserved the role of the Pharisaic avenger to themselves, although by the same token they became defenders of dissent
and the right to conscience. The South, to the extent that it
defended slavery, denied the concept of an open society which,
otherwise, states' rights required. Both positions were self-con-
tradictory and unrealistic. In their own uncompromising excesses, they crystallized life into brittle frailty. In the aftermath
of Civil War, both sides permitted themselves hypocritical

stances. Defeat became for the South its "Great Alibi," excusing all things and rendering its citizens playactors in the role of the pure victim. The North, meanwhile, has remained the "Treasury of Virtue" whose material prosperity has confirmed the sublime innocence which the self-righteous always find in themselves.

What has saved America from complete self-deception and the catastrophies attendant on living lies, Warren argues, is the development in certain men of a moral awareness responsive enough to inner contortions, to be able to find charity in the wilderness of war—the capacity to understand and to forgive. Lincoln had a laborious ethic—an appreciation of expediency but a delicacy also for the turn of consequences. The breakdown that he suffered before Gettysburg is to Lincoln's credit. Grant likewise, a former alcoholic, fought with dignity and magnanimity. The constitution of the Confederate States of America opposed further slave trade. There was such honor among enemies in battle, that we can view the Civil War now nostalgically. It has become a prototype for the ambivalence of love and hate in man: innocent men stumbled into the "crime of monstrous inhumanity," as surely as Adam did. But, however sobering, the war also presented lasting proof that we are not just victims of nature and history but salient participants in its movements. It is this faith, in the possibility of being instructed by suffering, that validates any meditation on the very real deaths of human beings. From this "image of the powerful, painful, grinding process by which an ideal emerges out of history," man can find dignity in his existence and even some grandeur. Perhaps, Warren says in *Legacy*, that is "what we yearn for after all." Ambition is man's hope, although, in excess, his flaw.

*Wilderness'* epigraph from Pascal is a continuation of the same thought: *Tout ces misères-là mêmes preuvent sa grandeur. Ce sont misères de grand seigneur, misères d'un roi dépossédé.* Here is the basic expression of the novel's faith; just as the other epigraph *Henry V*—so often human ends find imperfect means—states the condition preliminary to any faith. Accept the deformity, and many things are possible. *Wilderness* can be read as a dramatization of the ironies of the American Civil War, in which idealists had to hire foreign mercenaries or stoop to forceful conscription, and in which the freed slave remained a nonperson even to those allegedly dying in his cause. Yet such ironies are only symptoms of the whole agony of human existence, the essential tentativeness of knowledge and the recalcitrance of experience. Negro—or Jew—epitomizes reduction of the individual through abstraction, for example, through imposed specification. These are tactics of evasion natural to men who, deficient in comprehension or overproud, must invent simple explanations for the agony of life, including scapegoats for all error and annoyance. They must kill what is other. Evil becomes the exclusive property of some harassed and damnable few.

The method of the novel is, by poetic selectivity and specification, to translate *Legacy*'s discourse into narrative action and then to compress the moments of action further into decisive, living metaphors— vicarious gestures. In his longer novels Warren used to insert an *exemplum*, to inform anticipatorily on the distraught narrator's dilemma. *Wilderness* resembles just such an *exemplum*, expanded and extracted from its outer shell.[4] It is a play within a play removed; it is a metaphysical poem, deliberately freed from the high circumstance of history without sacrificing history's availability as myth. It is what any critic's reading of a worthy novel ought to be—one man's cautious record of the feel of an elephant in the dark.

4 At a reading of his poems at Boston College, April 12, 1962, Warren revealed that he suspended the writing of short stories when he realized that the abridged, graphic impulse which animates many of his stories was better suited to lyric poetry. Perhaps *Wilderness* marks an attempt to reverse this process: to restore partially the conditions of space and duration to otherwise essentially static poetic images.

# 13 · When All Is Said and Done:
## *Warren's* Flood

I

But I have done good things! is the agonized cry of one protagonist in *Flood* at the moment of final self-revelation. Mr.
Warren's new novel is subtitled "A Romance of Our Time"
and so deliberately runs the identical calculated risk which
dogged the reception of *World Enough and Time*. It is certain
to arouse the same obtuse misunderstanding in the bosoms of
the popular reviewers which the earlier romance had to live
down. On the surface, at the most obvious level, the novel is
pastoral and lyrical. Mr. Warren has been many things in his
time, but obvious is not one of them. Within the pastoral mode,
and with a strict economy of means, he has constructed a powerful and moving Divine Comedy of art, Daedalian man, holy
and profane love, damnation and redemption.

If the "romantic" intention of *World Enough and Time*
was essentially to dramatize the failure of a personal, subjective
ideal to become consonant with the realm of public life—the
world as it is—then it seems probable that *Flood*, by a partial
inversion of the coin, dramatizes the failure of a fragmented,
subjective life activity to become a lasting, adequate equivalent
for human fullness of being. The lonely passion of Jeremiah
Beaumont was often testily dismissed as a mere riotous excur-
sion into costume drama, and in some ways the era of Willie
Stark seems even more remote, if that is possible. But *Flood* is
explicitly a romance of our own time, and there can be no
blinking of what it brings home to us. The metaphysical dimen-

sion is all there; it is only in the ease and flow of the pastoral mode that the common reader may be slow to detect it.

Fiddlersburg is a small crossroads in Middle Tennessee, dating back a century and a half. When the floodgates of the new TVA dam are closed, the water will eventually cover Fiddlersburg. The characters of the novel are persons who are present in the town during the last year of its life. Most of them have lived there always; they will be relocated a few miles away and be generously compensated by the federal government. Others have come from Hollywood to make a documentary about the flooding of the town. When the year is over, they have all gone their separate ways. This is the *donnée*. There is little in such data to engage the passionate attention of serious readers. Fiddlersburg, a handful of people, and their various responses to its passing is all there is. Time span covers only the present generation. Mr. Warren has chosen just such a limited arena in which to illuminate his vision of human significance. His method is to establish the tensions and polarities between true and false in art, in aspiration and desire, in human love in all its manifestations, and ultimately to show how all our choices or rejections flow from a basic theological awareness or lack of it. The novel is infused with a powerful and desolate sense of alienation, but in every case the aloneness is what the actor has earned by his choice between flesh and spirit, the self and the other, the self and God.

In a year or two the town will vanish as though it had never been. This fact releases action on several levels—character for instance. The water is there, and its slow rising is freighted with images of both flooding and redemption. "I pray" says Brother Potts, the fundamentalist preacher who is trying not to die of cancer before he can lead the final memorial service for the town, "I pray to know that the lives we lived are blessed." Having this awareness is one acid test for each protagonist. Individual response to the passing of Fiddlersburg is another. Significantly enough, those who are indifferent to the death of the town have failed at every essential human effort. This is not to say that the town itself is sentimentalized. The shabbiness of what might be called its cultural resources is documented. ("Fiddlersburg," says the lawyer Cottshill, "is where God forgot to wind his watch.") Sentimental naturalism is parodied in the nastiness of some of the lower forms of human life who move and speak with all of Mr. Warren's customary brio of detail and dialogue. Thus, it is difficult to paraphrase adequately the exact nature of that blessedness which shines through the fabric of undistinguished mortality which is Fiddlersburg. None the less, it is there, and some feel it powerfully, even a stranger like Yasha Jones the Hollywood genius, who has never seen it before. Others, like Bradwell Tolliver, who grew up there, cannot feel it at all.

II

As Mr. Warren so often shows us, experience can be fulfilled and redeemed only in a maturity of realization and acceptance. A linear analysis such as the present one can do little more than suggest the intricate pattern of influence and counterinfluence in the lives of the major protagonists. The novel is rich in characterization, both in the individual and in a presentation that is truly ensemble playing. Some justice can be done to that richness by the technique of comparison and contrast. In such a presentation no one character can be designated as "the" protagonist. However, Bradwell Tolliver is most often the center of attention. His too is the most dramatic failure of fulfillment and redemption. Thus, he may serve as a paradigm for all, particularly as a measure of such tortured complexities as flesh and spirit, the self and the other.

Any human relationship, love for instance, is a joint relationship between the self and the other. But as Carson McCullers has shown so well, this does not mean that the experience is the same for both. In an age when the psychiatrist can say with the utmost seriousness that he cannot distinguish love from hate, we all know that any relationship mingling dependence, need, acceptance, and joy is unbearable to many. Even in some ultimate moment, physical love for instance, the other is still the other, and forever separate. The fascination of otherness may lead down many a twisted path: envy, emulation, aggrandizement, or the terrible need for approval. More than any one thing, *Flood* demonstrates the essential theological paradox that separateness is a necessary condition of being, that self may ultimately live only in that redemption which is the death of the self. By this measure human emptiness is gauged. Gratification is provided by the degree of overt approval, envy, or emulation, as the case may be.

Brad is drawn to Lettice Poindexter because of her beauty, her social position, her easy familiarity with all the places where the very rich go to be rich together. Lettice wants, in her poignantly human way, what any human wants; to be loved and valued as an individual. She hopes that Brad will be able to give her the gift of herself. Her conventional wish to be simply wife and mother is genuine enough, and but for the accident of settling on Brad, might have succeeded. But this is not the point: neither of them realizes the degree to which their love is a demanding rather than a giving.

The paradigm is seen even more clearly in the life of Brad's sister, Maggie, in her simplicity and her capacity for unselfish, undemanding love. At her moment of greatest happiness, so long delayed, Brad can respond only with the long-cherished feeling that her entire life has been a reproach to him. Maggie's rape and the subsequent murder of the assailant by her husband Cal was a direct result of a drunken brawl pitched by Brad. Cal is sentenced to life imprisonment in the state penitentiary, located in Fiddlersburg. He refuses to see or speak to Maggie; refusing to forgive her for what was done to her. She spends twenty years caring for Cal's elderly mother, but not seeming to regard this endless, deadening task as particularly extraordinary. It is clear that Cal's murder of Tuttle, his later near-murder of Yasha, and his treatment of Maggie are acts of retaliation; a punishment of others for injuring his image of himself. He clearly states that he attributes all of it to his attempt to emulate Brad. All the major figures except Brad will find some sort of redemption, a salvation of one sort or another. Lettice finds peace with herself and with God as a voluntary and happy menial with the Sisters of Charity, Cal on the other side of the nightmare of extended solitary confinement, and Maggie liberated at last into a nearly perfect marriage with Yasha Jones.

The parallels are many, and offer instructive contrasts.

Lettice, so startlingly beautiful, knows her body is her most impressive asset and spends hours tending and grooming it. Unconsciously, the urge is to gain attention and approval— the response of the other. Eventually, this emphasis on the physical means that her marriage to Brad has lust as its only basis, as is seen in his morbid interest in the detail of her past affairs. Only at the end of the novel, in the letter to Maggie, do we find how she was "goosed to God" and learned that bodily decrepitude is wisdom and grace. Maggie, by contrast, is not so beautiful by far, and has never given her body such elaborate, disproportionate attention. Their one joint attempt to glamorize Maggie leads to her marriage to Cal, and all that follows. Here also might be mentioned Leontine, the beautiful blind girl who can find her way about Fiddlersburg with ease, but who will be helpless anywhere else. Brad is so obsessed with the mystery of her difference, her "otherness," that he wants to marry her and cherish her helplessness forever, only to learn that she is the semiprofessional town whore, giving herself promiscuously as a compensation for the loneliness of her affliction.

Yasha Jones has achieved his condition of blessedness much earlier in life. Here too, his life is an instructive parallel to Brad's. Each is a creative artist; each has lived through combat and the constant danger of death. The single difference is that Yasha somehow has achieved the death of the self and Brad somehow has not. Each is talented, and each has had what seemed at the beginning to be a promising marriage. Brad begins with Lettice and all her potential, and ends by ruining her and driving her away through his wounded self-esteem. Yasha, conversely, deeply loved his wife, only to lose her in a violent accident. Yasha feels deeply that a man must be splendid when he has lived past his own death. Brad, living through many of the same experiences, has not known how to be splendid. This is why Yasha's art is pure and Brad's is corrupt. Yasha's creation is pure because his sole attention can be focused on perfecting the thing in itself. He no longer needs gratification or the spasm of envy in others. Brad does.

III

Bradwell Tolliver published his first book, a collection of stories about Fiddlersburg, before he had finished college. His only subsequent success has been Hollywood success. He is resentfully aware of his failure, but cannot discover where he has lost out or gone wrong. His basic defect is his inability to come into a right relation to the world around him and the people who live there. Brad cannot distinguish *thou* from *it*, or love from use. Thus his personal vision is clouded, and like a painter with one eye, he cannot tell because he cannot see. Every stick and stone, every soul, is precious in God's sight, and each is a unity that is separate and inviolable. The early stories were true and beautiful because at that period of relative innocence and wonder the human beings he created in his fiction had their own integrity and carried it over into the work itself. By the period of his Hollywood success, every stick and stone has become grist for his mill, and in the creative crisis of turning out a script about Fiddlersburg he can produce only the usual Hollywood clichés. He cannot see the "depth and shimmer," the uniqueness of place and moment which Yasha wants to get into the beautiful movie they hope to make. Brad cannot write it and Yasha will accept nothing less.

The failure of his art is merely the outward symptom of a deeper, more human failing. Brad has taken the Faustian, Daedalian gambit—he has jettisoned every human consideration in the effort to practice his creative art, a course he is not altogether equipped to pursue. In the purity of his early work the artist was very nearly invisible. At some point after that, the art of creation has given away to self-aggrandizement. Adrift in the world of publishing in New York, and understandably not sure how much of the surface glitter is spurious, he is troubled by his own provincial lack of ease, and haunted by a powerful sense of emptiness, of nonfulfillment. Seeing others move easily against the backdrop of history, he begins to fear he will turn out to have no history at all.

In his obsessive awareness of this emptiness, Brad is somewhat like Slim Sarrett in *At Heaven's Gate*. Convinced of the boring triviality of his own family background, Slim selects and plays out a role of his own choosing, even to the extent of con structing and offering to others a complete and more glamorous life history. But alike as these two are in their emptiness, their response is different. Brad's major life activity is not the playing out of a role, but rather the continuously baffling problem of trying to find a role to play. His nagging concern is not that his disguise will be penetrated, but rather that the world will sud- denly see that he is naked, without a disguise to assume. All history, including his own, is merely what happens, no matter how blank the happening. Hence his fear that he will turn out not to have a story at all. It is said of him that he did not know the real shame is in yearning for the false, not the true story. Seeking himself, he can define himself only in the reaction he produces in others: attraction, admiration, envy. Praise may be insincere, and silence implies reproach. Failure is always the fault of someone else.

This kink in his vision cuts both ways. The defect is a failure of apprehension; an inability to see what he is looking at. People are cut off from him; he is never able to establish what their reality is, what they really are in themselves. Sooner or later, the result is disaster, leading to paralysis in any effort he begins. When reality is read only in the baffled assessment of human reaction, then any human relationship is use, not love. Hence the outcome of his marriage. Hence also his impulse to marry Leontine and redeem *his* life, not hers. His decision to fight in the Spanish Civil War is triggered not by a powerful conviction of the rightness of a cause, but in the hope that the act of going will prove something about him to other people and perhaps to himself. Each gesture that he hopes is a truly gratuitous act, each noble project for the future is doomed before it can begin.

IV

On the day of the final memorial service for the town, Bradwell Tolliver tries to extract meaning from the insane se- quence of events which have allowed him to live past his second death. He has saved Yasha's life by lunging at the gun in Cal

Fiddler's hand, an act that seems to him as irrational as the rest
of it, since Cal then drops the pistol and saves Brad's life. In
the long nights of long months in the hospital, he has fought
the black beast of despair and suicidal rage; the frenzied *Why
me?* In all the forms of coming true, everyone seems to have
found a truth except himself. He goes back to the penitentiary
to see Cal, to hear him explain the truth he learned in the extended solitary confinement after the shooting:

> "In solitary you decide, well, I'll just shut my eyes, for only
> what you can think can truly exist. But then you shut your eyes and
> that thing that was unthinkable—it really does come true. It
> blazes up around you like a brush fire. It blazes up like spilled
> gasoline. It blazes in the dark inside your head. You realize in
> that flash that there is no *you* except in relation to all that un-
> thinkableness that the world is. And you yourself are. . . ."
> "But . . . suddenly you feel different. I felt different. It was
> like knowing that life, which I myself had never had, for a nerve
> had got cut or a wire short-circuited—like knowing . . . that life
> is beautiful. Beautiful—that's the only word I can find for it. . . .
> It was as though a ghost, invisible to the direst look of your eye,
> could be seen in the mirror as an image, a reflection, of some sort
> of—of misty beautifulness."
> ". . . That doesn't seem to say it," he decided.[1]

After he has left Cal, he watches the memorial service
from a distance, too far away to hear clearly. He sees Brother
Potts and Leontine in the crowd, but his alienation is as profound as ever. He thinks of a moment in Hollywood at the
beginning of an important sexual conquest: walled off, glassed
in inside a telephone booth after his conversation, he sees the
shabby specimens of humanity through the glass, totally cut
off from him in their misery. The people across the road from
him now are no more real. They have nothing to do with him.
Reading Lettice's letter which Maggie has passed on to him,
he learns of her religious conversion, and considers her generous
statement that she failed him, rather than he her. He still cannot fit meanings together. Watching Brother Potts, hearing
imperfectly the shouted words of blessedness, he cannot understand why Brother Potts has gained some sort of victory even

---

1 Robert Penn Warren, *Flood* (New York: Random House, 1964). All
quotations in this essay are from this edition.

though he will now die of cancer, while Bradwell Tolliver will have to go on, wearily performing over and over the trivial actions of physical life. In all his life, it seems to him, he has blamed Fiddlersburg because it was not the world, and so not real, and blamed the world because it was not Fiddlersburg, and so not real. He says, in his inwardness, " 'I cannot find the connection between what I was and what I am. I have not found the human necessity. . . .' "

However dimly, he sees the necessity is what he must find— the illumination that will make plain the place and the people who have made him what he is. He has come back to Fiddlersburg partly to make one last search for the grave of old Goldfarb, his earliest mentor. Suddenly he sees that moving the grave does not matter. It would be an empty gesture, a concern once more with the mereness of the physical. Goldfarb is where he wanted to be, above the flood or below it. Bradwell Tolliver could even come back some day to where the town once was. He could come back without guilt or pain to the edge of the water so long as he keeps Fiddlersburg, all of it, the good and evil, the living and dead, intact in his memory. *Mentre che la speranza ha fior del verde.*

*William C. Havard*

## *14* · The Burden of the Literary Mind:

### *Some Meditations on Robert Penn*

### *Warren As Historian*

I

THE OCTOBER 7, 1962, issue of the *New York Times Book Review* reported the answers of six prominent critics to the question, "Who's to take the place of Hemingway and Faulkner?" One of the respondents, W. M. Frohock, replied,

Obviously we are thinking about novelists. Otherwise I would take Robert Penn Warren. His reputation is entrenched: superior novelist, able poet, really fine critic. But don't the novels go down hill after *At Heaven's Gate* and *All the King's Men?*

The reply is perhaps typical of the critical attitude toward Warren; a profound respect for the diversity of his accomplishment is compromised by a skeptical attitude about the possibility that the man can really do so many things so well. The dubious compliment to Santayana which acknowledged him to be the best poet among philosophers and the ablest philospher among poets is implicitly applied to Warren in this reluctance to accept him as a master in any single literary genre. The reluctance to give Warren full marks is not, however, due solely to doubts about his omnicompetence. It derives in part from the accepted fact that Warren is a *philosophical* novelist. It is not sufficient for some commentators to assess the extent to which Warren's philosophical interests are intrusive and thereby tend to impair the quality of his fiction; a number of critics impugn the philosophical activity itself in the name of a purity which sparsely disguises a behavioral substitute for philosophy.

When Warren published his *Legacy of the Civil War*, in 1961, with the appropriate subtitle "Meditations on the Centennial," it soon became apparent that to his dimensions as a poet, novelist, and critic would have to be added his measure as a historian or philosopher of history. On the whole the historians have accepted his incursion with less equivocation than the literary critics. T. Harry Williams notes, for example, that

It is . . . a most valuable book, because these are the meditations or conclusions not only of a man who knows American history but of a sensitive literary artist who knows life. Mr. Warren has said more meaningful things about the central event in our national record than many an author has managed in thrice that spread.[1]

And C. Vann Woodward, who of all contemporary American historians has the closest affinity with Warren in terms of intellectual concerns, obligations arising from the conditions attached to being a southerner, and felicity of prose style, has received him graciously, and on Warren's own terms, into the professional guild. Woodward reminds us that

Warren was a historian before he was a poet or a novelist. His first book was a biography of John Brown. All of his novels and much of his poetry have dealt with historical themes or with characters and events in historical context. One of his major professional problems has been to define the relationship between history and poetry, to defend his use of both, and to reconcile the sorts of truth they seek and the kinds of sense they make.[2]

In assessing any philosopher's contribution a critical commentator will find it necessary to deal with his work as a whole, because philosophy is precisely the effort to synthesize diverse experiences and specialized knowledge at the highest level of generality. And so it must be with a philosophical novelist and quondam historian like Warren. This statement should not be taken, however, to imply either that there is no development in his work or that Warren is a self-consciously systematic philosopher. The first of these problems may be left to the literary critics. The second question—whether Warren is sys-

1 In a review in the Baton Rouge *Morning Advocate*, September 17, 1961.
2 C. Vann Woodward, "Reflections on a Centennial: The American Civil War," *The Yale Review*, L (1961), 483.

tematic in his philosophy—may not for our purposes be so easily
dismissed. Of course Warren is not a systematic philosopher in
the strict meaning of the term. In choosing the literary forms of
poetry and fiction as the media for his philosophical inquiry,
he implicitly spurns systematization because the special demands of these forms must take precedence over the traditional
forms of philosophy. Even so, the choice is in itself related to
the substance of his philosophical endeavor because it reveals
a point often made explicit in his work—the interconnectedness
of all things. In fine, certain philosophical truths, and these
perhaps the quintessential ones for Warren, can only be realized
and communicated through forms originating in the imaginative experiences of the poet or novelist. Richard Rovere has
identified the specific obligation which attaches to the artist
who approaches reality in this way: "In Warren's view, it is
man's thorny lot in life to pick up the tangled skein of good
and evil and untangle it as best he can. Warren also believes,
or writes as if he believes, that it is art's responsibility to lend
man, the untangler, a helping hand." [3]

Warren's uses of history bear a similar relation to the
whole. He is not a historical novelist who is also a philosophical
novelist; he is rather a novelist who accepts historical experience
as fundamental to philosophical understanding as that understanding is unfolded through the creative imagination. Robert
Heilman has stated this proposition more clearly in the following comment on World Enough and Time:

Warren sticks to the central method of his other three novels,
digging up a pretty well preserved skeleton of action from recent
history, covering it with the flesh of imaginatively conceived story,
and giving it the life of human (suprahistorical) meaning.[4]

By giving to history full human—or suprahistorical—meaning through the philosophical unification of different modes of
experience, Warren avoids the charge of historicism. It is possible to infer from Warren's repeated pessimistic treatment
of man's public life an acceptance of the idea that all collective

3 "Salute to Robert Penn Warren," Harper's Magazine, CCI (1950),
103.
4 "Tangled Web," Sewanee Review, LIX (1951), 107.

action eventuates in historically predetermined failure. The general feeling aroused by the novels that the introspective awareness of individual freedom of will is a delusion soon dissipated by contact with the intractable conditions of the world is often made explicit by one or another of the fictional characters who are protagonists in the philosophical dialogue. In the latest novel, *Wilderness*, for example, Aaron Blaustein represents this view. He defines himself as a worshiper of history, since all you can fall back on is history if you stop worshiping God. He then goes on to ask, "Do you know what History is? . . . It is the agony people have to go through . . . so that things will turn out as they would have turned out anyway."

Although Blaustein is clearly symbolic of the negative or pessimistic form of historicism—a *reductio ad absurdum* of Hegel and Marx—his is not the final word. That is left to the hero of the story, Adam Rosenzweig, the crippled Bavarian Jew who had come to America to fight in the Civil War for an ideal of freedom in the name of all mankind, who had been disillusioned at every point of contact with historical reality, and who yet maintained the core of his faith and his will to action, even though his choice of means and his ultimate expectations were modified by the wisdom of experience. Moreover, Adam does not emerge with a baseless existentialist conviction that man must simply endure. The hope survives, sustained by a glimmer of rationality, that meaning may be grasped. In Adam's words, " 'you have to know if there is a truth in the world.' " And in the affirmation that "others have been permitted" to know that truth, he wonders whether it will be vouchsafed to him. Is it not Warren's contention here that if the contingencies of existence and of knowledge are such that man cannot fully conquer history through an act of will based on understanding, man's nature is so ordered that it will not allow history to conquer life?

II

This interpretation of Warren's escape from historicism anticipates conclusions that are related to the wholeness of his

endeavor. When indicating something of his philosophical unity
in brief space, the temptation to take refuge in digression is great
because Warren's fictional materials are extraordinarily rich,
complex, and fraught with the tortuousness of life itself. As
Heilman puts it:

the total effect is one of a manically exhaustive ripping apart of
excuses, justifications, defenses, ruses, consolations; of a furious
burrowing into ever deeper layers of self-understanding until almost
every clarity becomes a puzzle and every dependability a delusion.[5]

The following remarks run a risk of oversimplification
because in the context no satisfactory attempt can be made to
examine the methods of the literary artistry through which
Warren embodies and embellishes his philosophical themes.
What is offered is an abstraction of the basic problems with
which he comes to grips, the logical connection of these problems, and some suggestions about the way in which he tentatively resolves them.

The striking feature of Warren's effort is the tremendous
scope of his quest; for his concern is nothing less than the
perennial problems of philosophy. If, because of his intense application to the fundamental question of being, good and evil,
knowledge, and justice, Warren sometimes fails, in Jamesian
terms, to make the most of his *donnée* as a novelist, it is a
noble failure.

The central problem—the core of Warren's burden—is
the self-understanding or self-identity of the individual. The
theme does not just hover around the action in the novels;
practically every central character and many of the supporting
ones raise it specifically to themselves or to others in the form
of the direct question, "Who or what am I?" Nor is the problem of Being raised in the abstract. The issue invariably arises
in the mind of the sensitive, introspective hero or heroine as
a result of a dramatic moral confrontation. The problem of
Being is brought to the surface of consciousness by the direct
experience of evil; the awareness of one's own participation
in evil forces the demand for self-recognition in the search for
the good. The beginning of wisdom is the rational perception

5 P. 109.

of the internal conflict between good and evil. The irony in Warren's novels arises because the confrontation so often occurs after it is too late to rectify the damages that have been done to one's self and to others. The understanding which results is that the individual must assume responsibility for his actions even when they were taken without awareness of either the moral issues involved or the practical consequences that these issues entailed. Only when this understanding is reached is it possible to perceive the limitations of both human action and human knowledge; and these limits, inherent in the nature of an imperfect world, define the rational bounds within which the means to human ends should be confined.

The historic implications are inseparable from these individual themes. The moral confrontation which motivates the inquiry into self-identity is contact with the world. Initial contact with the world does not ordinarily set off self-inquiry, although it may produce a self-interpretation or primitive mythic self-projection. All of us live in a world peopled by other human beings possessed by passions, moved by wills, and handicapped by the limitations of knowledge. Warren's highly differentiated characters are seldom merely allegorical figures, but it may be helpful to outline the broad range of moral types in his novels and suggest something of their relation to the world of evil and potential good.

At the bottom of the list are those characters so dominated by pride that they appear to be altogether lacking in moral sensitivity. These amoralists are the real villains in Warren's dramatic structures, or as some allege, in some of his lapses into melodrama. The prominent examples are Bogan Murdock, in *At Heaven's Gate*, and Jeremiah Beaumont's friend Wilkie Barron, in *World Enough and Time*. In their unalloyed egotism they have so completely embraced the corruption of the world that they have foreclosed the possibility of regenerative self-understanding. Devoid of all sense of responsibility and incapable of any love other than projected self-love, they either justify or even do not feel the need to justify their most capricious actions and the evils produced by the calculated means to their ends. Even in these cases the world exacts a justice that Warren leaves as devoid of explanation in human terms as Murdock and Barron are barren of internal life; Murdock's anticipated ruin and Barron's suicide are simply facts corresponding to the abstract inevitabilities of the world.

A second moral dimension is revealed in characters such as Percy Munn in *Night Rider*, Willie Stark in *All the King's Men*, and Jeremiah Beaumont in *World Enough and Time*. These are characters who are made forcibly aware of external evil and the injustices of the world. Their common moral defect, presumably the one which afflicts most of mankind, is failure to grasp the relation between the evils of the world and the inner conflict between good and evil in the individual. Self-identification, or mythical self-projection, takes the form of the avenger or rectifier of perceived wrongs. Starting with the erroneous conviction noted in *World Enough and Time* that "the idea in and of itself might redeem the world . . ." such a character moves to a second error expressed in the notion that "the world must redeem the idea." An act of will based on this moral necessity thrusts him into the use of "the means of the natural world, and its dark ways, to gain that end he names holy the idea, and ah! the terror of that, the terror of that."

In the act of rebellion against the evils of the world, the moral type obsessed with the ideal of total human justice or perfection loses the possibility of a true sense of self-identification. In this loss he connives at the corruption of his own ends through the unselective adoption of the world's means, and he contributes to his personal corruption and eventual destruction through the identification of himself with the idea to an extent which permits him to act entirely outside any moral restraints. He identifies his individual will with the absolute; in his angry virtue he excuses and justifies all. With Willie Stark the actions which result are not wholly destructive; the evils that he sees are real and he does not overly romanticize trivial or uncertain injustices in the manner of Jeremiah Beaumont. Stark's motives are not initially corrupt and his capacity for political action is not without potentiality for good. This potentiality rapidly dissipates, however, in the self-delusion which deadens the awareness of an internal personal conflict between good and evil.

The third type may be identified as Warren's modest version of the Aristotelian *spoudaios*, the morally mature man whose excellence introduces order into society. In Warren's treatment this is the prototypical character who has gone beyond the easy naturalistic openness to good and evil, has had some experience of the obsession with the "idea," and has confronted, without accompanying delusion or external projection, the dilemmas of existence, the universal tension between evil and good, the limits of human understanding, and the awesome burden of responsibility. The response to the moral confrontation in this type is a correct one with neither a turning to the "blank cup of nature" in search of innocence nor an act of wilful rebellion against the evil of the world. Finally, the attainment of the limited wisdom open to man does not force a retreat from the world, but demands that the life of action continue. Warren's affirmation of objective good, even though only limitedly attainable in the world, is the variously reiterated injunction against fleeing inward "into the ironies of history and knowledge, into that wisdom which is resignation." If the idea cannot redeem the world or the world the idea, neither can the attempt to realize some relation between the two be adandoned.

In *The Cave* Warren makes a dramatic adaptation of the famous Platonic parable. Plato used the symbol of the cave to illustrate the limited vision of reality open to most of humanity and the self-closure against the potentiality of a larger vision represented by the person who had been permitted to turn from the cave toward the light. Warren reverses this use of the cave symbol. In the novel, Jasper Harrick, a young backwoods Tennessee war hero, a "cave-crawler" to get away from the world and establish self-identity, is trapped in a cave. The ordeal of the attempted rescue culminates in the creation of a heroic myth whose effect on a variety of characters is developed in contrapuntal form. The heroic qualities of the myth, while founded on a falsehood contrived for worldy benefit, touch the core of reality. And through the common trauma of participation in the myth, each of the central characters, except for the doomed Isaac Sumpter, is brought to the recognition of his hitherto sublimated moral conflict, and from this recognition comes an enlarged capacity for fulfilling his obligations to himself and to the limited circle directly affected by his actions. *The Cave* is

Warren's most ambitious attempt to explore the essentially private implications of the moral dilemma in its multifold variations.

If *The Cave* is an exploration of the private aspect of the unfolding of fully developed moral character, *All the King's Men* is the definitive examination of the political implications of the search for self-understanding, obligation, and justice. Jack Burden, uneasy in the limited possibilities offered by his southern elite social heritage, becomes involved in Willie Stark's rebellion against the historical accretion of power symbolized by Burden's Landing. The combination of Stark's example as a political activist and Burden's participation in Stark's activities leads to personal tragedy which forces Burden to look inward for meaning to achieve the identity he has been seeking. The problem of action is resolved neither by naturalism nor by a genteel resignation which repudiates the world. Instead a morally mature Burden prepares to return to politics with the broader perspective and the more limited aspiration of his experience with history and a recognition of the unforeseen consequences of a blind striking out for the idea of justice.

### III

But what is the relation of Warren the historian to all of this? *The Legacy of the Civil War* in a sense brings Warren full circle. The biography of John Brown launched him into the imaginative exploration of certain basic themes in Brown's character and actions, within the historical circumstances which influenced Brown and were reciprocally influenced by him. These include practically all of the philosophical elements of the novels: the lonely search for self-identity, the compromise with the world, the commitment to the idea which justifies great evil in the name of the absolute elimination of evil, the irony of history whereby man sometimes reaches heroic proportions in a frame of action that is nonsensical, and the creation out of historical incidents of myths by which men live and die, myths whose components range over the whole scale of good and evil, of truth and falsehood, of reality and delusion. The novels explore these problems from the standpoint of universal man, mainly through the application to historical incidents of the intuitive insights and dramatic skills of the novelist, for well-handled fiction can evoke the sense of personal participation in event and plausibility of internal cause in a manner that is beyond the limits of the historian's materials and function. In *The Legacy of the Civil War*, Warren turns back to a commentary on history from the standpoint of philosophical understanding matured through the incarnation of individual and historical motivation in novel form. This little book is a summing up of Warren's reflection on man's universal problems within the particular context of American history. The themes are familiar to readers of the novels; now they are stated with the incisiveness of the thinker who has used all of his skills to master his materials through painstaking investigation and analysis.

With his opening sentence, "*The Civil War* is, for the American imagination, the greatest single event in our history," Warren joins the issue. In his view, "The Civil War is our only felt history—history lived in the national imagination"; before the war there was no American history in the "deepest and most inward sense." Apart from the important external facts of saving the South for the Union, freeing the slaves, and setting the nation on the new course of industrialism, what were its effects?

The first effect is the contribution of the war to the pragmatic bias of the nation. At first sight it may appear strange that Warren should embrace so morally neutral a doctrine as pragmatism. However, a reading in context reveals that this pragmatism is related less to a total relativity of existence than to the factors which limit the means to human ends, a theme much in evidence in the novels. Warren quotes with obvious approval the characterizations of Lincoln's pragmatism by T. Harry Williams and Sidney Hook. The former notes that "his [Lincoln's] personal or inner opinions were based on principle; his public or outer opinions were tempered by empiricism," while Hook indicates that Lincoln's course of action consisted in being "principled without being fanatical, and flexible without being opportunistic. . . ."

American pragmatism, fostered by the Civil War, is a

response to the two absolutes whose collision was an essential factor in the coming of the war, the "higher law" and "legalism." These designations apply respectively to Puritan, fanatical abolitionism, and to the rigid adherence of the slaveholders to the minor logic of legal instruments in defiance of all major logic. The "higher law" men, with their corner on truth by reason of divine revelation, end by denying the very concept of society in the name of absolute idea. If these men completely repudiated society in the name of an individual purity of conscience which rejected all responsibility, the legalists of the South denied the concept of life in the society which they sought to vindicate by refusing to allow, "through the inductive scrutiny of fact, for change, for the working of the life process through history." The trancendentalists repudiated social institutions; the South repudiated criticism. Both absolutes were accompanied by compromises with the world, by hypocrisies, and by self-justifications and internal contradictions.

As a result of the head-on conflict of the ideologies, and the eventual catastrophe that their rigidities promoted, Americans learned the political lesson that "logical parties may lead logically to logical shooting, and they had had enough of that." Through violent experience they learned respect for the non-logical arrangement of political parties and politics. Warren conveys the idea that politics is best conceived as the application of common sense to issues which arise within a working political tradition with the rationality of experience behind it. No one is absolutely satisfied with the settlement, but no one is committed to the destruction of the system through which the settlement was reached. Here is a pragmatism of political means without a total rejection of objective standards.

If the war brought certain benefits to the psychology of Americans, it also levied some psychological costs. Warren notes that these costs were different for the two sides and sums up these differences in two labels which attaches to the respective attitudes. For the South the war produced the "Great Alibi," and to the North it gave the "Treasury of Virtue."

By the Great Alibi the South explains, condones and transmutes everything. . . . By the Great Alibi pellagra, hookworms, and illiteracy are all explained. . . . Laziness becomes the aesthetic sense, blood-lust rising from a matrix of boredom and resentful misery becomes a high sense of honor, and ignorance becomes divine revelation. . . . By the Great Alibi the Southerner makes his big medicine. He turns defeat into victory, defects into virtues.

The Great Alibi has broadest application to the race issue. Seeing the situation as one in which history has trapped him, the southerner is powerless to confront the internal conflict that arises from his treatment of the Negro as something other than human. This moral quandary is the focus of Warren's earlier short book on *Segregation,* appropriately subtitled "The Inner Conflict in the South." *Segregation* is Warren's interview with the people of the South in an attempt to bring the conflict to the level of consciousness and to achieve a rational self-identity which may free the South from the mental and moral paralysis induced by the ironies of history and the uses of self-justification to which these ironies may be put. In the delineation of the Great Alibi he returns to the problem of the debasement of the noble and courageous elements in southern history by the obscene parody on that history reflected in contemporary racial incidents. Warren asks, "Can the man howling in the mob imagine General R. E. Lee, CSA, shaking hands with Orval Faubus, Governor of Arkansas?"

If, according to the Great Alibi, the southerner is trapped by history, the northerner is automatically redeemed because history has conferred the Treasury of Virtue on him, and with it "a plenary indulgence . . . for all sins past, present and future." Forgotten and forgiven is the culpability that the North shares with the South for the war; excused, too, are the failures of responsibility to act on avowed principles in regard to race and the Union. The North also avoided the internal moral struggle in the Puritanical acceptance of external success as a sign of monopolized virtue. Like the race issue in the South, the Treasury of Virtue continues to be a corruptor which takes the form of "moral narcissism." American illusions of national innocence and virtue have produced a self-righteousness in relation to internal and foreign policy which enables us to condemn others and suggest the means to their spiritual regeneration with no apparent awareness that our own souls may be in jeopardy.

One recognizes in this brief summary of Warren's fully developed and image-dominated presentation of the symbols of American self-interpretation the ubiquity of the problem of the refuges available to those who refuse to confront the moral difficulties of existence and the consequences which flow from evasion of responsibility. The negative function of the myth is also made more precise at this point, for Warren asserts that, even though the Great Alibi and the Treasury of Virtue both serve deep needs of human nature, in the absence of historical realism and criticism they merely help compound the "old inherited delusions which our weakness craves."

There are, on the other hand, positive functions of the symbolic myth, because the war furnishes an image of life which condenses many kinds of meanings. The first of its offerings is a

gallery of great human images for our contemplation . . . , a dazzling array of figures, noble in proportion yet human, caught out of Time as in a frieze, in stances so profoundly touching or powerfully mythic that they move us in a way no mere consideration of "historical importance" ever could. . . . This was our Homeric period, and the figures loom up only a little less than gods, but even so, we recognize the lineaments and passions of men, and by that recognition of common kinship share in their grandeur.

The interest and meaning go deeper, for the war revealed a starkly realistic inner conflict. Despite southern nationalism and southern preference for the "War Between the States," the Civil War was, after all, a civil war. The ambivalence of love and hate, the guilts and the self-division "within individuals becomes a series of mirrors in which the plight of the country is reflected, and the self-division of the country a great mirror in which the individual may see imaged his own deep conflicts. . . . " The inwardness of the experience of the Civil War, both in individuals and in the nation, constitutes the drama which painfully forces self-identification and furnishes experiential possibility for acting on a different level of rationality. Here again is the central theme of the search for identity, followed by a moral confrontation forced by tragedy, and eventuating in a moral awareness which provides the potential for matured self-interpretation.

The internal divisions were present in both sectors, but the South confronted a greater moral dilemma than the North because it had to deny so many of the things it shared with the North to confirm its slaveholding identity. The South shared not only adherence to the Union, but the "universalist conception of freedom based on natural law. . . , Jacksonian democracy and Christian doctrine. . . ." In this brief list Warren affirms that the American tradition embodies a measure of objective moral good. If this interpretation is correct, Warren's seemingly ambivalent emphasis of pragmatism is clarified, because the limitations of existence require acceptance of pragmatic action within the framework of a prevailing tradition which experience has confirmed as good. The attempt to transmute that good into perfection by forcibly attacking the institutions through which it is effected and the counterattempt to repudiate the obligations that the tradition imposes are both acts of destruction. Proper action is limited to the pragmatic attempt to realize the tradition more fully as our failings and shortcomings are manifested in history. As Warren had previously made clear in *Segregation:* "Gradualism is all you'll get. History, like nature, knows no jumps. Except the jump backward, maybe."

In the larger sense neither the evitablity nor the inevitability theory of the Civil War is historically important, for both can work to the same happy end of diminishing guilt. The experience itself and what we make of it is the important thing. In a phrase which recalls the full import of the novels, Warren notes that we should "seek to end the obscene gratifications of history, and try to learn what the contemplation of the past, conducted with psychological depth and humane breadth, can do for us." While history cannot give us a program for the future, it "may help us to understand, even to frame, the logic of experience to which we shall submit . . . ; it can give us a fuller understanding of ourselves, and of our common humanity, so that we can better face the future."

The Civil War was a tragedy. "It is the story of a crime of monstrous inhumanity, into which almost innocently men stumbled. . . ." The entanglements increased until the powers of reason and its virtues were perverted, but, ironically and redeemingly, nobility could still be discerned through the murk,

and in the conclusion there is "a reconciliation by human recognition." We have not, however, been adequately instructed by
that "catharsis of pity and terror. . . ." We have not achieved
justice, created a full sense of community, or resolved our deep
dubieties or self-deceptions. "In other words, we are sadly human, and in our contemplation of the Civil War we see a dramatization of our humanity. . . ." Beyond all of the false
comfort we may derive from the event—the satisfactions of
rancor, self-righteousness, spite, pride, armchair blood lust, and
complacency—"we can yet see in the Civil War an image of
the powerful, painful, grinding process by which an ideal
emerges out of history." This should teach us humility and at
the same time draw us "to the glory of the human effort to
win meaning from the complex and confused motives of men
and the blind ruck of event." So much for the bare bone summary of Warren's moving and profound reaffirmation of the
historical meaning conveyed by the Civil War.

IV

At the outset of this essay the question was raised whether,
in uniting philosophical concerns, fiction, and history, Warren
is engaged in a valid function. Alfred Kazin recently pinpointed
the problem in a decidedly negative review of *The Legacy of
the Civl War*.[6] Kazin's treatment is elliptical, for the argument
is by implication *ad hominem*, in the apparent attempt to
avoid direct commitment to consideration of the philosophical
problems that Warren poses. Running through the entire review—starting with the title, "City of the Soul," a phrase Warren uses to delineate the southern ethos—is a rebuke to Warren
for being a southerner and for taking the primordial struggle
of the South seriously. An answer to this form of criticism can
be offered in terms of Warren's own categories. The psychology
of the "Treasury of Virtue" obviously has such a strong hold
on Kazin that in his identification with the war's outcome he

6 *The Reporter*, XXIV (June 8, 1961), 40, 42–44. For a devastating
rebuttal see Louis D. Rubin, Jr., "Theories of Human Nature: Kazin or
Warren?" *The Sewanee Review*, LXIX (1961), 501.

has overlooked the shoddiness that accompanies all real socially beneficial change.

Kazin petulantly complains that he cannot see anything new in the book and expresses wonder "that Warren can take up so cursorily a subject that requires so much detailed handling." Words cannot be minced in regard to this statement: it is made either as part of a pattern of deliberate obscurantism or is arrant nonsense. *The Legacy of the Civil War* is a lesson in the sources pertinent to the interpretation of the war's meaning. Warren's obvious acquaintance with historical literature, his choice of quotations, the serious attention accorded the book by professional historians, and the earlier research that went into *John Brown* are sufficient testimony to the technical competence of the author.[7] By no means a cursory handling of an enormous subject, Warren's discussion is a distillation of more than thirty years of research and soul-searching reflection on American history. His compact essay is a calm philosophical summing up of a system of ideas which has been mastered and refined by prodigious mental and moral effort.

Kazin's central objection is to Warren's philosophical orientation. He agrees with the emphasis on pragmatism, but he sees in Warren's sudden enthusiasm for the term "what it is about his novels and poems that so often bothers me." In his view Warren is too much concerned with *theories* of human nature to be a good novelist or poet. These theories ought not to interest a novelist so much, for

the truth is that no matter what philosophy of life a novelist may claim, no matter how astringent or realistic or "pragmatic" he may set himself up to be, literature itself consists in saying "Yes" to life—not just to the "open" life that Warren praises, but to the life in every man. . . .

The naturalism which Kazin espouses in opposition to Warren's dedication to ideas may very well be the literary man's synonym for the social scientist's affinity with "behaviorism." If so, I must take my stand with Warren, who looks for meaning not solely to the external record of man but to his internal

7 See Heilman, p. 108, for a testimonial to Warren's care in handling historical problems.

capacity for feeling, thinking, willing, and acting. The philosophical problems of existence, purpose, good and evil, truth,
justice, freedom and determinism, human limits and potentiality, and their tentative resolution have been the central
concerns of the philosophical and religious traditions of this
civilization and of its greatest literary expressions. If history
is more than an interest in antique gossip, literature more than
an elegant renditon of an emotive reaction to external stimuli,
and both history and literature more than the "register of the
crimes, follies, and misfortunes of mankind," neither the historian nor the novelist can afford to ignore such questions.

*Part Three*     *Poetry*

# *15* · Psychology and Theme in

## *Brother to Dragons*

WARREN's novel in verse, *Brother to Dragons*, is most notable in its philosophy and psychology and summarizes vividly his continuing metaphysical and ethical themes. Aware in his moralist's zeal "that poetry is more than fantasy and is committed to the obligation of trying to say something about the human condition," Warren is in this work more than ever haunted by an anguished sense of the disparity in man between recurrent beatific vision and the ubiquitous evil which blights it. Accounting for the force of the book are Warren's realization of character, his flair for the arresting image and apt phrase, his evocation of situation and atmosphere, and his instinct for the telling structural contrast. Indispensable as are these aspects of literary talent to the precise rendition of value through form, they are all subordinate to Warren's tense brooding over human motivation and human destiny.

Despite his cavils against oversimplified abstract thinking in his critique of "The Ancient Mariner" and elsewhere, abstract speculation has come to absorb Warren. He has, however, eschewed the dangers he warns against—the abstract, the general, the universal is always related forcibly, even violently, to the concrete, the particular, the local. Warren achieves a sensible, sometimes drily pragmatic balance, then, between the relative and the absolute, the mutable and the permanent, the fact and the archetype. In *Brother to Dragons*, the combined reflections of the several interested persons, including the author as R. P. W., yield a valid disinterested truth, since its roots are in their

immediate experience. The localizng of his narratives in history
achieves a similar purpose. Viewing dispassionately the dilemmas of individuals in history, Warren has a specific perspective
upon which to focus his ranging intelligence. To reach exact
definitons of elusive moral and metaphysical values, to reach
befitting conclusions as to the provenance of good and evil,
Warren also utilizes in *Brother to Dragons* an incident from out
of the past, one drawn from the annals of the Jefferson family.

The central figure in this episode is Jefferson's nephew,
Lilburn Lewis, who, after his mother's death, butchers his
Negro valet, George, when the latter breaks a pitcher once belonging to the mother. Since a maniacal self-love and a maniacal
Oedipus complex consume him, Lilburn must at all costs secure
vengeance for an imputed spiteful violation of his mother's
memory by George and the other household Negroes. The
senselessness of Lilburn's crime and the sinister forces it epitomizes all but overwhelm the hapless idealist, Thomas Jefferson,
who had not, in his aspiration, fully considered the evil in all
men. With his eventual if somewhat reluctant attainment of a
more valid knowledge—presupposing right reason, infused by the
spirit, or else creative imagination, informed by the sense of
fact—he is then able to effect a fruitful reconciliation between
aspiration and reality, between the disparities, in general, of his
experience. As a result, he achieves wholeness of spirit.

Warren is even more insistent in *Brother to Dragons* than
in his other work upon the transforming influence of the true
spiritual principle and the nefarious influence of perverted
spirituality. Both Lilburn and the early Jefferson illustrate a
familiar pattern in Warren's work: the individual's search for
spiritual peace by side-stepping his inner difficulties and by
subservience to an abstract ideal only indirectly related to them.
Unable to find peace within, through his lack of internal resources and through his too easy disregard of the truths to be
found in religious tradition, such an individual searches for it too
aggressively outside the self—in the empirically derived configurations of his experience or in nature. From these sources,
he seeks some kind of absolute which can always command allegiance, but an absolute personally defined and designed to
further his own interested motives, whether he will admit to

this tacit hypocrisy or not. Such anodyne for inner insecurity is only temporary since too much is expected from it. Unless conversion to a different mode of being has finally occurred, disillusionment and violence rather than meaningful insights into reality result from a quest thus histrionically self-centered and self-sufficiently pursued. The aborted spirituality which may derive from such activity often has dire consequences, since if prideful man alone provides the measure for all values there is nothing to prevent him from going to any length, even to crime, to make his vision prevail. Barring a conversion from such self-righteousness, the typical Warren character is unable—or unwilling—to lose his soul to find it.

In purport *Brother to Dragons* does not depart markedly from Warren's previous work, but its exacerbated tone and persistent undercurrents of violence reveal Warren's increasingly urgent sense that the provenance of original sin is universal and that it is inescapable. The potential acedia of spirit resulting from our possible despair at such a prospect Warren condemns, however, at the same time that he shows how little room there can be for complacent acceptance of human nature as it is. If human nature in itself is seen to be ultimately monstrous, and if we are lost in its labyrinthine fastnesses, there can also transpire, through the accession of Grace, an enlargement of our possibilities beyond those predicated by any superficially optimistic philosophy. The succinct definition of these possibilities and of the positive values that man, in his fallen condition, may yet embrace is Warren's most distinctive achievement in *Brother to Dragons*.

I

A psychology which distorts the facts of experience by assimilating them into a self-generated obsession betrays Lilburn Lewis. Consumed by Oedipal attraction, he idealizes Lucy Lewis and makes of mother love a worshipful abstraction, to be put forward regardless of the consequences. This intense, abstract benevolence ultimately leads to crime, enforcing Warren's judgment that this is a tragedy of "our sad virtues." In Lilburn we see the most frightening aspect of our moral history, that

all too often "evil's done for good, and in good's name" and
that a single-faceted idealism can be tragic. Lilburn has made no
compact with the devil, Warren says—he has not had to go
that far afield. He has only had to follow the good impulse, love
of his mother, to be corrupted. If, after his mother's death, Lilburn had been humble in his sufferings, he might have escaped
the degradation which ensues when he insists that all others
revere his mother's memory as he does. When the household
Negroes, in particular, seem to forget Lucy Lewis, Lilburn's
fury works at odds with the affection that prompts it. He finds
to his horror that love diminishes to the degree that he asserts
it strenuously and desires to preserve it intact. In its place, injured pride and fear lest the organizing principle of his life be
destroyed now fanatically motivate him. Like the Ancient Mariner in Warren's interpretation, Lilburn is the victim of self-
deception as to his own motives, judging the morality of an act
in terms of its advantage to him while pretending to be dispassionate. The good impulse, conceived in self-interest apart
from Christian restraints, can become through its induced intensity more uncontrollable than calculated evil and eventually
more destructive. When self-knowledge or "definition" eludes
Lilburn, he adheres to his mistaken idea of the good and does
the worst. Following a reductive principle, Lilburn tries, with
fearful results, to define the human, to give order, violently, to
chaotic flux. In such wrenching of the spirit to preconceived
ends, all hint of humility evaporates. Such eager defense of his
self-locked love for his mother from contamination in the outside world blinds Lilburn to his mother's greatness of soul and
causes him more and more to fix upon the letter of his affection
for her.

To implement this ruling devotion to his mother's memory,
Lilburn develops a passion for the pure act motivated by the
pure idea and untouched by embarrassing reality. Afraid that
the facts might rout his cherished ideal, he raises it above them
to an absolute and assures himself that its importance justifies
his realization of it beyond the limits of the ethically permis-
sible. "The dear redemption of simplicity" in such abstracted
activity becomes his solace despite its untruth and the anguish
it fosters. To others, the gratuitous act inspired by unreasoned

fervor is forcible but not ethically justifiable. When they then react sharply against it, Lilburn is only the more confirmed in his self-righteous vision.

Lilburn's desire for others to meet his impossible standards prevents, first of all, a normal sexual relationship with Laetitia. Something she describes as "awful" transpires in their relationship shortly after their marriage. Though we are not told definitely what has happened, some sort of sexual violence has undoubtedly occurred. Lilburn seems to force the apparently inexperienced Laetitia against her will and then holds this fact against her, particularly after he compels her the next night to tell what she thinks has happened. Irrationally, he resents the fact that she is spoiled at his own hands and would not remain "pure" despite her helplessness before his violence. His "angelic" Laetitia is an ordinary mortal after all; she has, he is sure, liked stepping in "dung." Shock from her violent experience deepens in Laetitia to frigidity, so that, after the mockery of their marriage, she cannot respond to the husband whose contempt for her increases nor help him when he most needs her.

Because obsessive love for his mother excludes the possibility of other emotional commitments, Lilburn uproots the love that might have steadied him after death. After he spurns Laetitia, he becomes yet more tortured, more unfeeling, more inhumane. He beats his servant George, whom Lucy sent out to bring him home following a three-day drunk when Laetitia had disappointed him. Having resisted the affection of Laetitia and George before Lucy's death, he is led, in his overwrought fixation upon his mother, to repudiate, after her death, both Aunt Cat and his hound. Since these two love him most unquestioningly, he derives sadistic pleasure from senselessly repulsing them. Poetic justice is served when they betray him after his crime—though such betrayal is paradoxically also Lilburn's "deepest will"—the dog unwittingly, Aunt Cat by clever design. By killing love, Lilburn attains "the desiderated and ice-locked anguish of isolation" which then frightens him, a security breeding insecurity. He asks love, yet he cannot bear to be loved, since it magnifies his guilt; he must then destroy what disturbs him. Symbolic of his confusion and incipient degradation is Lilburn's hatred at his mother's grave for the encroaching grass which destroys her memory among men. In view of the raw, cold, cruel, pure fact of his love, he wishes her grave to remain bare and open as a fresh wound, to be a perpetual reminder to him of his loss.

In order to break through to a reality whose force, however, diminishes in proportion to his frantic efforts to reach it, Lilburn is led, Macbeth-like, from one crime against man and nature to others still more harrowing. Now that any other love except that for his mother seems desecration to him, he instinctively kicks the hound which comes fawning to him at the grave. The resulting rapture of conflicting joy and sorrow brings catharsis in cruelty for his festering grief. When he kicks the hound the second time, Lilburn is not surprised but soothed. Distraught by his mother's image, he feels no joy "of the soul's restoration" in reconciliation with the hound. Terror and violence besiege the homestead, while the Negro victims counter with supernal cunning. He rages inwardly and broods upon insatiate revenge, trusting that inward force will vindicate the self by vindicating what the self most reveres.

At no time does Lilburn question the rightness of his acts, since their absolute rationale forbids any vacillation. The only necessity he now feels is to remain true to the light within, to a self-appointed destiny. Defining thus expeditiously his own necessity, Lilburn resembles Warren's other uncritically self-confident characters like Slim Sarrett in *At Heaven's Gate*, Willie Stark and Adam Stanton in *All the King's Men*, and Jeremiah Beaumont in *World Enough and Time*. Like them, once Lilburn tastes the spiritual security inherent in a self-generated absolute principle, he has no power to remain aloof from its demands. To compensate for deficient inner resources, which had earlier made him discontented with the frontier, he now enshrines at all costs the ideal which orders his life. In contrast with his previous states of incertitude, Lilburn is now perfectly adjusted, if occasionally still unsure of himself. As he waits for the "thrilling absoluteness / Of the pure act to come," Lilburn is unaware of the price he has paid for this assurance, the snuffing out of intervening benevolent instincts. Forcible and self-willed, he abrogates the intelligence and attains to a ruminative peace like that which any monster might feel, sunk deep in nature, such peace as Warren depicts in his poem "Crime" as "past despair and past the uncouth / Violation." Linked to Lilburn's suprahuman surety is the motionless, insensate catfish with its brute face and complacent adaptation to the channel-mud as it hibernates under the Mississippi ice. In his complete harmony with amoral nature, of Lilburn as well as of the catfish it might be said, "How can there be / Sensation where there is perfect adjustment?" The result is that Lilburn is unconscious of the barbarity of his crime, since his own nature justifies it.

His crime moves him one step nearer a more perfect realization of self as he has been able, delusively, to define it. The fact that he has now completely left the world of actuality behind him is implied in his inability to kill a huge moth which comes in the window and which distracts him only momentarily from concentrating upon his vision of his self-imagined destiny. With the help of Isham after the crime, he awaits then, in his half-joyful abandonment to the currents of the self, the grand hour when he can still more completely fulfill his nature, "the hour of the Pentecostal intuition." In his impatience, he moves to bring this time about more quickly when he gets Isham to agree to a mutual death pact. Because Lilburn savors the full pleasure of this abstracted moment—the grandest of moments because the farthest removed from the distracting realities of life—and because he wishes to enjoy to the full his "sweet alienation" and the sense of injustice done him previously, he counts slowly while Isham stands before him with a pistol. He then betrays Isham by himself not firing, since he knows that the law will take care of Isham. Monomania induces the "death of the heart," despite the fact that a heart too sensitive to confront the reality had induced the monomania.

II

At a more intellectual level, Thomas Jefferson in Warren's view is also initially motivated by the oversimplified abstraction. His ruling passion is the idealistic destiny he foresees for man, for he grasps the fact that man in his median position between God and beast aspires to the God-like. He is too anxious, however, to believe this aspiration exists pure, and he discounts too readily and vehemently the beast-like within man, as he himself admits later. Subscribing to this self-defined "rational hope" and leaping beyond man's "natural bourne and constitution" to envisage his glorious future, Jefferson denies, until too late, the discomfiting reality. At first, he looks upon the evil in man as a blot upon his shining nature, which the centuries have all but erased. With its clean lines and simple harmonies, the Romanesque cathedral at Nîmes is a symbol of ideal human fulfillment and of Jefferson's noble vision. If man would but strike off his shackles, his divine innocence would then "dance" amid the oppressive realities of the world which tend to stifle it. Because one must struggle with some of the realities of the world to attain to inner integrity, one cannot, as Jefferson tends to do, deny them all. "The eternal / Light of just proportion and the heart's harmony," which Jefferson so insatiably hungers for, is, accordingly, ironically extinguished in his fanatical craving to achieve it. As Warren presents him, Jefferson is, in his early phase, as fervent in his idealism and as insensitive to pragmatic realities as Jeremiah Beaumont in *World Enough and Time*. As a result, Jefferson cannot see that he desires too unmixed a good, impossible under the imperfect conditions of this world, just as Jeremiah Beaumont cannot see that if his antagonist, Cassius Fort, once did evil he might yet be, on the whole, a good man. Neither character realizes until he has been inexorably reoriented by tragedy that beatitude for man—a partial realization at best of all that he aspires to—is possible only through humble contrition and dispassionate love. Such a transcendence of reality must be earned through suffering, through divine Grace, instead of merely being asserted by the intellect as a cherished aim.

Warren shows how close Jefferson's psychology is to Lilburn's, despite their different purposes in life. Both seek to define the human through the self-determined abstraction, and both wish to assert an innocence consonant with it. Both lack in large part a sense for tangible realities, and both become enslaved to an overpowering vision. Both are romantic in that they tend to transform by wishful thinking things as they are into what they are not. As with so many of Warren's misguided characters, they both wish a too easily attained coherent explanation for an essentially incoherent world. Hate, the result of a naive emotionalism in Lilburn's case, and nobilty, the result of a misguided intellectuality in Jefferson's, are, as Warren explains, but different "thrust[s] toward Timelessness, in Time." The only valid motivation, Warren implies, is just the opposite: with one's intuited sense of the eternal, one must work toward time, the actual, the objective, and bring one's sense of the ideal always back to the reality. Life without saving illusion is a mockery, but a life given over to furthering at all costs the self-righteous illusion can be calamitous. Neither Jefferson of the early hopeful stage nor Lilburn could realize that the "impalpable" is not the ideal and that the ideal, in becoming too nebulous and disembodied, is in danger of being distorted.

The difference between Jefferson and Lilburn is in sensitivity, the contrast Warren had made memorable in *World Enough and Time* between Jeremiah Beaumont and Skrogg. Despite the fact that he meets a violent death, Jeremiah could ultimately be saved in a spiritual sense after a wasted life because he had spiritual receptivity, whereas Skrogg had deliberately snuffed out his soul. This kind of sensitivity also underlies the bluff exterior of Jack Burden in *All the King's Men* and allows him finally to decide between the conflicting claims of the illusion and the reality, of the self and the world of other men. The education of a misguided protagonist to the truth is thus a constant theme in Warren. In *Brother to Dragons* both Lucy Lewis and Jefferson are educated by tragedy, Jefferson the more slowly because his mistaken vision is so inflexible. Jefferson's conversion from a restrictive idealism to a more integral view of life is the chief situation explored in this verse-novel. It is significant that Lucy Lewis, reborn through her death—the result of her inability to cope with reality—redeems Jefferson by making him aware of realities outside those apparent to the intellect when it perceives only what it is interested in perceiving. For most of the novel, Jefferson is in the first period of his redemption—when he has become disillusioned with his earlier ideals and has come to realize the universality of evil in men. Only at its end, through Lucy's intervention, does he reach a decisive spiritual poise and the second period of his redemption

—when he can acknowledge original sin without recrimination.

In the first stage, Jefferson is haunted by the fact that human nature too often turns its back upon the glories of which it is capable to revel instead in the evil act. Like Lilburn, Jefferson lacks to a large degree the spiritual reserves, the stabilizing philosophy he needs to combat the evil which destroys his perfectibilist vision. Heartfelt joy in his vision leads to Jefferson's sense of betrayal, then, when one of his own blood, through the absolutely evil act, extinguishes it. Trying to order reality according to his own ideals, Jefferson continually fails to grasp the circumstances under which it may be ordered. Like Jeremiah Beaumont or Adam Stanton, Jefferson at this point both both overemphasizes and underplays the intellect: he worships an intellectualized abstraction while disregarding the critical function of reason except as it reinforces his interested idealism. Jefferson becomes bewildered, disillusioned, almost cynical in outlook. In this phase, this induced pessimism is so powerful as to becloud his earlier humanism. In a world where evil is apparently supreme and obliterates by greater force the serene good, Jefferson even comes to feel that violence alone gives truth. He now assumes that "all values are abrogated in blankness," and he reproves his sister for not having struck George after he had returned from Lilburn's beating. At this stage, Jefferson does not understand how close this counsel is to that suggested to Lilburn by his own unleashed nature before the crime. From Lilburn's brand of violence Jefferson had, indeed, recoiled in loathing. The fact that redemption often derives from violence through the polar connection existing between a strongly negative evil and a strongly positive good does not justify this counsel of Jefferson's to Lucy, although he is right in feeling that the violence he recommends is preferable to the inertia of Charles Lewis, for example. Jefferson does not perceive, moreover, that Lucy's inability at this point to conquer pride and assert the love which inwardly prompts her is her real sin and the ultimate cause of her son's tragedy.

In his first stage of regeneration, Jefferson cannot see past the fact of human evil, which has paralyzed his soul. In his obsession with its prevalence, he is as unreasoning in his denial of aspiration as he had been devoted to it previously. At a time of crisis, the inflexible philosophy of life, whether it stresses demonic pride in Lilburn or angelic aspiration in Jefferson, fails to comprehend the complexities of experience. In recoil from the reality he misunderstood, Jefferson now condemns love as "but a mask to hide the brute face of fact, / And that face is the immitigable ferocity of self." Unrealistic also is his present despair over humanity itself: "I'd said there's no defense of the human definition." This agonized pessimism is actually as intense and as uncritical as the optimism of his unregenerate days had been.

Since he has had to relinquish the perfectionist enthusiasm which motivated him at the First Continental Congress, Jefferson now recognizes "the darkness of the self" and its labyrinthine wilderness. At the height of his dreams, he had been realist enough to acknowledge the fact of evil, but he had tried to minimize it. He knew from his reading of history, for instance, that there lurked horror in its "farther room" and that the act and the motive are not always ballasted by the good deed and the good intention respectively. He also had known that all men are not innocent despite his belief in innocence as an ideal. His disillusion, however, makes him perceptive where he had been merely suspicious. Correctly but reluctantly gauging evil, even if unnerved by it to an unreasoned denial of the good, he now sees that it can be passive, since all things come to it and seek it out in magnetic attraction. He sees the lurking beast within us all, a minotaur to be found at the last turn of the spirit's labyrinth. This beast, "our brother, our darling brother," is not, in Warren's view, to be denied by any mere effort of the will; his insidious promptings can be finally overcome only by effort of the will if one can force himself to make it. Like Pasiphaë with her unnatural lust, we can become enamored of our evil. This Jefferson now sees. At the height of indulgence, we catch, like her, in the same sneaking way, a glimpse of our beatific innocence in childhood, and thereby rationalize our evil acts. Except for the reductive premises in each case, Jefferson's initial vision of man's preternatural innocence was the obverse of Pasiphaë's. She was evil but rationalized her evil by the fleeting vision of the innocent good, while Jefferson thought of man as innocent only to find him besmirched with evil. Thus the lie was given to Jefferson's earlier "towering definition, angelic, arrogant, abstract, / Greaved in glory, thewed with light." That earth's monsters are innocent in their lack of knowledge Jefferson had always realized; but that man, capable of knowledge and self-definition, could be a "master-monster" and exhibit only a blank, ignorant innocence Jefferson had not realized. Neither had his nephew, Meriwether Lewis, comprehended "the tracklessness of the human heart" until the facts of experience forced him to do so.

Now that his original conception of man has been proved wrong, Jefferson would have stressed the truth about man at all costs, he asserts, had he known then what he knows now: he would have run with "the hot coals" of that truth till they had burned through his flesh to the bone. That evil is progressive, that one deed of horror can poison all else, is Jefferson's sickening conclusion. When he still tries to cling tenaciously to "the general human fulfillment," he finds that violent evil obtrudes in his thoughts and proliferates emotionally. In his near-hysteria, therefore, Jefferson looks upon Lilburn's deed as the reigning archetype of human psychology, as the microcosm of the evil which infects all hope and which lies like a cloud and curse over the land he had once loved. To Jefferson, all social injustice and all crime are, in fact, somehow inherent in the fall of the meat axe, in the fact that his nephew could commit his crime and that other people might commit similar crimes. That one must not only shudder at evil but try actively to understand it Jefferson doesn't realize until later, nor the fact that suffering, in some degree, atones for it. He is impatient at its persistence, failing to see that it can be only partly overcome and that one must not shirk the struggle to master it.

The second stage of Jefferson's education provides the poem with its central meaning. Under the guidance of Lucy Lewis, Jefferson accommodates his original resplendent vision of man's nobility to the actual facts of human existence, especially to the cardinal fact of original sin, and mitigates the harsh abstractness of this ideal with the exertion of his sensibility. A grander nobility than Jefferson's initial conception consists, Lucy claims, in testing that conception in the world. His redemption is assured when his faith in the Idea is renewed, once a "deep distress" has humanized it and once he relates it

to mankind. The dream—or idea—of the future, Jefferson concludes, requires for complement the fact of the past:

> Now I should hope to find the courage to say
> That the dream of the future is not
> Better than the fact of the past, no matter how terrible
> For without the fact of the past we cannot dream the future.[1]

Since lack of self-knowledge is original sin in either Lilburn
or Jefferson, and since complete self-knowledge is impossible,
original sin is universal, and we are all implicated in it and with
each other. As a gesture indicating he now understands that he
and all men are involved in Lilburn's crime, Lucy insists that
Jefferson take his hand. Evasion will no longer do, for Jefferson
can't escape our universal complicity in sin, "our common
crime," as Warren phrases it in "End of Summer." As commentator on the action, R. P. W. stresses throughout our complicity in the tragedy. It contains us, he says, and it "is contained
by us," for we in our fallen condition are all guilty of it in being
human. We are guilty, furthermore, in being too complacent
about evil, since we are only too anxious to adjust ourselves
comfortably and snugly to it. As to the crime which so un-
nerves Jefferson, R. P. W. explains that it is not so special as
he thinks. It is but one episode in the long pageant of man's
sinfulness down the ages and is "impressive chiefly for its senselessness" as all evil acts tend to be. The earthquake which followed the crime struck fear into the hearts of guilty men who
had no knowledge of Lilburn's act—they were simply guilty of it
by extension, by being human, and by being capable in their worst
moments of kindred atrocity. Guilt is common enough, therefore, to make any one day appropriate for the Judgment,
even as this present hour would be. R. P. W. expresses, however,
the ironical fear that the modern age might be too "advanced"
to pray for deliverance from its guilt or to fear God's wrath,
just as men in 1811 had got used both to the repeated quakes
and to the "horror" of being men. In any event, Jefferson's complicity in original sin through his use of black labor to build
that citadel of freedom, Monticello, is real, if at first unacknowl-

[1] Robert Penn Warren, *Brother to Dragons* (New York: Random
House, 1953). All quotations are from this edition.

edged by him. The fact that evil exits should not attract us nor repel us, but should interest us since we all are, for better or worse, involved in it. When the evil is done is the question R. P. W. would explore, for all who face up bravely to life must solve that question, must analyze the anguish and the agony involved in bringing the evil act to its full birth. Unless we have that curiosity, we can never attain to saving knowledge, R. P. W. would insist.

In a noble speech Lucy tells Jefferson that she in her love brought disaster to her son, just as he in his aspiration brought disaster to Meriwether Lewis. "Our best gifts," she says, carry some ineradicable taint, and we corrupt even as we freely give—Jefferson like Lilburn has done evil in the name of good by interfusing his altruism with pride of self. This burden of our shame should always confront us, and while it should not inhibit us, it should make us bestow our gifts with humility. Lilburn's face, Jefferson must realize, is but a "mirror of your possibilities." To the criminal we are linked by the terror we all must feel at our own demonic propensities which, without our careful scrutiny, will project outward into the evil act: Lilburn's last indefensible hour is simply "the sum of all the defensible hours / We have lived through." Jefferson has squelched his fear that he, too, might be capable of all evil in being capable of any evil. As R. P. W. expresses it, Jefferson had forgotten that even the wicked man seeks God according to his own lights and fulfillment as he can find it. Along with his disillusion and his cynicism, Jefferson is forced to see that his rejection of Lilburn is too summary. Now that his confidence in himself and in his Utopian dreams has been shaken through Lilburn's crime, Jefferson rejects his nephew principally out of pique. There is some truth, then, to Meriwether's charge that Jefferson had originally contrived his "noble lie" for his own comfort and to feed his own vanity. Jefferson has a sure sense for the horror of Lilburn's crime, but hardly sees, in his revulsion, its application to himself:

> For Lilburn is an absolute of our essential
> Condition, and as such, would ingurgitate
> All, and all you'd give, all hope, all heart,
> Would only be disbursed down that rat hole
> of the ultimate horror.

In commenting upon the action and characters, R. P. W. insists that evil—at least its germ—is universal. Modern Smithland, a village near the site of decayed Rocky Hill, is to Warren a symbol for universal sin and universal suffering, by virtue of the sin and suffering it does contain. The minotaur-in-labyrinth image, so forcibly presented by Jefferson early in the poem, also becomes a symbol which dominates the poem in vividly suggesting the lurking evil in the dark heart of man. In greater or less degree, all the characters in the poem sin, and they all suffer because they cannot transcend their failings and emerge completely from the darkness of their inner selves. None of them are as wholly innocent and glorious as Jefferson had initially imagined the men at the First Continental Congress to be; rather they all resemble his colleagues as Jefferson describes them in a revised estimate:

> lost
> Each man lost in some blind lobby, hall, enclave,
> Crank cul-de-sac, couloir, or corridor of Time.
> Of time. Or self: and in that dark no thread . . .

Lucy Lewis, radiant as she is, is prevented by pride from making toward George in his suffering the spontaneous gesture which would alleviate it and result in her own fulfillment: "the small / Obligation fulfilled had swayed the weight of the world." Similarly, Laetitia is prevented from making toward Lilburn at Lucy's death the gesture which would gain his love forever through her willingness to forgive his past violence to her. Actually, Laetitia had in part willed Lilburn's violation of her, and in one sense, therefore, merits the scorn of her husband for imputed impurity—at least she could not, and hardly wanted to, tell Lilburn to stop. Betrayed by her innocence into a fascination with the evil she shrinks from, Laetitia in her psychology at the time of her defilement by Lilburn is not unlike Pasiphaë, as Warren describes her, at the time of her submission to the plunging bull.

Our common complicity in evil Warren elaborates upon still further in his analysis of Laetitia's brother, of Isham, of Aunt Cat, and of George. Laetitia's brother is indignant when he learns that Lilburn had forcibly used Laetitia, and he proclaims loudly how sweeping would have been his revenge if

he had known. Laetitia acutely says that he would not have
avenged her out of love, but out of pride at accomplishing the
deed—at best, out of desire to protect the family honor. Aunt
Cat, Lilburn's colored mammy, really loves him, but in her
love there is calculation too, manifested for years in the silent
but tense struggle between her and Lucy Lewis for Lilburn's
affection. To a degree she also merits what she gets when Lilburn, in a fit of fury at the time of his mother's death, pretends
to disgorge the black milk he had been nursed upon. Isham,
too, is as guilty of George's butchering as his brother, for Isham
knew instinctively what was going to happen and did nothing
to prevent it. In that he seemed half-willing to meet his fate,
George was, in some part, an accomplice in the deed. He almost
wills, with obscene pleasure, the fatal stroke, and seems more
in love with the "sweet injustice to himself" than fearful of
death. Even though he keeps running away, George is also
drawn back hypnotically again and again to Lilburn in a continuing attraction-repulsion pattern. R. P. W. admits this notion
of George's complicity is, in some degree, fantastical, since
nothing can really excuse Lilburn's crime. But R. P. W.'s ob-
servations are true, he would assert, to the extent that "we're
all each other's victim. / Potentially, at least."

III

Jefferson has failed to see, in short, that positive good
presupposes positive evil, that the two are closely related, and
that Lilburn's motivation is really the need, as R. P. W. maintains, "to name his evil good." That moral and psychological
values are complex Jefferson is unwilling to admit, because of
his zeal to preserve the integrity of his vision. That ambiguity is
the indispensable feature of the moral life, that philosophical
truth is to be measured in terms of an adjustment of the dis-
cordancies of experience, that illusion must be squared with
a multiform actuality has somehow escaped Jefferson, as it had
also escaped the unintellectual Lilburn. In describing the crime,
R. P. W. had addressed the night as a symbol of the absoluteness of vision that Lilburn—and Jefferson—aspired toward. The

night would obliterate in its uniform blackness "the impudent daylight's velleities," that is, the concrete actualities of our experience. Once they are obscured, it is tempting to define the Absolute by an interested exertion of the will alone rather than by the vigorous reconciliation of the many to the one. The mixture of good and evil in humanity is something that Jefferson had realized in his intellect, but he had not given the concept his emotional assent. Jefferson's psychology is essentially too simple—in his disillusion he rejects, for instance, the innocence of the newborn babe because of the evil that human nature can also perpetrate. He then denies the generous act because it can never exist pure, because it is always tainted inescapably by the self. The omnipresence of malignant evil disturbs his inner poise to the extent that he all but denies the worth of the ideals he had once cherished. Though love, for example, has an admixture of pride in it and is scarcely ever disinterested, Jefferson fails to see, notwithstanding, that it is truly estimable. The all-or-none point of view is thus pernicious in overlooking the truth that every act and emotion carries within it not only its own impulsions but its contrary possibility. A fervently accepted good, therefore, has more possible evil in it than a lukewarm virtue, while an unabashed evil carries within it latent violences that augur the possibility of heartfelt conversion.

Every act, moreover, implies a choice among motives for it to become the act, implies a resolving of "the essential polarity of possibility" contained within it. The act has a finality "in the mere fact of achieved definition," therefore, a degree of purity and simplification at variance with its confused intent. Even though such choice among motives is made and a large degree of purity is thereby attained, the act still carries within its secret core other latent impulsions. If it represents a simplification of our swarming experience, the origins of the act are never clearcut, but rather a "hell-broth of paradox and internecine / Complex of motive." It must, accordingly, be exhaustively analyzed, not merely accepted at its apparent value for the relief it brings the doer. Lilburn's evil deed, for instance, must be judged not only for its destructiveness but also as misguided creation. The wicked man, says R. P. W., is, after all, but seeking for his crimes some outward rationale which the good man would term God.

The paradoxical substratum underlying all our acts is variously emphasized in the poem. One aspect of the tangled nature of reality is suggested by Charles Lewis—though Warren shows more contempt for him than for anyone else—the fact that madness is "the cancer of truth" and has more affinity with the actuality than has a deadened complacency. For this same reason, Warren values violence more highly than timid conformity to convention. Even Jefferson realizes this truth when in his disillusion he says that "all truth is bought with blood," except that he then is too much obsessed with the blood to realize that violence is only one avenue to renewal. At the very least, violence will exorcize unreality, will expose the fraudulence of "the pious mind" to whom "our history's nothing if not refined." Only when violence is pursued with self-interest, as with Lilburn, does it become the supreme evil. Since reality is thus elusive and multiple, R. P. W. maintains that a balance of qualities, educed by the supple intelligence, is the essential of wisdom. Grace, pity, and charity we all need from God, but that does not mean that free-will can be set aside. The glorious possibility acknowledges the despair which hems it round, and derives its strength from that honesty. But it does not give in to this pessimism. The complexity of existence is again emphasized when R. P. W. asserts that it is through isolation that we grasp "the human bond" and at length define the self—in "separateness," Warren has declared in his poem "Revelation," "does love learn definition"—while at our peril we reject our fellow man completely. If we withdraw from society to gain a greater inner irradiation, we must, thus fortified, return to it and seek our place in it. Failure to see that a personally determined moral code has weight only when it comprehends the self in relation to other men was, after all, Jefferson's original mistake as it had also been Lilburn's.

Of the many ambiguities explored in the poem, the most striking concerns the natural world. On the one hand, Warren stresses the malignancy and impersonality of nature. The fact that the white inhabitants have unfairly wrested the land from the Indians places a curse upon it, so that moral unhealth hangs like miasma over the wilderness, and its shadows enter the souls of the pioneers. Both sons of Lucy Lewis come under its dark spell; both have become victims of "the ignorant torpor / That breathed from the dark land." After his crime, moreover, Lilburn feels only at home in "the unredeemed dark of the wild land." Raised on the edge of the wilderness, Jefferson had also come to feel over and through him "the shadow of the forest," sinister and foreboding. Even then, he had felt that man must redeem nature, for nature is too harsh and unfeeling for it to serve as moral ministrant to erring, aspiring man. As she did in 1811, nature will likely as not visit mankind with earthquakes, floods, and sickness to add to his discomfort and perplexity. As measure of her hostility to living creatures, she causes the dog-fox to drown in protracted agony in a flood, or she causes the oak tree, like Jacob, to struggle all night in anguish with "the incessant / And pitiless angel of air." In a perfect adjustment to nature, there is either overplus of misdirected feeling or inability to feel at all. In its "idiot-ignorance" nature obliterates the purely human and the moral law which alone can educe the human. Feeling strongly this need for other than naturalistic values in their undiluted form, Warren asserted in his poem "Monologue at Midnight" that "Our mathematic yet has use / For the integers of blessedness." The grandeur of nature, Warren maintains in the concluding lines of the verse-novel, can give us an "image" only for our destiny, but can in no sense give us a "confirmation" of it. That must be sought from within the soul itself.

If nature "as an image of lethal purity" is a symbol of evil, it is also a symbol of reality and truth; it is both malignant and beautiful, soul-benumbing and life-inspiriting, giving rise to heartfelt joy despite the infinite darkness at its heart, as Warren also tells us in "Picnic Remembered." The beauty of the springtide upon the untracked forest, its "heart-breaking new delicacy of green," is an emblem of such ambiguity. If we follow the promptings of nature too closely, we can lose our humanity; but, paradoxically, it can also assuage our sufferings deriving from the evils which follow the loss in others of that humanity. By making such men contemptible and insignificant in comparison with its power, it can comfort us for the violence and cruelty they may instigate. It can bedwarf even the monstrous and endow us with the vital energy that can alone enable us to transcend the "human trauma." Lilburn is as if driven onward by the raging wind, as if in the whirlwind of senseless force. Yet if he is so closely part of nature, it is only by escaping from him out into "the glimmering night scene" that we can regain proportion and sanity. After his crime Lilburn, so much a part of nature in his unrestrained violence, can no longer respond to its spiritual influence. He inhabits then a somber inner landscape "of forms fixed and hieratic," and abjures the promiscuous promise of joy in newly wakening nature.

Nature is in essence spiritual and a source for deep reality provided its power is used to strengthen the innately spiritual and not substituted for it. Warren can say, therefore, that in spite of "all naturalistic considerations" or because of them, we must believe in virtue—nature can both extinguish the human impulse and reinforce it. We ought not to regard nature abstractly by naming its objects out of their context, for they are more than mere names: they are symbols of inner spiritual facts, so that a snake is really a symbol of evil, violence, darkness, and terror, though science would call it only *Elaphe obsoleta obsoleta*. Such a rationalist approach to nature impoverishes it, yet Warren's earlier emotional fervor for it, as recounted in the poem, is also unreal. The joy he had felt as a boy in holding tight the objects of the sense provides an easy faith that cannot last. Neither an easy nor an exclusive faith in nature is tenable, yet Warren does quote Lucretius to the effect that the order underlying nature, the ranging of natural phenomena under natural law, may dispel the "darkness of the mind" and lead to inner light. A true knowledge of nature, fortified by our sense of the human, can dispel our morbid fears and the darkness and terror that haunt the innermost soul of man, while an unconditioned emotional response to its promptings can intensify those fears and that darkness and terror. Man is at once part of nature and above it, and should, in his adjustments to it, be mindful of this paradox. A security or joy obtained, like Jefferson's, by a denial of inconvenient natural fact is as reprehensible as Lilburn's blind immersion in nature.

IV

More than any of his other poems, *Brother to Dragons* represents a mature if sometimes muted statement of Warren's own values. From his narrative Warren elicits certain conclusions about human life which he is always careful to clothe, however, in the specific symbol or to educe from the concrete situation. While for Warren the absolutes of tradition have an independent existence, he avoids sentimentality and provides for their inevitable definition by allowing them to emerge from a specific milieu.

Chief among these positive values is glory, which alone makes life worthwhile, fearful as the experience of it may become. It is a dynamic spiritual harmony, the exaltation attendant upon salvation, the sense of being attuned to both the natural and the supernatural. Failing to cultivate such a mystique as it illuminates his experiences, man fails to live as deeply as he could, Warren asserts. Despite this truth, it is with reluctance that we face the necessity of being saved, of surrendering ourselves to the radiance of glory and permitting it to determine the quality of our lives. As the chief reality in our lives to be reverenced, glory will, once its provenance is admitted, reorient us positively: "for it knocks society's values to a cocked hat." Glory is what the soul is best capable of, contrasting with the abstract idealism which becomes hardened to formula and withers rather than elicits the potentialities of the soul. If we are identified with all other men in guilt, we are also identified with them in their troubled aspirations after glory.

To know the farthest reaches of the spirit demands an emotional sensitivity toward others, a realization that it is fatal only to love and to love well, and not to love well enough. In these terms Lucy Lewis describes her own failure with respect to the family tragedy. Unable because of fear to extend her hand to George in kindness and love, she soon collapses physically and morally. Her death retributively follows her inability to live the life her instincts countenance. Because she fails in love toward George, she fails in love toward her son. She learns that love is the most valuable human trait and represents "definition"; once expressed it can never again be denied, unless one would die spiritually, the same point that Warren had made in his poem "Love's Parable." As we have seen, Laetitia does not love Lilburn enough, either, to minister to him at the time of Lucy's death. She is right in feeling that a change of heart in herself would have availed her husband; in her pride, however, she is unregenerate and cannot attain to selfless love. Lilburn is in a sense betrayed by the women who love him—Lucy, Laetitia, and Aunt Cat—because they do not love him strongly enough to stand by him when he needs them most and to instruct him in "the mystery of the heart." In the modern age, we also deny ourselves too often to others. As we speed down the highway, we can too easily forget, for instance, the loveless eye, which glares at us from a hovel and reminds us of our inhumanity; we merely press the accelerator "and quick you're gone/Beyond forgiveness, pity, hope, hate, love."

Closely allied to Warren's reverence for both love and glory is that for virtue and its concomitant, humility. There is no possibility of our not believing in virtue, for our conscience is always with us and will not be silenced, Warren asserts. Virtue is tougher and more "remorseless" than any of our other attributes, for it isolates the human amongst the other forms of life. Virtue, if disregarded, will lie in wait murderously, like "the lethal mantis at his prayer," to pounce upon the heart that denies it. It is also the necessary rationale for all human anguish. Without anguish, virtue could not be so clearly delimited as to command our absolute allegiance: anguish gives to virtue its local habitation so that it does not become intolerably abstracted from reality:

> I think I begin to see the forging of the future.
> It will be forged beneath the hammer of truth
> On the anvil of our anguish. We shall be forged
> Beneath the hammer of truth on the anvil of anguish.
> It would be terrible to think that truth is lost.
> It would be worse to think that anguish is lost, ever.

Virtue purifies from pride and induces in the more sensitive characters of the poem needed humility, a sacramental vision of the universe such as the regenerate Ancient Mariner also embraces in Warren's interpretation of the poem. Through thus dying to the self, real selfhood alone will be achieved, says Warren in his own poem. As to Jefferson, he remains cynical until Lucy can prevail upon him to cease dwelling upon the outrage of Lilburn's crime and to accept him. When he finally acknowledges Lilburn, the pride inseparable from the judging of another by one's own standards disappears. Jefferson then attains the humility needed for the inner balance his near-hysteria had heretofore destroyed. The other chief characters, Laetitia, Lucy, and Aunt Cat, are, as we have seen, all prevented by varying kinds of pride from being true to their instinctive sympathies. Only when they accept in humility rather than reject in pride are they serene. The forms of pride, Warren argues, are many and treacherous. Even the act of forgiveness stems in large part from injured self-esteem, and allows us to placate the wounded self. Heroism, declares the knowledgeful Jefferson, this time speaking for Warren, is more often motivated by pride in putting down the monster than by any altruism. The usual hero is potentially more evil than the monsters he vanquishes, because vainglory encourages him to reject normal human limitations in an aggrandizement of self: "man puts down the bad and then feels good," says Warren. The black snake that R. P. W. sees outside at Rocky Hill is not only the traditional symbol for the evil and violence that have brooded there, but it is conversely a symbol of the fact that forgiveness for such evil is necessary, of the fact that by humility and love we gain wisdom to oppose the influence of furtive evil. Like man at his ideal moral and spiritual fulfillment, the snake both forgives and asks forgiveness.

An activist cluster of values also informs the poem. As members of the human race, Warren insists, we must be morally responsible—our connections with other men are so subtle and so pervasive that we deny them at our peril. Because we are all in some degree the victims of history and of our environment, we have no right, Warren alleges, to disavow responsibility:

> For if responsibility is not
> The thing given but the thing to be achieved,
> There is still no way out of the responsibility
> Of trying to achieve responsibility
> So like it or lump it, you are stuck.

Jefferson's rejection of Lilburn is simply his rejection of what is unpleasant, says Lucy, Warren's mouthpiece. In his presentation of Charles Lewis, Warren even more directly inculcates the need to assume gratefully and without evasion our responsibilities. Lewis had fled his moral obligations in Virginia in the hope of finding peace in a new land; but since he brought his inner weakness and hollowness with him, he is, if anything, more at loose ends on the frontier than he had been in Virginia. By his repudiation of family responsibility, his descendants are left, without light, to degenerate on the frontier.

Coming to Kentucky to seek reality, to become once more "part of human effort and man's hope," Charles does not find it because his soul is shrivelled. After Lucy's death, Charles in fact sometimes thinks he is empty so that he is surprised to find his footprint in the earth. At that time he feels relief, as well as sorrow, that he need no longer seek reality. It demands too much uncomfortable effort now that the one person to whom he was in any way real has gone. He hopes that her remains will rot quickly "into the absolute oblivion" and that she may soon be the nothingness he has already become. He goes back to Virginia to fulfill a barren, hollow destiny amid the artifices of civilization where the reality—as well as the stark evil—of the dark land will not so rudely challenge him, where he will be safe from disturbing violence, and where he can pursue, unimpeded, a materialist "success." Like his nephew Meriwether, Charles Lewis had also found that the foulness of savage men had more vitality than the artifice of "civilized" man, but Charles lacks the vigor to break out of his moral torpor. He cannot escape the lie he lives because he brings it with him from Virginia to the Kentucky wilderness. The milieu he fled, he sees, is intolerable simply because it had nothing intolerable in it. His desire to find some new "tension and test, perhaps terror" in the West is thwarted because he tells the only lie that a man cannot embrace and still live, "the lie that justifies." Lilburn and Jefferson—and in his wake, Meriwether Lewis—also tell the lie that justifies. Tragic violence, disheartening disillusion, and suicide are the respective results. This kind of lie is simply a rationale for irresponsibility: in each case, the critical sense, or, as R. P. W. calls it, "a certain pragmatic perspective," is lacking.

The effort of the will to achieve definition is ultimately necessary if the individual is to attain spiritual clarity. One cannot arrive at the reasons for George's anguish and Lilburn's degradation by thought alone, says the reborn Jefferson, but one must create the possibility for such a reason by a directed resolution, wherein strength is modulated by charity. This, the only knowledge worth possessing, is so elusive as to be almost impossible to possess fully. Understanding—even understanding a crime—requires an active exertion of the will, not merely a passive analysis by the intellect. One cannot define abstractly the inscrutable, but one must participate, at least vicariously, in its manifestations: "what is any knowledge / Without the intrinsic mediation of the heart?" Above all, we have to realize that such intuitive sympathy demands that we also acknowledge, unflinchingly, the worst that can happen:

We must strike the steel of wrath on the stone of guilt,
And hope to provoke, thus, in the midst of our coiling darkness
The incandescence of the heart's great flare.
And in that illumination I should hope to see
How all creation validates itself,
For whatever you create, you create yourself by it,
And in creating yourself you will create
The whole wide world and gleaming West anew.

To translate idea into action demands a courage which Warren's characters do not usually possess, though they may recognize its desirability. Lucy and Laetitia, for example, are unable to realize in actuality what their hearts tell them is right. Warren says that bravery is the quality which counts most, for only those who meet moral tests without cowering have a true knowledge of life. The reasons which prompt the Lilburns to evil will become apparent alone to those who have striven, for they alone will be aware of the suffering involved in translating the evil impulse into the actual evil act. Warren, as we have seen, quotes Lucretius to the effect that, in dispelling the "darkness of the mind," the law and aspect of nature is needed: this implies a patient perusal and endurance of the tests it offers. Stoic endurance is also necessary for the expunging of vanities: it is needed, for example, says Warren, in accepting our fathers' reconciliations to experience, which we can do only when we do not set ourselves above our fathers and when we can accept our own failure to achieve their triumphs. Recounting his experiences in the West, Meriwether Lewis stresses how greatly fortitude was required, a quality, moreover, which eluded him in his own adjustments of life. His sentiment that "pride in endurance is one pride that shall not be denied men" is surely, in its clear emphasis, Warren's own. Aunt Cat also illustrates the tenacious fortitude that Warren values so highly, for she has the stability which permits her to survive to a ripe old age, to outlast the rest of the people at Rocky Hill who are either physically dead or blighted inwardly.

Warren is poised in his general view of things between an outright pessimism, which is most intense when due to self-dramatized frustrations, and a too easy optimism, which feels it can control to its own advantage the conditions of life. Warren is pessimistic to the degree that he feels life is possible only because we do not have to face realities too often. He condemns both Lilburn and the earlier Jefferson for not facing them at all, yet he knows also that mankind cannot stand too much reality. Life is possible only because of its "discontinuity." A partial glimpse of the truth is about all that we can ordinarily endure. Otherwise the pressures upon us might cause us to go mad. In the conduct of life, discretion is all-important, for it is an outward sign of inner balance. Jefferson's ultimate reasoned position and, by extension, Warren's own is a qualified optimism or a meliorative pessimism: "we are condemned to some hope," says Jefferson at the last to contrast with the fulsomeness of his earlier utterances and with the blackness of his intervening despair. The fact that Grace is possible, that a modicum of knowledge may be attained, that tentative definition is possible implies that a constructive point of view is, in part, valid. Extreme optimism or extreme pessimism are both false since they both falsify the facts. Warren is not sure, however, how far he ought to stand from either pole. Lucy Lewis is his avatar: the spaciousness of her personality, superior to both transient enthusiasm and soured despair, induced in the slaves under her control an enthusiastic loyalty which to them—and to Warren— represented a serenity that transcended in value their love for her and her love for them.

# *16*·The Recent Poetry
## of Robert Penn Warren

> So you didn't know? Well, it's time you
> did—though one shuns to acknowledge
> the root from which one's own virtue
> mounts.
> Robert Penn Warren—"Clearly About You"

IF YOU CHOOSE to begin with 1935, the year of publication of
Warren's *Thirty-six Poems,* then it is simple enough to state that
for thirty years he has been writing poetry of distinction and
importance. Including his book length narrative in verse,
*Brother To Dragons* (1953), there have been six books of poetry, and during that time Warren's poems have received a good
deal of critical attention. He has won many awards and honors—
the Pulitzer Prize, the National Book Award, the Shelley Memorial Award, and others. He has served as Consultant in Poetry
at the Library of Congress. All of which adds up to a simple
fact. Even if the poetry of Robert Penn Warren were to be
considered in abstraction from his closely related achievements
as novelist and short story writer, as critic, editor, and teacher,
still he would obviously have to be counted among the very
small number of outstanding and genuinely productive poets
of our time.

Judged by that second and much less frequently invoked
standard of judgment, productivity, the continuing creation of
poems of high quality over a considerable period of time, Warren's achievement is more rare. He stands almost alone in the

sense of continued growth and change in his poetry. Most of
our poets have chosen to reflect the specialization of industry
and the age, no matter how much they howl against it. Each
finds his particular way, what the peer group prefers to call "his
own voice," and then proceeds to cultivate and exploit it with
the single-minded devotion of the mythical manufacturer of
Brand X. Perhaps closer to the mark, each imitates the insistence
of the latest popular crooner whose sighs, groans, bumps, and
grinds are immediately identifiable to the most careless listener
and which, through the bounties of success, may eventually be
called a "style." Take yet another image for the American
poetic scene. The young poet begins as a sharecropper, hoeing
his hard row, living in relative squalor at the fringes of a large
plantation at the center of which stands a sort of Selznik-style
mansion house, a kind of national monument, museum, and
tourist attraction where only a few, widely recognized, very
important poets live. These are chiefly those who have long
since laid down the shovel and the hoe of hard labor and, while
waiting for a first-class chariot ride, are willing to settle for clean
fingernails, uncalloused palms, the sweatless and riskless roles of
lecturer, reviewer, critic, and sometime judge for one of the
prizes and grants which are available, able to be tossed with
benevolent *noblesse oblige* to the most obedient and best-be-
haved youngsters and the faithful middle-aged who know their
place. For that young poet out there in the hot sun the ideal,
the dream of glory is, of course, to get out of it, to escape the
weather, the work, the danger, and to move into the comfortable shade and dignity of the old manse. And, like ambitious
young men since time began, they are willing to polish any
number of boots, to kiss any number of famous and ample
posteriors, because that beats staggering along behind a mule
and a plough.

Our present poetic situation is not conductive to growth
or change. In the past twenty years, years some have called afflu-
ent, it has become a kind of dancing court, a splendid hall of
mirrors ("Mirror, mirror, on the wall/Who is Donald Andrew
Hall?"), a genteel society of mutual admiration and profound
self-esteem. It should be added that there is always at least one
chamber reserved for those distorted and disturbing mirrors
which are intended to make us all appreciate, even more than

we naturally do already, the essential symmetry of our natural selves. Here the well-paid, well-fed jesters, wearing traditional cap and bells, play in happy mockery, the kind of mockery whose sole purpose is to emphasize the altogether enviable status of the *status quo*.

The American poetic *status quo* is conservative (a little to the right of Ivan the Terrible) in literary matters and takes a dim view of productivity. The prolific, the versatile, the *changing*, are more feared by the establishment than the world, the flesh, and the devil combined.

Paradoxically, Warren began his poetic career with the assurance of a decent place within a respectable group in the hierarchy. He was an acceptable young "fugitive." The influence of this small group, small in number and even smaller in gross product, can hardly be overestimated. It is not only critically, as has been widely allowed, but also by the example of their work and success, that this little group has been so influential. This is a little surprising, for the essentials of good, sound fugitive verse, exemplified at its best by the best of Ransom and Tate, are traditional and traditionally southern. Their verse is formal and, for the most part, shuns innovation in language, form, and subject matter as if it were a social disease. Their work is deeply rooted in the old, historical southern assumption that there is a clear-cut boundary, formidable as any curtain of iron or bamboo, between the proper precincts of prose and poetry. Viewed against the backdrop of southern literary history, the very slight changes effected by the fugitives in poetry or prose are as negligible as the works of man considered in the context of geologic time. In poetry there was a mild increase in the intellectual surface and content, which has sometimes been advertised as "obscurity," and there was the admission into the realm of the acceptably poetic a gentle irony which might be called a kind of academic gag writing. Taking a signal from T. S. Eliot's brief, though famous bow in the general direction of John Donne, they quickly codified a set of laws and bylaws of poetry and fiction; then, with almost missionary zeal, they became fugitive indeed, all but a few of them fleeing the benighted South for the security and culture of the suburban North.

In some of his earliest poems Warren demonstrated his

ability to turn this kind of poem almost to perfection. And, ironically, it is by these poems that he is usually represented in the anthologies today. The familiar final quatrain of "Bearded Oaks" is a really marvelous example of Marvell translated into twentieth-century English:

> We live in time so little time
> And we learn all so painfully,
> That we may spare this hour's term
> To practice for eternity.[1]

"Love's Parable" is pure Donne and shows its origin proudly in its syntax, deliberate inversions and archaisms, and here, for example, in the dominant image of the opening stanza:

> As kingdoms after civil broil,
> Long faction-bit and sore unmanned,
> Unlaced, unthewed by lawless toil,
> Will welcome to the cheering strand
> A prince whose tongue, not understood,
> Yet frames a new felicity,
> And alien, seals domestic good:
> Once each to each, such aliens, we.[1]

Warren might easily have stopped right there, and not without some honor; but he is gifted as a superb storyteller, and he is also more deeply related to the living heart and guts of the southern tradition than any of his mentors. Even among his early poems there are ones which break the rules and have a very different kind of validity and excitement. The variety is clearly evident in *Selected Poems 1923–1943*. There is "The Ballad of Billie Potts," a sustained narrative poem which is particular and concrete, exactly local, and riddled with homely imagery, some of it part of the folk tradition, some designed and contrived as a close approximation of it.

> Little Billie was full of piss and vinegar,
> And full of sap as a maple tree.
> And full of tricks as a lop-eared pup.[2]

In a group of poems with a Mexican setting he had begun to show an ability to handle the concrete scene and real action in

---

1 Robert Penn Warren, *Thirty-six Poems* (New York: Alcestis Press, 1935). All quotations from *Thirty-six Poems* are from this edition.

verse that could rival his abilities in prose. For example, this
flashing, cinematic moment from "The World Comes Gal-
loping":

> Then at the foot of that long street
> Between the pastel stucco and the feathery pepper trees,
> Horse and horseman, sudden as light, and loud,
> Appeared,
> And up the rise, banging the cobbles like castanets,
> Lashed in their fury and fever,
> Plunged:
> Wall-eyed and wheezing, the lurching hammer-head,
> The swaying youth, and flapping from bare heels
> The great wheel spurs of the Conquistador.
> Plunged past us, and were gone:
> The crow-bait mount, the fly-bit man.[2]

Not many of our poets could write down a gallop like that one.
*Selected Poems* shows a mature and gifted poet, able to use
various voices and ways, some apparently inconsistent with each
other if one accepts the dictum of the Establishment and looks
for one voice only.

Then came *Brother to Dragons: A Tale in Verse and Voices*
(1953). The critical debate about this poem goes on, and no
doubt it will continue. It ought to, for in *Brother to Dragons*
Warren did what everyone had declared impossible. He wrote a
book-length narrative poem, highly original in many aspects of
both form and content; and he sustained it with power and
grace, *as a poem,* from beginning to end. More than anything
else, this work managed to bring together the concerns and
themes which had separately haunted his poetry and his prose.
For any study of his whole work it is crucial. For a consideration
of Warren as poet, it marks a turning point, proof positive that
the stuff of prose and the stuff of poetry could, in fact, be
wedded and live happily together. In a sense, then, after *Brother
to Dragons,* Warren was liberated, free to turn to something
new if he chose to, equally free to carry along with him whatever he wished from his own poetic experience.

*Promises: Poems 1954–1956* let us see what the direction

2 Robert Penn Warren, *Selected Poems 1923–1943* (New York: Harcourt, Brace, 1944). All poems from *Selected Poems 1923–1943* are from
this edition.

would be. It is technically different, with new, rolling, long lines based often on stresses and speech rhythm, and new and interesting variations on traditional stanzaic forms. The *language* is different, able now in simulataneity to encompass the prosaic and the "poetic" to create of out of disparate parts a total effect of poetry. The earlier virtuosity is here replaced by the much harder trick of surface simplicity and an easy and familiar mystery of the whole range of the living language, from commonplace to "highfaluting" rhetoric. Nothing, no subject, no word, no notion, is to be cast aside as "unpoetic." It is an explosive book and a bold one. A declaration of independence. To those who had counseled reticence and rigor it must have seemed that he was speaking to and of them in the little poem "Work":

> The hand that aches for the pitchfork heft
> Heaves sheaf from the shock's rich disrepair.
> The wagoner snags it in mid-air,
> Says, "Boy, save your strength, 'fore you got none left,"
> And grins and wipes the sweat from his hair." [3]

*Promises* has poems set in Italy, in history, in the South, and in the country of the imagination, but it is a deeply southern book and more inclusively southern than any of the work of the celebrated fugitives. It belongs to what might be called the grand tradition of southern writing, the one which includes so much more than our schoolmarms and schoolmasters (our own Ichabod Cranes), the one which includes our novelists, our backwoods humorists, our lawyers, politicians, and preachers. There are many things which come together in that tradition. Briefly, some of them are: a love of the land which was, and is still in many places, a *beautiful* land, a sense of its history, a strong bond of family, a sense of humor which bubbles out of the ground like fresh springwater in surprising places, and a way with language.

In literature it is this last quality which most clearly distinguishes the southern writer from any other. It is a legitimate child of the tradition of southern rhetoric in life—religious rhetoric, and more specifically political and legal speech. From

---

3 Robert Penn Warren, *Promises* (New York: Random House, 1957). All quotations from *Promises* are from this edition.

the beginning of this nation until now, the New England writers have *preached* at people. The more recently arrived, the sophisticated urban writers, learned to talk English from James Cagney movies—out of the sides of their mouths, lively, nervous, and never quite at home with the idiom. The southern writer comes from a race of talkers of another kind. He loves rhetoric for its own sake and without embarassment. He has a fine, given tradition of it: pulpit rhetoric, grave or comic, calm or evangelical; political oratory, the sounds, not always empty for being stentorian, of a rip-roaring, stumping, and stomping political campaign, a firing-off of rockets, roman candles, catherine wheels, and sparklers in a dazzling display of truth and falsehood; and the long, honored tradition of courthouse rhetoric, great speakers and great men who first voiced this nation's aspirations and follies, our ideals and vices, who once for the pure joy and hell of it would battle as fiercely over the ownership of a hog as the rights of man, seeing no incongruity there, Stump or pulpit, bench and bar, they loved the English language, and they taught it to perform, to turn somersaults and to jump through hoops of fire. This love of language long since found its place in southern prose, including the prose of Warren. But until *Promises* it was strictly segregated, separate and utterly unequal, from the world of poetry. In *Promises* Warren achieved a graceful integration.

Now place the book in a scene. The literary scene in which the literary stockbrokers and entrepreneurs were asking themselves: "What will Lowell do next?" "What will become of Richard Wilbur?" "Do you suppose the Beats really *have* anything?" "What will Ciardi think about all this?" "What will James Dickey say?" "Who will get Archie's High Chair at Harvard?" and, above all, "Do we dare to eat a peach?" Into this piddling and unimportant scene came *Promises*, perhaps inimitable, yet offering the example of a poet going his own way at a time when conformity was (and still is) not only expected but also demanded, an experienced poet making a bold sight change and hitting the target again and again while the others were (and still are) trying to learn the basic manual of arms. The poems of *Promises* were different from the earlier poems, yet withal a natural development, spun out of personal need and experience, clearly impossible without much milage and all the earlier work behind them, clearly the work of a finished poet who was not a victim of the General Motors mentality—a new model every year, nor even, a self-made success through the success of his fiction, evidently much concerned about his place at the establishment feeding trough.

For himself *Promises* must have marked a new sense of freedom and expansion. One which, for a literary parallel, can only be compared to that last astounding harvest of W. B. Yeats. For the young writer it should stand as a living example of the real dream of every real artist, that vision of a late-blooming garden which grows not by hothouse care and protection, not by a florist's dutiful, commercial urging, but richly from the sparse, sandy soil of patience, courage, and fortitude. The baffled Establishment, busily preparing its annual hooprolling contest and daisy chain, threw up its hands and awarded Warren the prizes for the year. Then promptly forgot the whole affair. Rushed off with a sigh of relief to the nearest newsstand to pick up the latest *New Yorker* and see what their friends (each other) were up to. There is a fine madness to the poems of *Promises*. None of its poems ever appeared in the *New Yorker*.

There are many interesting and original qualities evident in the poems of *Promises*. Some of these call for special emphasis because they point toward a new direction, one which has, in fact, been followed by Warren in his most recent collection, *You, Emperors, and Others: Poems 1957–1960*. In form and language Warren shows himself more truly a child of the metaphysical poets in these new poems than in the earlier, more obviously and strictly imitative examples. Here, without trying to imitate the language, style, or imagery, he demonstrates a kinship with the whole manner and substance of the metaphysical poem. The metaphysicals, as we all know too well, have been celebrated for the power and originality of their controlled incongruity, for seemingly unrelated ideas and images judiciously "yoked by violence together." It is, then, the absence of a strict decorum which marks their poems; or, when a surface decorum is observed, there is, as in Marvell, an ironic, sometimes mocking attitude toward the observance and, thus, the form itself. The former quality shows itself in the ready mixture of high, low, and middle voices, in a range of speech which may, within the same verse unit, jump from high oratory to slang and right back again. And speech is a key word, the viability and excitement of the spoken language as well as the literary tongue. Along with this, inevitably, goes a certain deliberate roughness of form. And all this, whether a literary fashion or an articulate esthetic (let scholars fight *that* one out) becomes important in its result or effect. Which is the *dramatization* of the mind, body, and spirit, the sensibility, of the poet (or speaker in the case of a dramatic monologue) in action. It is the dramatic presentation of the action in progress, rather than the after-the-fact, lyric evocation of a real or imagined experience. This method, then, is daring, has great risks. For the action of the poet's sensibility, exposed in the very act of groping to create the poem, itself becoming the poem which the reader is experiencing and, thus, remaining unfinished until the experience of the poem is finished, this action must be interesting in and of itself. One gains small insight and less pleasure from watching a sensibility of limited interest groping toward an obvious conclusion.

This, in turn, means a number of things. The poet who would try to write metaphysical verse, then as now, must be a man of the world, experienced both as a man and as a poet-rhetorician. In the best sense he must be sophisticated. It is not, then, a method for the young. Moreover, the method implies that parts and pieces of the well-wrought poem, whether single images, lines, or stanzas, are in themselves meaningless and without interest, however striking, when abstracted from the whole poem. The poem is the unit, not its parts. It shouldn't be necessary to add here that this method goes directly against the grain of much modern critical theory. All those poets and critics who judge by looking for the validity of the line as unit or the realized stanza are, right or wrong, barking up a very different tree.

So it follows, quite naturally (*organically*, one of the fugitives might say) that Warren would experiment with new verse forms as well as play around with old and honored ones. And it follows that, as he found his way, the units would become larger and larger, looking beyond the individual poem to the entire sequence or the book, which, however various, would itself be yoked together. This can be clearly seen in the fact that in these two most recent books Warren has grouped more and more poems together as subunits under one title.

This new method is begun in *Promises* and superbly realized in *You, Emperors, and Others* whose book jacket (*mirabilis!*) for once honestly and simply states that it is "an extension of the lyric voice which made *Promises* such an important literary event." The voice is not a *new* voice. It is a development, a unified version of all the separate, earlier voices into one strain. Image and symbol detectives will easily find the evidence, many of the same images and symbols revised and recurring, to relate the later and earlier poems. Many of the themes and subjects are, of course, the same. The most obvious difference is in the form, in the toughness and verbal activeness of the lines, in the full use of strong, hard-textured, often "unpoetic" words and sounds. For example, the opening stanza of "Gull's Cry" from *Promises*:

> White goose by palm tree, palm ragged, among stones the
> white oleander,
> And the she-goat, brown, under pink oleander, waits.
> I do not think anything in the world will move, not goat, not
> gander.

Goat droppings are fresh in the hot dust; not yet the beetle; the sun beats. It is not just the clear-cut scene nor the *things* which evoke it, but it is also the words themselves, as things with sound and texture, which work here for the hard, clear, clean effect. The intrusion of the speaker in the third line, which might be deplored in a lesser poet as distracting from the scene, works. And the sensitive reader will notice that the end rhymes in this quatrain are not intended to ring like little bells. On the page they are decorative. In the listening experience of the inner ear they serve almost as internal rhyme. For a superb example of the ability of Warren to cram extraordinary variety into small space, to keep both the inner and outer life fully dramatized, look at the concluding couplet of "The Child Next Door," which deals with a retarded peasant child:

> I think of your goldness, of joy, how empires grind, stars are
> hurled.
> I smile stiff, saying *ciao*, saying *ciao*, and think: this is the
> world.

One should not ignore the importance of Warren's new direction and achievement within the current literary scene. For more years than it's worth worrying about, modern poets have been trying to find some way to do exactly what Warren has done—to find form, manner, and voice able to contain at once a whole sensibility, a whole spectrum of thought and feeling, faithful to the multiplicity of both the outer and the inner life. Theodore Roethke came as close as anyone in some of his finest poems. But what was presented was an irrational sensibility, one which could communicate, but only by means of shards and fragments painfully dug from the dark strata of the unconscious. Where Roethke might have gone is a moot point, now that he is dead. In some of his recent poems Robert Lowell has shown an inclination to move in this direction; but, for all his energy and power and for all the seeming candor of his confessions, there is one essential quality missing—coarseness, a healthy vulgarity which might relate his experience to that of another human being. This base and simple element is essential to the alloy which is a whole sensibility. Lowell is painfully conscious of and articulates the vulgarities of the world he lives in, but some inhibition, perhaps the inevitable result of the urban-intellectual *milieu*, the *literary* world, prevents him doing more than naming the parts. Which, after all, any *New Yorker* writer could do, always implying in the very act of naming that "all this has nothing to do with the real *me*."

Younger poets, too, have been conscious of and chafed against the limitations of the modern lyric mode. But not having lived long enough or learned enough to be interesting, they seem to be left with the alternative of joining either the nose-thumbing, clever crowd, the so-called Beats, or returning to basics, to what might be called "candid camera poetry," as exemplified by the recent verses of Robert Bly, James Wright, and Louis Simpson.

I mention these things, relating Warren's work to the literary scene, the current fashion show, to point out that whether or not the establishment knows it or likes it, Warren's recent poetry is a very important part of that scene. The poems are important and successful because the poet has all the qualities needed to make them work. He has intellect, sensitivity, and critical acumen; he has extra literary experience as a storyteller and dramatist; he belongs to a strong, vital literary tradition; and he has deep roots, has kept alive a healthy memory of the dirt farm. In short, unlike many of his contemporaries, he can tell the difference between horse manure and shinola without running a lab test.

Using a wide variety of verse forms, ancient, modern, and original, and treating a variety of subjects, Warren has one central theme in *You, Emperors, and Others* which gives the book the unity and coherence of a single poem. The voice is that of an older man, looking back with some nostalgia, viewing the present with intelligent skepticism and sometimes satirical distaste, glimpsing the future, which includes the brute, simple fact of death, with anxiety. The subject or theme of all the poems is classical—the tears of things. Yet this ancient and honorable theme is raised to a higher power by a strongly Christian sense of joy. Along with "history," the word "joy" occurs over and over again in the resolution of these poems and serves to link the poems together. Whether the poem is an elegy for a boy who fell off a freight train or a ruminative treatment of a Roman emperor, the method is much the same: a long, hard, unblinking look at the naked truth as he sees it, by which exercise and vision is earned a brief vision of the ineffable truth. This is nowhere more explicitly evident than in the final unit in the book, "Nursery Rhymes," tough and sardonic songs of experience, clad in the pleasant rhythms of familiar children's poems. There is something in these poems of the feeling of that masterpiece of modern film art, Fellini's 8½ (Warren's book like Fellini's film is at once deeply autobiographical and wildly imaginative) where, at the lowest point, all illusions of Marcello having been stripped away, all losses named and known now to be irrecoverable, with blank despair apparently the only logical conclusion, there is the sudden, earned moment of pure vision. Here, for example, are the last stanzas of "Mother Makes the Biscuits," a *peripatea* immediately following a catalog of worldly afflictions:

> Clap hands, children,
> Clap hands and sing!
> Hold hands together, children,
> And dance in a ring.

For the green worm sings on the leaf,
The black beetle folds hands to pray,
And the stones in the field wash their faces clean
To meet the break of day.

But we may see this only
Because all night we have stared
At the black miles past where stars are
Till the stars disappeared.

With a very few exceptions (I think, for example, of the poems of John Hall Wheelock and Babette Deutsch), we have not had the good fortune to witness the continued development of an American poet from youth to old age and, with age a certain wisdom. Most of our poets finished, *as poets*, young, left us the undeniable virtuosity of their youthful, lyric voices; a condition so emphatic that many have come to believe that only the young lyric voice is the truly poetic. One might call up Yeats as a poet in English who had a sudden surplus of energy and wrote magnificent poems out of the bone-vexing times of decay and long shadows. I have no hesitation in suggesting that Warren's later poems, in the full power and energy of his hard-earned liberation, in the full freedom of language and form, which exploded in *Promises* and has been consolidated in *You, Emperors, and Others*, are more important to us than the late poems of Yeats. One need not accept wholly and whole cloth his vision. Indeed, that would be impossible without first having lived and worked as long. But for anyone interested in the art of poetry these late poems are important. We have a modern poet whose career and history show a steady growth and blooming which can be compared to those of Picasso and Stravinsky. Quite suddenly the whole history of the establishment seems unimportant, trivial. For poetry is not written by schools or establishments, but by single, lonely poets. If Warren were to conclude now with this final book it would be enough. But in another of the final nursery rhymes, "Cricket, On Kitchen Floor, Enters History," Warren offers us at least the promise of more poems, Lord willing and himself alive and able:

History, shaped like white hen,
Walked in the kitchen door.
Beak clicked once on stone floor.

Out door walked hen then;
But will, no doubt, come again.

Though the texture is dry, the texture of old bones pared down
fine from the last fat, those who care about American poetry
are grateful that one man has come this far. Will be more
grateful if he will come again.

# 17·Knowledge and the Image of Man

OUR GENERAL TOPIC is Man's Right to Knowledge. To put my cart before the horse, the conclusion before the discussion, and let the cat out of the bag, I'll assert that to say man's right to knowledge is simply a way of saying man's right to exist, to be himself, to be a man.

That, of course, is the premise of our society—man's right to exist as a man, as a uniquely defined individual. Our society, we know well, violates this premise every day, but it remains fundamental to our democratic western world.

We must distinguish this idea from the idea of the sanctity of life as such. More frequently in other societies than ours has the saint or sage turned from the caterpillar in the path or shrunk to pluck the lettuce for fear of the unhearable scream. No, we have limited and revised the idea of the sanctity of life. Human life we mean in our world, and human life not as existence but as the individual's right to exist as himself, the right to the hazards and glories of trying to develop most fully as himself.

I suppose that this notion of personality—the right to define oneself—despite all the distortions it has suffered from forces like Machiavellianism, Manchester economics, the winning of the west, and progressive education, is a heritage of Christianity. Every soul is valuable in God's sight, and the story of every soul is the story of its self-definition for good or evil, salvation or damnation. Every soul is valuable in God's sight. Or, with the secularization of things, we may say: every soul is valuable in man's sight.

If we accept this notion, then we are committed to recognize the right of every soul to that knowledge necessary for its best fulfillment.

At this point, however, someone may object to the statement that man's right to knowledge, in our society at least, derives from, or is related to, our Christian history. The objector may recollect that every Christian church has, at one time or another, opposed the extension of knowledge. To this objection one may say that the various churches are of this world and have made their worldly errors, and that opposition to the extension of knowledge, in any given instance, was accidental and not essential to Christianity; and one could paraphrase Jacques Maritain in another context: the glory of God does not demand that man go on all fours.

To be a man, to keep from going on all fours, implies the right to knowledge. But it is a sad fact that, though the glory of God does not demand that man go on all fours the glory of our democracy, by a last perversion, sometimes seems to make that demand. Since I am about to refer to the age of the common man, I shall hasten to say that I was a New Dealer, with as few reservations and heart burnings as one can reasonably expect about a political process, and I don't take it back now. But one of the heart burnings I did have was precisely about common man-ism of the sort the New Deal *sometimes* promoted.

The prophets of the common man might have spoken gloriously—if they had really believed that that fellow-citizen whom they called common man was really as good as they, the prophets, too often took themselves to be. But no, they often spoke with a nauseous condescension, and it was not glorious. They might have said something like this: As men we have in common certain capacities that make us men, the capacity to envisage ourselves in relation to nature and other men, the capacity for self-criticism, the capacity for a disinterested love of excellence. Let us try, therefore, to create a society in which each man may develop as far as possible those capacities that distinguish his manhood, and in which each man will accept his responsibility for trying to realize his common humanity at its highest.

Perhaps some of the prophets did speak gloriously, but their voices were generally drowned out by voices that in declaring the age of the common man uttered a doctrine of complacency. These voices, by implication at least, denied that democracy should mean the opportunity—and the responsibility —for the development of excellence, and uttered a doctrine carrying at its core the appalling convictions that the undeveloped, the unaspiring, the frustrated, the un-responsible, is somehow mystically superior to the excellent, and that a refusal of effort toward excellence is a gesture of moral worth.

In reading the history of our country we have met all too often this same old notion, the glorification of the unexcellent, this conviction that a mystic worth attaches to ignorance. Sometimes this was, we know, a way of pitting the honest coonskin cap against crowns and coronets, an honest faith in democracy against Norman blood. But looking back on our forefathers, we know, too, that they were not above the human frailty of an awkward and strident defensiveness in the face of the learning, grace, and achievement of the old world, and that, to keep their courage up, they whistled a little in the dark of their own heads.

Looking back, we can applaud the sturdy independence, the faith in democracy and destiny, and the lethal efficiency of the long-rifle leveled at a Redcoat. We can relish the juicy rambunctiousness and wild poetry and courage of the frontier, and see the pathos of its loneliness, malaria, and degradation. But this does not mean that, in the end, we have to take Davy Crockett as a philosopher superior to Immanuel Kant.

This isn't quite what happened in 1933, but it is uncomfortably close. And part of the sad comedy was that one of the places where the process flourished most rankly was in some classrooms of literature, especially of American literature, and in learned books on that subject. To study our culture sometimes meant to seek out documentations of common man-ism. I am not referring merely to those students of our culture who made a holy alliance with Stalin and interpreted our history as a blundering and uninstructed provincial attempt to be Russian. No, I am referring to that far greater number who were devoted to the American dream and the American mission, but whose devotion manifested itself as an easy and sometimes false documentation of common man-ism, a process that took the place of the investigation of all other values, and I do not mean what it was sometimes fashionable to refer to as "merely literary values." I mean all values, including those of common sense and simple honesty.

Whitman was split down the middle and the part of his work that is humanly full was rejected for what was politically viable. Flaubert had nothing to tell us in an age of crisis. Down with Hardy and up with Ruth Suckow and Rölvaag or Grace Lumpkin. "Snowbound" is a great poem, and Henry James betrayed America. Conrad is not socially relevant, for he merely treats of man against geography. Faulkner is a Gothic fascist and hates Negroes.

Most of the people who adopted these views were simply innocent, with decent human sympathies, but their very virtues made it possible in that context to accept the fashionable thing, and the fashionable thing simply amounted to the notion that only the easy and immediate is valuable. The spirit of God may not be in you, but the spirit of democracy sure is, and if you are a common man, all things shall be added unto you, without your turning a hand, and anyway you've probably already got everything worth having. So the right to knowledge, which should have meant the glorification of our common human capacity to move toward excellence, to define ourselves in a communal aspiration, was betrayed by the prophets of common man-ism.

Not only was the right to knowledge betrayed. There was an even more gross betrayal. The complacency fostered by the doctrine of common man-ism belied and betrayed that aspiration to excellence that is really in our midst, that has always marked much of our history, an aspiration that is sometimes blundering and confused but is indomitable and indestructible. It must be indestructible, more indestructible even than the cat in the adage, for it has survived even the attempt of the New Deal to choke it with butter.

All this has been, in a way, an aside, the self-indulgent venting of old spleen, but too, I trust, a description of one extreme threat to the right to knowledge—the threat from well-meaning friends. We have less to fear sometimes from the powers of darkness than from would-be angels of light, and the would-be angels of light change their plumage from time to time. Right now the fashionable cut in wings and haloes is not that of the New Deal.

Let us come back to our beginning, the statement that the right to exist as a man assumes the right to knowledge.

It assumes the right because only by knowledge does man achieve his identity. I do not mean that the mere implements of knowledge—books, libraries, laboratories, seminars—distinguish man from the brute. No, knowledge gives him his identity because it gives him the image of himself. And the image of himself necessarily has a foreground and a background, for man is in the world not as a billiard ball placed on a table, not even as a ship on the ocean with location determinable by latitude and longitude, He is, rather, in the world with continual and intimate interpenetration, an inevitable osmosis of being, which in the end does not deny, but affirms, his identity. It affirms it, for out of a progressive understanding of this interpenetration, this texture of relations, man creates new perspectives, discovers new values—that is, a new self—and so the identity is a continually emerging, an unfolding, a self-affirming and, we hope, a self-corrective creation.

Despite this osmosis of being to which I have referred, man's process of self-definition means that he distinguishes himself from the world and from other men. He disintegrates his primal instinctive sense of unity, he discovers separateness. In this process he discovers the pain of self-criticism and the pain of isolation. But the pain may, if he is fortunate, develop its own worth, work its own homeopathic cure. In the pain of self-criticism he may develop an ideal of excellence, and an ideal of excellence, once established, implies a depersonalized communion in that ideal. In the pain of isolation he may achieve the courage and clarity of mind to envisage the tragic pathos of life, and once he realizes that the tragic experience is universal and a corollary of man's place in nature, he may return to a communion with man and nature.

Man can return to his lost unity, and if that return is fitful and precarious, if the foliage and flower of the innocent garden are now somewhat browned by a late season, all is the more precious for the fact, for what is now achieved has been achieved by a growth of moral awareness. The return to nature and man is the discovery of love, and law. But love through separateness, and law through rebellion. Man eats of the fruit of the tree of knowledge, and falls. But if he takes another bite, he may get at least a sort of redemption. And a precious redemption. His unity with nature will not now be that of a drop of water in the ocean; it is, rather, the unity of the lover with the beloved, a unity presupposing separateness. His unity with mankind will not now be the unity of a member of the tribal horde with that pullulating mass; his unity will be that of a member of sweet society.

I suppose that the ultimate unity of knowledge is in the image of himself that man creates through knowledge, the image of his destiny, the mask he stares at. This would mean that manipulative knowledge, as well as knowledge of vision, calculation as well as conception—to take Shelley's distinction—works toward the creation of that image. Or to take another set of distinctions, the knowledge of *make*, that of *do*, that of *see*, that of *be*, however sharply we may distinguish them for various purposes, ultimately interfuse in our life process. Any change of environment—including any making—creates a new relation between man and his world, and other men. Any doing changes the doer. Any seeing changes the see-er. And any knowledge one has of his own being modifies that being, re-creates it, and thus changes the quality of making, doing, seeing.

Here let us remind ourselves most emphatically that a change in man's image of himself is not necessarily for the better. We do not ride a gravy train. We have seen, and see, in our own time, certain self-images of Frankensteinian horror that have captured the imagination of whole peoples. So new knowledge may give us new images absurd or dangerous, or may inadequately revise an old image so that it becomes absurd or dangerous, an anachronism. An intimate knowledge of fruit flies may lead us to think of human needs and values at the level of the fruit fly. A knowledge of the domestic arrangements of ancient royal houses of Egypt, or of Shelley's idea that incest is

the most poetic of subjects, may lead us to a new admiration
for the goings-on of the Jukeses and Kallikaks. And a knowledge
of the structure of the atom may lead us to destroy ourselves. I
say that knowledge *may* lead us to such unfortunate conclusions.
But need it? And if it does, must we blame knowledge? No, we
should blame incompleteness of knowledge—the fact that
knowledge of human nature, human needs, human values, has
not kept pace with knowledge of fruit flies and atoms, the fact
that we have not achieved balance and responsibility in the ever-
unfolding process of self-definition.

When we ourselves must combat the force of some absurd
or dangerous image of man—the image of man, say, that stood
behind Nazism—we run the risk of assimilating the horror in
the very act of wrestling with it. We run that risk because such
an image, horrible though it may be, could not exist at all, or
compel the imagination of millions, if it did not spring from,
and satisfy, certain human needs, and give scope for certain
human virtues. By our own similar needs and similar virtues we
are vulnerable to the temptation of that image. As Coleridge
says, all beliefs are true; at least, the fact of their existence
proves that there is a kind of truth in them. To say this is not
to condone a horror, but to realize its fullness in the fact that
its energies of evil are a perversion of energies potential for
good, that the will for destruction is but the will for creation
swayed from its proper end.

And I am reminded here of the profound passage in Conrad's *Lord Jim*, when Marlow comments on the apparently
aimless massacre by the brigand Brown:

> Thus Brown balanced his account with the evil fortune.
> Notice that even in his awful outbreak there is a superiority as
> of a man who carries right—the abstract thing—within the en-
> velope of his common desires. It was not a vulgar and treacherous
> massacre; it was a lesson, a retribution—a demonstration of some
> obscure and awful attribute of our nature which, I am afraid, is
> not so very far under the surface as we like to think.

Even in the act seemingly most brutal and gratuitous,
Brown has, somehow, in a last distortion, affirmed himself as
human, not brute, has affirmed, paradoxically, the human need
for moral vindication. And let us not forget that Jim, the re-

deemed, had confronted Brown, the damned, in a dark dialogue of communion and complicity delivered back and forth across a jungle creek.

Each of us longs for full balance and responsibility in self-knowledge, in a recognition and harmonious acceptance of our destiny. Saints and sages may achieve that harmonious sense of destiny, or the hero at the cannon-mouth, or the famous sergeant of Belleau Wood. But we lesser and more fumbling mortals may find at least some intimation of it in the unfolding pattern, however modest, of our own effort toward knowledge.

I know that this has been a congress of philosophers, and I have a becoming diffidence about offering my amateur and homemade product after the three-day exhibit of glittering articles. If I am invited here at all, it is with the credentials of one who tries to write novels and poems and not of one who tries to philosophize. And that would suggest that the thing I was supposed to do in the first place was to remark on what relation I find between my own profession and the topic of this meeting. So I'll say my say, though I find myself saying it in the last, not the first, place. But last place may be best, for what has gone before, if it has accomplished anything, will explain what now I try to say.

I'll start by making one of the most debatable statements one can make: poetry—that is, literature as a dimension of the creative imagination—is knowledge.

In accidental or incidental ways, poetry may, of course, give knowledge, even very important knowledge, but I do not mean such accidental or incidental knowledge. I do not mean, for instance, the absurdity I now shall tell you about, an absurdity we have all encountered in many places but which I have most recently encountered in a philosophical journal. The author of this absurdity, who no doubt embarrasses his friends, announces himself as a logical positivist, then argues that the novel is the most valuable form of art, for some novels give valid historical, sociological, and psychological knowledge. True, all novels report human motives and actions, and the settings, spatial, temporal, and social, in which those actions take place. But such reports occur much more systematically in works of history, geography, psychology, and so on, and most certainly cannot be taken as the thing that characterizes and differentiates the novel as an art form. No, the novel, as novel, as art form, is not reporting anything—how to drive chariots or govern cities. It is using certain materials, which may include valid knowledge of chariot-driving or city-government, for its characteristic purposes, and so on. There is no use to pursue the argument. Let us blush, avert our eyes, and pass on from this scene of logical naiveté and terminological carnage and Hobbesian nonsense. In other words, knowledge by report is not the kind of knowledge I mean in this discussion.

Nor do I mean what, for lack of a better term, we may call knowledge by symptom, the knowledge we may get from a work by regarding it as a cultural or linguistic symptom, or the symptom of its age or author. True, we may learn much by regarding poetry as symptom—for example, about an age or author, if we know how to take the deep ambivalences, the condensations, the subtle distortions and essential purgations of an age or personality. But again, such knowledge is not characteristic or differentiating.

If knowledge by report and knowledge by symptom, however valuable and interesting such knowledge may be, are not characteristic and differentiating, then what kind of knowledge am I talking about? I should say: knowledge by form. No, knowledge *of* form.

By this I mean the furthest thing possible from any doctrine that might go as sheer formalism. I mean the organic relation among all the elements of the work, including, *most emphatically*, those elements drawn from the actual world and charged with all the urgencies of actuality, urgencies not to be denied but transmuted—as we are told Tintoretto transmuted the gamin divers of the Venetian canals into the angels of his painting. The form is a vision of experience, but of experience fulfilled and redeemed in knowledge, the ugly with the beautiful, the slayer with the slain, what was known as shape now known as time, what was known in time now known as shape, a new knowledge. It is not a thing detached from the world but a thing springing from the deep engagement of spirit with the world. This engagement may involve not only love for the world, but also fear and disgust, but the conquest, in form, of fear and disgust means such a sublimation that the world which once provoked the fear and disgust may now be totally loved in the fullness of contemplation. The form is the flowering of that deep engagement of spirit, the discovery of its rhythm. And the form is known, by creator or appreciator, only by experiencing it, by submitting to its characteristic rhythm.

With this word *rhythm*, I am reminded of the necessary question: how does the knowledge of form give man an image of himself?

It does so insofar as it gives the image of experience being brought to order and harmony, the image of a dance on the high wire over an abyss. The rhythm is, as it were, a myth of order, or fulfillment, an affirmation that our being may move in its totality toward meaning. The soul faces some potentiality of experience, drawn from actuality, and the form is the flowing vibration of the soul, the abstraction of experience by imagination. The form gives man an image of himself, for it gives him his mode of experiencing, a paradigm of his inner life, his rhythm of destiny, his tonality of fate. And this evocation, confrontation, and definition of our deepest life gives us, in new self-awareness, a yet deeper life to live.

But not merely the life of contemplation, for the soul does not sit in self-regarding trance, like Rachel before her mirror all the day, in Dante's *Purgatorio*. No, that gazing prepares for the moment of action, of creation, in our world of contingency. It is, as Yeats puts it,

> . . . our secret discipline
> Wherein the gazing soul doubles her might.

The might is there for the moment when the soul lifts her head.

LEONARD CASPER'S *Robert Penn Warren: The Dark and Bloody Ground* is indispensable for many reasons. It publishes the only exhaustive Warren bibliography so far in print. It is especially useful for the chronological checklist of Warren's own publications, listing some eighteen items under "Short Fiction and Excerpts" and some eighty-three signed items under "Reviews and Articles." "Poetry" lists sixty-five entries, each listing publication of one or more poems in periodicals.

*Modern Fiction Studies* VI (Spring, 1960); The Robert Penn Warren Special Number. Seven essays (including two by Casper and Longley reprinted in the present collection) plus a bibliography of reviews and criticism which is broken down into studies of the individual works.

West, Paul. *Robert Penn Warren.* University of Minnesota Pamphlets on American Writers; No. 44. 1964. Bibliography of works complete for books only. List of critical studies on Warren is selective.

### PRINCIPAL WORKS OF ROBERT PENN WARREN

*Poetry*
*Thirty-six* Poems. New York: Alcestis Press, 1935.
*Eleven Poems on the Same Theme.* Norfolk, Conn.: New Directions, 1942.

*Selected Poems, 1923–1943.* New York: Harcourt, Brace, 1944.

*Brother to Dragons: A Tale in Verse and Voices.* New York: Random House, 1953.

*Promises: Poems 1954–1956.* New York: Random House, 1957.

*You, Emperors, and Others: Poems 1957–1960.* New York: Random House, 1960.

*Novels and Short Stories*

*Night Rider,* Boston: Houghton Mifflin, 1939.

*At Heaven's Gate.* New York: Harcourt, Brace, 1943.

*All the King's Men.* New York: Harcourt, Brace, 1946.

*Blackberry Winter.* Cummington, Mass.: Cummington Press, 1946.

*The Circus in the Attic and Other Stories.* New York: Harcourt, Brace, 1948.

*World Enough and Time: A Romantic Novel.* New York: Random House, 1950.

*Band of Angels.* New York: Random House, 1955.

*The Cave.* New York: Random House, 1959.

*Wilderness.* New York: Random House, 1961.

*Flood.* New York: Random House, 1964.


*Plays*

"Proud Flesh." Unpublished, 1939. (First performed, 1946.)

"All the King's Men." Unpublished, 1947.

*All the King's Men.* New York: Random House, 1960.


*Nonfiction*

*John Brown: The Making of a Martyr.* New York: Payson and Clarke, 1929.

"The Briar Patch," in *I'll Take My Stand,* by Twelve Southerners. New York: Harper, 1930.

*Understanding Poetry,* edited by Cleanth Brooks and R. P. Warren, 1st ed., New York: Holt, 1938; 2nd ed., 1951.

*Understanding Fiction,* edited by Cleanth Brooks and R. P. Warren. 1st ed., New York: Appleton-Century-Crofts, 1943; 2nd ed., 1959; 3rd ed., 1960.

*Segregation: The Inner Conflict in the South.* New York: Random House, 1956.

*Selected Essays.* New York: Random House, 1958.

*Remember the Alamo!* (Landmark children's book.) New York: Random House, 1958.

*The Gods of Mount Olympus.* (Legacy children's book.) New York: Random House, 1959.

*The Legacy of the Civil War: Meditations on the Centennial.* New York: Random House, 1961.

*Current American Reprints*

*All the King's Men.* New York: Bantam. $.75.

*At Heaven's Gate.* New York: Signet (New American Library). $.75.

*Band of Angels.* New York: Signet. $.75.

*The Cave.* New York: Signet. $.75.

*Segregation.* New York: Vintage (Knopf). $.95.

*Wilderness.* New York: Signet. $.60.

SELECTED CRITICISM

Anderson, Charles R. "Violence and Order in the Novels of Robert Penn Warren," *Hopkins Review*, VI (Winter, 1953), 88–105. Reprinted in *Southern Renascence: The Literature of the Modern South*, ed. Louis D. Rubin, Jr. and Robert D. Jacobs. Baltimore: Johns Hopkins Press, 1953, 207–24.

Antonini, Giacomo. "Il mito della dignità umana. Penn Warren: Nostaliga per il vecchio Sud," *La fiera letteraria*, January 22, 1956, 1–2.

———. "Penn Warren e il primato dello stile," *La fiera letteraria*, January 12, 1955, 5–6.

Bennett, John. The Iron Beach: A Study of the Poetry of Robert Penn Warren. M.A. Thesis, Vanderbilt University, 1948.

Bentley, Eric. "All the King's Men," *Theatre Arts*, XXXI (November, 1947), 72–73.

———. "The Meaning of Robert Penn Warren's Novels," *Kenyon Review*, X (Summer, 1948), 407–24.

Blonski, Jan. "Robert Penn Warren," *Tworczosc* (Warsaw) (March, 1956), 164–67.

Blum, Morgan. "Promises as Fulfillment," *Kenyon Review*, XXI (Winter, 1959), 97–120. Review of *Promises*.

Bradbury, John M. *The Fugitives: A Critical Account*. Chapel
    Hill: University of North Carolina Press, 1958.
———. "Robert Penn Warren's Novels: The Symbolic and
    Textural Patterns," *Accent*, XIII (Spring, 1953), 77–89.
Brantley, Frederick. "The Achievement of Robert Penn War-
    ren," in *Modern American Poetry*, ed. B. Rajan. London:
    Dennis Dobson Ltd., 1950, 66–80.
Breit, Harvey. "Talk with Mr. Warren," *New York Times Book
    Review*, June 25, 1950, p. 20. Reprinted in *The Writer
    Observed*. New York: World Publishing Co., 1956, 131–
    33.
Brooks, Cleanth. *The Hidden God*. New Haven, Conn.: Yale
    University Press, 1963.
———. *Modern Poetry and the Tradition*. Chapel Hill: Univer-
    sity of North Carolina Press, 1939.
Byrne, Clifford M. "The Philosophical Development in Four of
    Robert Penn Warren's Novels," *McNeese Review*, IX
    (Winter, 1957), 56–58.
Campbell, Harry Modean. "Warren as Philosopher in *World
    Enough and Time*," *Hopkins Review*, VI (Winter, 1953),
    106–16. Reprinted in *Southern Renascence: The Literature
    of the Modern South*, ed. Louis D. Rubin, Jr. and Robert
    D. Jacobs. Baltimore: Johns Hopkins Press, 1953, 225–35.
Cargill, Oscar. "Anatomist of Monsters," *College English*, IX
    (October, 1947), 1–8.
Casper, Leonard, *Robert Penn Warren: The Dark and Bloody
    Ground*. Seattle: University of Washington Press, 1960.
———. "The Founding Fathers," *Western Review*, XXII (Au-
    tumn, 1957), 69–71. Review of *Promises*.
———. Loss of the Sense of Community and the Role of the
    Artist in Robert Penn Warren. Ph.D. dissertation, Univer-
    sity of Wisconsin, 1953.
———. "The New Criticism and Southern Agrarianism," *Dili-
    man Review* (Philippines), II (April, 1954), 136–49.
———. "Robert Penn Warren: an Assessment," *Diliman Re-
    view*, II (October, 1954), 400–24.
———. "Robert Penn Warren: Method and Canon," *Diliman
    Review*, II (July, 1954), 263–92.
Clark, Marden J. Symbolic Structure in the Novels of Robert

Penn Warren. Ph.D. dissertation, University of Washington, 1957.

Coleman, Thomas Emmett, Jr. Form as Function in the Novels of Robert Penn Warren. M.A. thesis, University of Louisville, 1950.

Cottrell, Beekman W. "Cass Mastern and the Awful Responsibility of Time," in *All the King's Men: A Symposium*, ed. A. Fred Sochatoff *et al.* Pittsburgh: Carnegie Press, 1957, 39–49.

Cowan, Louise. *The Fugitive Group: A Literary History*. Baton Rouge: Louisiana State University Press, 1959.

Cowley, Malcolm. "Luke Lea's Empire," *New Republic*, CIX (August 23, 1943), 258. Review of *At Heaven's Gate*.

Craib, Roderick. "A Novel on Freedom," *New Leader*, XXXVIII (September 26, 1955), 24–25. Review of *Band of Angels*.

Curtiss, Mina. "Tragedy of a Liberal," *Nation*, CXLVIII (April 29, 1939), 507–8. Review of *Night Rider*.

Davidson, Donald. "The Thankless Muse and Her Fugitive Poets," *Sewanee Review*, LXVI (Spring, 1958), 201–28.

Deutsch, Babette. "Poetry Chronicle," *Yale Review*, XLIII (Winter, 1954), pp. 277–78. Review of *Brother to Dragons*.

———. "Robert Penn Warren's Savage Poem: Old Murder, Modern Overtones," *New York Herald Tribune Book Review*, August 23, 1953, p. 3. Review of *Brother to Dragons*.

Dickey, James. "In the Presence of Anthologies," *Sewanee Review*, LXVI (Spring, 1958), 307–9. Review of *Promises*.

Dupee, F. W. "Robert Penn Warren and Others," *Nation*, CLIX (November 25, 1944), 660, 662. Review of *Selected Poems: 1923–1943*.

Ellison, Ralph, and Eugene Walter. "The Art of Fiction XVIII: Robert Penn Warren," *Paris Review*, IV (Spring-Summer, 1957), 112–40. Reprinted in *Writers at Work: The Paris Review Interviews*, ed. Malcolm Cowley. New York: Viking, 1958, pp. 183–207.

Fergusson, Francis. "Three Novels," *Perspectives U.S.A.*, VI (Winter, 1954), pp. 30–44. Review of *All the King's Men*.

Fiedler, Leslie A. "On Two Frontiers," *Partisan Review*, XVII (September-October, 1950), 739–43.

————. "Romance in the Operatic Manner," *New Republic*, CXXXIII (September 26, 1955), 28–30. Review of *Band of Angels*.

————. "Seneca in the Meat House," *Partisan Review*, XXI (March-April, 1954), 208–12. Review of *Brother to Dragons*.

Fitts, Dudley. "Of Tragic Stature," *Poetry*, LXV (November, 1944), 94–101. Review of *Selected Poems*.

————. "A Power Reaffirmed," *New York Times Book Review*, August 18, 1957, 6, 20. Review of *Promises*.

Fjelde, Rolf. "The Ruined Stone and the Sea-Reaches," *Poetry*, XCII (April, 1958), 49–52. Review of *Promises*.

Flint, F. Cudworth. "Five Poets," *Southern Review*, I (Winter, 1936), 650–74. Review of *Thirty-six Poems*.

————. "Mr. Warren and the Reviewers," *Sewanee Review*, LXIV (Autumn, 1956), 632–45.

————. "Poetic Accomplishment and Expectation," *Virginia Quarterly Review*, XXXIV (Winter, 1958), 118–19. Review of *Promises*.

————. "Robert Penn Warren," *American Oxonian*, XXXIV (April, 1947), 67–79.

————. "Search for a Meaning," *Virginia Quarterly Review*, XXX (Winter, 1954), 143–48. Review of *Brother to Dragons*.

Ford, Newell F. "Kenneth Burke and Robert Penn Warren: Criticism by Obsessive Metaphor," *Journal of English and Germanic Philology*, LIII (April, 1954), 172–77.

Forgotson, E. S. "The Poetic Method of Robert Penn Warren," *American Prefaces*, VI (Winter, 1941), 130–46.

Frank, Joseph. "Romanticism and Reality in Robert Penn Warren," *Hudson Review*, IV (Summer, 1951), 248–58.

Frank, William. "Warren's Achievement," *College English*, XIX (May, 1958), 365–66.

Garrett, George Palmer. *The Georgia Review*, XII (Spring, 1958), 106–8. Review of *Promises*.

————. "The Function of the Pasiphae Myth in *Brother to Dragons*," *Modern Language Notes*, LXXIV (April, 1959), 311–13.

Garrigue, Jean. "Many Ways of Evil," *Kenyon Review*, VI (Winter, 1944), 135–38. Review of *At Heaven's Gate*.

Girault, Norton R. "The Narrator's Mind as Symbol: an Analysis of *All the King's Men*," *Accent*, VII (Summer, 1947), 220–34.

Gordon, Clifford M. "Original Sin: A Short Story," *Explicator*, IX (December, 1950), 21.

Gregory, Horace. "Of Vitality, Regionalism, and Satire in Recent American Poetry," *Sewanee Review*, LII (Autumn, 1944), 572–93. Review of *Selected Poems*.

Gross, Seymour L. "The Achievement of Robert Penn Warren," *College English*, XIX (May, 1958), 361–65.

————. "Conrad and *All the King's Men*," *Twentieth Century Literature*, III (April, 1957), 27–32.

————. "Laurence Sterne and Eliot's 'Prufrock': an Object Lesson in Explication," *College English*, XIX (November, 1957), 72–73.

Havard, William C. "The Burden of the Literary Mind: Some Meditations on Robert Penn Warren as Historian." *The South Atlantic Quarterly*, LXIII (Autumn, 1963), 516–31.

Heilman, Robert B. "Melpomene as Wallflower; or, The Reading of Tragedy," *Sewanee Review*, LV (January-March, 1947), 154–66.

————. "The Tangled Web," *Sewanee Review*, LIX (Summer, 1951), 107–19.

Hendry, Irene. "The Regional Novel: the Example of Robert Penn Warren," *Sewanee Review*, LIII (Winter, 1945), 84–102.

Herschberger, Ruth. "Poised between the two alarms . . ." *Accent*, IV (Summer, 1944), 240–46. Review of *Selected Poems*.

Hoffman, Frederick J. *The Modern Novel in America, 1900–1950*. Chicago: Henry Regnery, 1951.

Humboldt, Charles. "The Lost Cause of Robert Penn Warren," *Masses and Mainstream*, I (July, 1948), 8–20.

Hynes, Sam. The Poet as Dramatist: Robert Penn Warren and Some Predecessors. M.A. thesis, Columbia University, 1948.

————. "Robert Penn Warren: The Symbolic Journey," *University of Kansas City Review*, XVII (Summer, 1951), 279–85.

Isherwood, Christopher. "Tragic Liberal," *New Republic*,

LXXXXIX (May 31, 1939), 108. Review of *Night Rider*.

Janeway, Elizabeth. "Man in Conflict, Mind in Torment," *New York Times Book Review*, June 25, 1950, 1, 22. Review of *World Enough and Time*.

Jarrell, Randall. "On the Underside of the Stone," *New York Times Book Review*, August 23, 1953, p. 6. Review of *Brother to Dragons*.

Jones, Ernest. "Through a Glass, Darkly," *Nation*, CLXXI (July 8, 1950), 42. Review of *World Enough and Time*.

Joost, Nicholas. "The Movement toward Fulfillment," *Commonweal*, LIX (December 4, 1953), 231–32. Review of *Brother to Dragons*.

———. " 'Was All for Naught?': Robert Penn Warren and New Directions in the Novel," in *Fifty Years of the American Novel—a Christian Appraisal*, ed. Harold C. Gardiner, S. J. New York: Scribner's, 1951, 273–91.

Kenner, Hugh. Omnibus review of poetry textbooks, *Poetry*, LXXXIV (April, 1954), 43–53. Review of *Understanding Poetry*.

———. "Something Nasty in the Meat-House," *Hudson Review*, VI (Winter, 1954), 605–10. Review of *Brother to Dragons*.

King, Roma A., Jr. "Time and Structure in the Early Novels of Robert Penn Warren," *South Atlantic Quarterly*, LVI (Autumn, 1957), 486–93.

Kristol, Irving. "American Ghosts," *Encounter*, III (July, 1954), 73–75. Review of *Brother to Dragons*.

Lane, Calvin M. Narrative Art and History in Robert Penn Warren's *World Enough and Time*. Ph.D. dissertation, University of Michigan, 1956.

Létargeez, J. "Robert Penn Warren's Views of History," *Revue des langues vivantes*, XXII (1956), 533–43.

Linenthal, Mark, Jr. Robert Penn Warren and the Southern Agrarians. Ph.D. dissertation, Stanford University, 1957.

Lowell, Robert. "Prose Genius in Verse," *Kenyon Review*, XV (Autumn, 1953), 619–25. Review of *Brother to Dragons*.

MacDonald, William. *Nation*, CXXXI (July 2, 1930), 22–23. Review of *John Brown: Making of a Martyr*.

Magmer, James, S. J. "Robert Penn Warren's Quest for an

Angel," *Catholic World*, CLXXXIII (June, 1956), 179–83.

Matthiessen, F. O. "American Poetry Now," *Kenyon Review*, VI (Autumn, 1944), 683–96.

McCormick, John. "White Does and Dragons," *Western Review*, XVIII (Winter, 1954), 163–67. Review of *Brother to Dragons*.

McDowell, Frederick P. W. "Psychology and Theme in *Brother to Dragons*," *PMLA*, LXX (September, 1955), 565–86.

———. "Robert Penn Warren's Criticism," *Accent*, XV (Summer, 1955), 173–96.

———. "The Romantic Tragedy of Self in *World Enough and Time*," *Critique: Studies in Modern Fiction*, I (Summer, 1957), 34–49.

Mizener, Arthur. "Amphibium in Old Kentucky," *Kenyon Review*, XII (Autumn, 1950), 697–701.

———. "A Nature Divided Against Itself," *New York Times Book Review*, August 21, 1955, 1, 18. Review of *Band of Angels*.

———. "The Uncorrupted Consciousness." *Sewanee Review*, LXXII (Autumn, 1964), 690–698. (Essay-review of *Flood*.)

Mohrt, Michel. "Robert Penn Warren and the Myth of the Outlaw," *Yale French Studies*, No. 10 (1953), 70–84, translation by Beth Brombert of "Robert Penn Warren ou le mythe du hors-la-loi," *Le nouveau roman americain*. Paris: Gallimard, 1955. Pp. 207–23.

Nemerov, Howard. "*All the King's Men*," *Furioso*, II (Fall, 1946), 69–71.

———. "The Phoenix in the World," *Furioso*, III (Spring, 1948), 36–46.

O'Connor, William Van. *An Age of Criticism: 1900–1950*. Chicago: Henry Regnery, 1951.

———. "Robert Penn Warren: 'Provincial' Poet," in *A Southern Vanguard: the John Peale Bishop Memorial Volume*, ed. Allen Tate. New York: Prentice-Hall, 1947, 92–99.

———. "Robert Penn Warren's Short Fiction," *Western Review*, XII (Summer, 1948), 251–53.

Olson, Elder. "A Symbolic Reading of the *Ancient Mariner*," in *Critics and Criticism: Ancient and Modern*, ed. R. S. Crane. Chicago: University of Chicago Press, 1952, 138–44.

Phillips, William. "Coils of the Past," *Nation*, CLVII (August 28, 1943), 243–44. Review of *At Heaven's Gate*.

Pulos, C. E. "Warren as Critic," *Prairie Schooner*, XXXIII (Spring, 1959), 1–2. Review of *Selected Essays*.

Purdy, Rob Roy, ed. *Fugitives' Reunion: Conversations at Vanderbilt*. Nashville, Tenn.: Vanderbilt University Press, 1959.

Raben, Joseph. "*All the King's Men*: A Symposium," *Folio*, XV (May, 1950), 14–18.

Raiziss, Sona. *The Metaphysical Passion: Seven Modern American Poets and the Seventeenth Century Tradition*. Philadelphia: University of Pennsylvania Press, 1952.

Ransom, John Crowe. "*All the King's Men*: A Symposium," *Folio*, XV (May, 1950), 2–3.

———. "The Inklings of 'Original Sin,' " *Saturday Review of Literature*, XXVII (May 20, 1944), 10–11.

R. G. "Biographical Sketch," *Saturday Review of Literature*, XXXIII (June 24, 1950), 12.

Ridgely, Joseph V. "Tragedy in Kentucky," *Hopkins Review*, IV (Autumn, 1950), 61–63. Review of *World Enough and Time*.

Rubin, Louis D., Jr. "All the King's Meanings," *Georgia Review*, VIII (Winter, 1954), 422–34.

———. "The Eye of Time: Religious Themes in Robert Penn Warren's Poetry," *Diliman Review*, IV (July, 1958), 215–37.

———. *The Faraway Country: Writers of the Modern South*. University of Washington Press, 1963.

———. "Theories of Human Nature: Kazin or Warren?" *Sewanee Review*, LXIX (1961).

Ruoff, James. "Humpty Dumpty and *All the King's Men*: A Note on Robert Penn Warren's Teleology," *Twentieth Century Literature*, III (October, 1957), 128–34.

Satterwhite, Joseph N. "Robert Penn Warren and Emily Dickinson," *Modern Language Notes*, LXXI (May, 1956), 347–49.

Schwartz, Delmore. "The Dragon of Guilt," *New Republic*, CXXIX (September 14, 1953), 17–18. Review of *Brother to Dragons*.

Sillars, Malcolm O. "Warren's *All the King's Men*: A Study in

Populism," *American Quarterly*, IX (Autumn, 1957), 345–53.

Southard, W. P. "The Religious Poetry of Robert Penn Warren," *Kenyon Review*, VII (Autumn, 1945), 653–76.

Southworth, James G. *More Modern American Poets*. Oxford: Basil Blackwell, 1954.

Stewart, John L. "The Achievement of Robert Penn Warren," *South Atlantic Quarterly*, XLVII (October, 1948), 562–79.

——. The Fugitive-Agrarian Writers: A History and a Criticism. Ph.D. dissertation, Ohio State University, 1947.

——. "Robert Penn Warren and the Knot of History," *ELH*, XXVI (March, 1959), 102–36.

Tate, Allen. "*The Fugitive*, 1922–1925," *Princeton University Library Chronicles*, III (April, 1942), 75–84.

Wasserstrom, William. "Robert Penn Warren: From Paleface to Redskin," *Prairie Schooner*, XXXI (Winter, 1957), 323–33.

——. "Warren's New Poems," *Prairie Schooner*, XXXII (Spring, 1958), 67–69. Review of *Promises*.

Watkins, Floyd C. "Billie Potts at the Fall of Time," *Mississippi Quarterly*, XI (Winter, 1958), 19–29.

——. "Thomas Wolfe and the Nashville Agrarians," *Georgia Review*, VII (Winter, 1953), 410–23.

Welker, Robert. The Underlying Philosophy of Robert Penn Warren: A Study of the Poetic Attitude. M.A. thesis, Vanderbilt University, 1952.

White, Robert. "Robert Penn Warren and the Myth of the Garden," *Faulkner Studies*, III (Winter, 1954), 59–67.

Whittemore, Reed. "Five Old Masters and Their Sensibilities," *Yale Review*, XLVII (Winter, 1958), 281–88. Review of *Promises*.

Wilson, Angus. "The Fires of Violence," *Encounter*, IV (May, 1955), 75–78. Review of *Night Rider*.

JOHN M. BRADBURY is Professor of English at Union College. He is the author of *The Fugitives: A Critical Account* and *Renaissance in the South: A Critical History of the Literature, 1920–1960.*

LEONARD CASPER is Associate Professor of English at Boston College. His *Robert Penn Warren: The Dark and Bloody Ground* is the first book-length study of Warren's work to appear. In addition to his own poetry and fiction, he has also edited *Modern Philippine Short Stories.*

RALPH ELLISON is the author of the distinguished novel, *Invisible Man.* A collection of essays, *Shadow and Act,* was published in 1964. His long-promised second novel is eagerly awaited.

F. CUDWORTH FLINT is Professor Emeritus and former Head of the Department of English at Dartmouth.

GEORGE P. GARRETT is Associate Professor of English at the University of Virginia, currently at Princeton for a year. He has published three volumes of poetry, two novels, two collections of short stories, plus his most recent collection, *Cold Ground Was My Bed Last Night.* He has been awarded a *Sewanee Review* Fellowship in Poetry, The Grand Prix de Rome of the American Academy of Arts and Letters, and a Ford Fellowship in Drama.

WILLIAM C. HAVARD is Professor and Chairman of the Department of Government at Louisiana State University. He is the author (with Loren P. Beth) of *The Politics of Misrepresentation*.

ROBERT B. HEILMAN is Professor and Chairman of the Department at the University of Washington. He is as well known for his many books of Elizabethan criticism as for his continuing interest in contemporary literature.

JOHN LEWIS LONGLEY, JR. is Associate Professor of Humanities at the University of Virginia. He has published essays in various areas of modern literature. One chapter of *The Tragic Mask: A Study of Faulkner's Heroes* was earlier awarded the Emily Clark Balch Prize. He has lectured frequently on Faulkner and Warren at other universities, and was in 1961–1962 Fulbright Professor of Contemporary Literature at the University of Freiburg.

FREDERICK W. P. MCDOWELL is Professor of English at the University of Iowa. He has published studies of Ellen Glasgow and Elizabeth Maddox Roberts.

ALVAN S. RYAN is Professor and Chairman of the Department of English at Notre Dame. In 1961–1962 he was Fulbright Professor at the University of Saarbrücken.

EUGENE WALTER is now living in Rome. His novel, published this year, is entitled *Love You Good, See You Later*.

# THE GOTHAM LIBRARY

Oscar Cargill, General Editor

Robert J. Clements, Associate Editor for Modern Languages

*A paperback series devoted to major figures in world literature and topics of enduring importance*

*If these titles are not available at your bookstore, you may order them by sending a check or money order direct to:* New York University Press, 32 Washington Place, New York 3, New York. *The Press will pay postage.*

73464

**DATE DUE**